A Modern Reader's Guide
to Dante's *Inferno*

American University Studies

Series II
Romance Languages and Literature
Vol. 191

PETER LANG
New York • San Francisco • Bern • Baltimore
Frankfurt am Main • Berlin • Wien • Paris

Rodney J. Payton

A Modern Reader's Guide
to Dante's *Inferno*

PETER LANG
New York • San Francisco • Bern • Baltimore
Frankfurt am Main • Berlin • Wien • Paris

Library of Congress Cataloging-in-Publication Data

Payton, Rodney Johns.
  A modern reader's guide to Dante's Inferno / Rodney J. Payton.
    p. cm. — (American university studies. Series II, Romance
languages and literature : vol. 191)
  Intended for beginning and intermediate readers of the Inferno in
English translation.
  Includes bibliographical references
  1. Dante Alighieri, 1265-1321. Inferno. I. Title. II. Series.
PQ4443.P38   1992   851'.1—dc20   91-43149
ISBN 0-8204-1827-7   CIP
ISSN 0740-9257

Die Deutsche Bibliothek-CIP-Einheitsaufnahme

Payton, Rodney J.:
A modern reader's guide to Dante's Inferno / Rodney J. Payton.—
New York; Berlin; Bern; Frankfurt/M.; Paris; Wien; Lang, 1992
  (American university studies : Ser. 2, Romance languages and
literature ; Vol. 191)
    ISBN 0-8204-1827-7
NE: American university studies/02

PQ
4443
.P38
1992

The paper in this book meets the guidelines for permanence and
durability of the Committee on Production Guidelines for
Book Longevity of the Council on Library Resources.

© Peter Lang Publishing, Inc., New York 1992

Printed in the United States of America.

ACKNOWLEDGMENTS

The following publishers have generously given permission to use extended quotations from copyrighted works: From Dante Alighieri, Charles S. Singleton, translator, *The Divine Comedy*, vols. I, II, III, Bollingen Series LXXX, Copyright © 1970, 1973, 1975 by Princeton University Press. Reprinted by permission of Princeton University Press. Reprinted by permission of the publishers and the Loeb Classical Library from Virgil: *Aenid*, vol. I, translated by H. Rushton Fairclough, Cambridge, Mass.: Harvard University Press, 1916; from Virgil: *Eclogues*, translated by H. Rushton Fairclough, Cambridge, Mass.: Harvard University Press, 1916; from Statius: *Thebiad*, vol. I, translated by J. H. Mozley, Cambridge, Mass.: Harvard University Press, 1928; from Statius: *Achilleid*, translated by J. H. Mozley, Cambridge, Mass.: Harvard University Press, 1928; from Lucan: *The Civil War*, translated by J. D. Duff, Cambridge, Mass.: Harvard University Press, 1928; from Ovid: *Metamorphosis*, vol. II, translated by Frank Justus Miller, Cambridge, Mass.: Harvard University Press, 1916; from Ovid: *The Art of Love*, translated by J. H. Mozley, Cambridge Mass.: Harvard Univesity Press, 1929. From Thomas Aquinas, *Summa Theologica*, Cambridge: Cambridge University Press. From John of Salisbury, John Dickinson, translator, *The Statesman's Book of John of Salisbury*, Englewood Cliffs, N.J.: Prentice Hall, 1963. Excerpts from the *Acts* of Peter are translated by Robert Stoops and taken from the *New Testament Apocrypha* and are reprinted by permission of Polebridge Press.

Table of Contents

PREFACE

This book is intended for either beginning or "intermediate" readers of the *Inferno*, that is, those who are just beginning to read the poem or those who have read it and now want to learn more about it. I assume that you are reading the poem in English.

There is a lot of information about *Inferno* available, as people have been writing about the poem ever since it appeared more than 600 years ago. However, much of the available information is diffused in scholarly journals which are difficult for most people to obtain. Most of this writing is the work of professional critics and academics and while much of it, especially recent work, is superb scholarship, it makes few concessions to readers who are not specialists or who are not competent in several foreign and ancient languages. This book draws heavily on these sources, but I have tried to put the arguments and insights of the scholars into everyday language. I have included my own thinking about the poem, ideas which have developed in eighteen years of reading and discussing Dante with my students.

Every modern English edition of *Inferno* includes a set of notes by the translator. In general, these notes are very good. The problem is that they are usually too brief. A deeper understanding of the poem requires more information than space allows the translators to include. There is another problem with "notes." Notes are keyed to the line numbers of the poem and are usually on a different page than the text itself. Nothing on the page with text refers the reader to the page with notes. New readers have no way of knowing when they should look at the notes and not recognizing a problem in the text, people tend to miss the explanation of it. This book avoids this problem by presenting a discursive discussion of each canto or group of cantos and, to the best of my knowledge and ability, brings the issues contained in the text to the attention of the reader with a longer discussion than a brief note can contain.

What translation should beginning readers use? Many are excellent. I am very fond of John Ciardi's, published by Bantam, for its beauty and cleverness. However, Ciardi sometimes does more of a paraphrase than a translation and readers can be mislead into thinking Dante said something that he didn't. Further, the edition of Ciardi's translation does not include the original Italian text. I think you should read a bilingual edition as a smattering of Italian or even a knowledge of French will go a long way towards unlocking the beauty of the original which a translation unavoidably loses. A bilingual edition can even help teach the serious student literary Italian. For these reasons and because it is a literal translation, not a paraphrase, I suggest the translation by Charles S. Singleton published by Princeton University Press. Singleton's notes are comprehensive. Like the notes in other translations, they are keyed to the line numbers and suffer from the difficulty explained above, but they are the best source of information about specific lines in the poem available to English readers. Like other scholarly work, however, the notes are intended for a professional audience although Singleton does translate all the foreign language sources he cites into English.

This book is an introduction to the *Inferno* and also to modern scholarly opinion about it. I have included a bibliography of books and articles in English for the benefit of those who wish to read further. I have tried not to clutter the text with too much documentation, although I think the references provided will lead the student to the appropriate scholarly sources. Inclusion in the bibliography should be taken as the acknowledgment of my intellectual debt to the scholars who are cited. All of those cited there have had a role in forming my thinking about the text. If I have misrepresented their conclusions or suggestions, I apologize.

In addition to my debts to those scholars and to my students, I owe a debt to my colleagues in the Department of Liberal Studies at Western Washington University: Professors William K. B. Stoever, Ulrich H. R. Mammitzsch, William Ladson Wallace, Michael Fisher and Robert Stoops. All have shared their knowledge with me and Dr. Stoops has significantly clarified my thinking. Dr. Albert Froderberg of Mathematics, Dr. George Mariz of History and Dr. Gerard Rutan of Political Science all read the manuscript and made welcome criticisms. My family, Sandra, Gwendolyn and Elspeth, have been appropriately enthusiastic. Gwendolyn, too, read the manuscript. I am grateful for research grants on several occasions during the development of the text from the Bureau for Faculty Research here at Western and for further support through the kind offices of Dean Peter Elich of the College of Arts and Sciences. The book would not exist save for the kindness, patience and skill of Phyllis Graham and Linda Pettigrew.

CHAPTER 1

Introduction

Dante Alighieri's *Comedy* is a poem of great length and stupendous complexity. The key to unraveling it is an understanding of some concepts which are characteristic of the culture in which it was written and some which are central features of the mind of Dante himself. These introductory comments will describe these important features of thought in order to prepare for an intelligent reading of the poem.

Although the idea of describing a mind such as Dante's, one of the authentic geniuses of history, is a daunting and perplexing task, it is a surprisingly grateful undertaking, at least in its broader strokes, since the mind of Dante is so gratifyingly logical. The simple basic ideas we have to grasp lead to some breathtakingly complex constructs in the poem, but the ideas themselves are not complex and remain stable reference points to which we can always refer. Of course, to say that Dante's thinking is logical is not to imply that his logic is the same as that of the Twentieth Century, rather it only means that if we understand the premises with which Dante begins, we can understand how he reaches his conclusions even if we cannot always agree with them.

A preliminary concept which we must address is so basic that some may wonder at the necessity of mentioning it at all: It is simply that Dante's age was, more than anything else, a religious age. Dante and almost all of the people he knew believed in God and thought of Him in much the same way. The religious diversity of our time was not characteristic of his. Although Dante does mention some heretics in *Inferno*, they were much rarer in his time than skeptics are in ours. The reason why it is necessary to start with this is because no one will go very far in understanding Dante's poem who chooses to quarrel with his belief in God. It is not necessary to *share* Dante's medieval Christianity to feel the power of his work, but the reader must *accede* to it for the time he or she is with Dante in the poem. For some, this will be no problem at all, others will have to make some effort to enter Dante's world fully. This book, to keep things as simple as possible, will speak as if the things Dante says about God are true. Readers should understand that this does not mean that I think they necessarily share Dante's beliefs, nor should you think that of me.

Not only did Dante believe in God, he lived at a time when one of the major tasks of serious thought was to determine the nature of that God. A favorite definition of God at the time was "That being than which there can be nothing greater than" and from this definition will flow much of what we need to say in this sketch.

I have followed the following organization: First, to speak of Dante's ideas of the ethical organization of the universe, the Great Chain of Being. This will lead to the principles of plenitude and correspondence. Second, it is necessary to describe Dante's theory of literature and what he thought a text like the Divine Comedy should do. Third, I will discuss Dante's conception of history, including the principle of authority; next, the physical nature of Dante's cosmos, the Ptolemaic Universe, and finally the nature of some of Dante's other works.

The term "Great Chain of Being" (Lovejoy 1964) refers to one of the central features of Dante's universe, that is, that it is arranged as an ethical hierarchy. All beings and substances in the universe have a value which locates them on a continuum of existence which stretches from the being with the most value, God, (that which there can be nothing greater than) down through the ranks of angels (from the most noble Seraphim to the least noble, simply called Angels), through the ranks of mankind (divisible by social rank and function from the pope through kings down to the most menial serf) and through the ranks of animals and substances (gold possessing, for instance, more virtue than silver or iron). This continuum can be visualized as a chain of interlocking links. In a chain, obviously, each link is necessary for the whole. The relationship of one thing to another can be precisely demonstrated by the use of this image. Man, for instance, occupies a very special place in the Chain for he possesses characteristics which are shared, on the one hand, by the creatures below him and, on the other, by those above. In addition, man has characteristics which are uniquely his. Like the creatures below, man is mortal and must suffer death. Unlike no other mortal creature, but like the beings above him in the Chain, God and the Angels, man has an immortal soul for which he can obtain salvation and whether he does so or not determines the conditions under which that immortal part will continue to exist. Like the beings above, and unlike the creatures below, man possesses reason, which can be used to obtain salvation for the soul. Other things can be similarly located on the

Chain, but clearly the central issue is the relationship of man to God and the other created things in the universe.

How many things are there on the Chain? Which is another way of asking how many things are there in the universe? The answer is "as many things as there can be." Since God is defined as "that which there can be nothing greater than," it follows that He is self-sufficient. Being self-sufficient (having no need of anything else), he is incapable of being jealous of the being of anything else. Therefore it follows, to the medieval mind at least, that God will not deny existence to anything which can exist. This conclusion is generally called "the principle of plenitude" and means, among other things, that there are no "voids" or unused, useless places in the universe since, if there is a location, there must be, given the perfection of God, something to occupy it.

The reasoning that we have followed to reach our conclusion in the preceding paragraph is *deductive* in nature. We began with a general principle (the necessary perfection of God) and reasoned from there to a specific fact (that the universe has no waste places). All people frequently think in a deductive manner, and it is the mode of sophisticated mathematics where particular cases are compared to general principles. But please note that modern scientific thinking is very frequently *inductive* in the experimental stage before the general principles are established. We modern people tend to begin with a specific fact or observation (the ball falls to the floor when released) and reason from that to a general conclusion about the universe (there is an attractive force between all masses in the universe). To us, the scientific frame of mind requires that general conclusions about the universe always be open to question. Dante's thinking, and the thinking of his era is much more likely to be deductive than inductive and the deductive principles with which thinking starts are far less likely to be questioned than they are in our own time. Anselm's definition of God, "that being than which there can be nothing greater than," is a good example of a deductive principle which came to be taken for granted. Intellectuals would try to make any other "facts" about the universe which they might observe agree with that deductive principle rather than challenge it as modern science might do. This is why Dante's age is such an age of orthodoxy.

You can see how the principle of plenitude is a deduction from the definition of God. Like it, the principle of correspondence follows from the definition of God and deals with the relationship between things in the continuum of existence. It works like this: God creates all things in the universe out of his goodness. Therefore all things in the universe share, inasmuch as they are able, in that goodness. It follows (deductive logic again, God's creation is all good) that nothing in the universe is in and of itself bad, merely that some things share less of God's goodness than others. God does not, for instance, deny existence to poisonous snakes simply because they are not capable of sharing very much in His goodness. This important idea explains why there is evil in a world created by a perfectly good God. Evil is merely a lack of goodness, rather than a thing in itself. In addition, to Dante and his age, the whole created universe, since all things in it are more or less good, is capable of reminding or teaching man of the absolute goodness of God. Man can experience the material universe around him (see its goodness) and through it be brought to contemplate the immaterial spiritual universe which he cannot experience directly. Everything in the material portion of the Chain of Being *corresponds* to some aspect of the spiritual portion and, ultimately, to some aspect of God. In a way, the universe is a *mirror* of God. Here is a familiar example: Man, says the Bible, was made in the image of God. Therefore, to Dante's time the physical aspect of mankind was a visible reminder of the being of God. In a similar way, the ideal state (for Dante a monarchy, ruled by a king who has everything and therefore no desires) is a model (imperfect, because man is fallen) of the government of Heaven itself. Here is how a twelfth century Bishop, John of Salisbury, combines these two correspondences to speak of proper government and social order and their relationship to divinity. At the same time, he lays out the chain of man's social being and shows how it corresponds to the Great Chain of Being which is found reflected in the organization of the human body:

> A commonwealth, according to Plutarch, is a certain body which is endowed with life by the benefit of divine favor, which acts at the prompting of the highest equity, and is ruled by what may be called the moderating power of reason. Those things which establish and implant in us the practice of religion and transmit to us the worship of God...fill the place of the soul in the body of the commonwealth. And therefore those who preside over the practice of religion should be looked up to and venerated as the soul of the body. For who doubts that the ministers of God's

holiness are his representatives? Furthermore, since the soul is, as it were, the prince of the body, and has rulership over the whole thereof, so those whom our author calls the prefects of religion preside over the entire body...The place of the head in the body of the commonwealth is filled by the prince, who is subject only to God and to those who exercise His office and who represent Him on earth, even as in the human body the head is quickened and governed by the soul. The place of the heart is filled by the senate, from which proceeds the initiation of good works and ill. The duties of ears, eyes and tongue are claimed by the judges and governors of provinces. Officials and soldiers correspond to the hands. Those who always attend upon the prince are likened to the sides. Financial officers and keepers...may be compared with the stomach and intestines, which if they become congested through excessive avidity, and retain too tenaciously their accumulations, generate innumerable and incurable diseases, so that through their ailment the whole body is threatened with destruction. The husbandmen correspond to the feet, which always cleave to the soil, and need the more especially the care and foresight of the head, since while they walk upon the earth doing service with their bodies, they meet the more often with stones of stumbling, and therefore deserve aid and protection all the more justly since it is they who raise, sustain, and move forward the weight of the entire body.

In John's simple example, the whole theory of proper government can be reviewed merely by thinking through the structure of the body. This technique of remembering things is called a "place memory system" (in such a system one relates important things one wants to remember to physical locations) and was common in Dante's time. In fact, the Comedy is a giant place memory system as we shall see.

Because of the principle of correspondence, Dante's cosmos was filled with signs and visible manifestations of divinity. Confronted with so many reminders, human reason, one of man's Godlike characteristics, should lead him to seek to approach that divinity and seek salvation. In this sense, the *Inferno* is a drama of how the God-given gift of reason awakens man's conscience and works to move him towards salvation.

The principle of correspondence is important to an understanding of what Dante thought a work of literature should do. It follows from the preceding discussion that if man is an imperfect reflection of God himself, then man's works are an imperfect imitation of God's works. Dante's *Divine Comedy* is a cosmos unto itself; it describes the workings of the entire universe. It is not God's universe, as becomes clear as we read the poem, but it corresponds to God's real universe. Another way of saying this is to say that Dante's universe which he depicts in the *Comedy* is an analog of the real universe. Dante's analogous universe exhibits a kind of plenitude in that it is like a catalog which enumerates and demonstrates the relationships between the things it lists, so that it has internal correspondences. As the reader progresses through the "catalog" of the *Divine Comedy* each part illuminates previously dark aspects of other parts in a process of continuous discovery. Furthermore, meaning in Dante's poem exhibits a hierarchy of ethical value which is similar to the hierarchical nature of the Great Chain. Dante said that his text in the *Divine Comedy* was like the text of the Bible itself in that it functions on four ascending levels of meaning. The first level is the literal where words mean exactly what they say. When, in the first canto of *Inferno* Dante writes that he saw a little hill with the light shining on it, and that he felt that ascending the hill would lead him to safety, we can take that exactly as any newspaper report in our own time. But the second level of meaning for Dante is the allegorical which is related to the principle of correspondence in that everything in the text can point outside itself to something else. This proceeds according to a system of iconology, a kind of vocabulary of symbols, which is well understood even today. In this example, it is safe to take light to stand for knowledge. To climb the hill, to get into the light, is to obtain knowledge or wisdom. Likewise the direction of motion, up, signifies improvement since God is "up" both in location and in value from man. Our little example then can be seen as a simple allegory of striving to obtain knowledge to make oneself safe from ignorance. The next level of meaning is a moral level. Here perhaps that people automatically know they *should* strive after knowledge. The fourth level is the anagogic or spiritual level of meaning in which we are to understand that the text tells us something of a spiritual or transcendent nature. This level is the most difficult and it may be that our example is too simple to contain such a meaning (Dante doesn't claim that all parts of his texts contain all four levels). Much of the enjoyment of reading the *Divine Comedy* consists in unraveling such mysteries.

There is a third deductive principle to which we now must turn, the principle of authority. To Dante, there were certain figures in human history who represented the peaks of human achievement and to whose opinions and works much deference was to be shown. It is not that such figures were incapable of error since, being human, they surely could err, it is that Dante took these outstanding people to be particular instruments of the will of God and, therefore, they were to be treated with the greatest respect. In the *Inferno*, the most important authorities are Aristotle, the Greek philosopher, and Virgil, the Roman poet. It is important to see that these two figures, both pagans, are part of God's plan which culminates in Christianity and the Church of Rome. Dante claims in his *Convivio* that David (out of whose line Christ was to come) was born in the same year that Aeneas (the hero of Virgil's epic *Aeneid*) set sail from Troy to Italy where he was to found the city of Rome which was to become the seat of Christianity. Thus history has two tributaries: a pagan Greek and Roman stream merges with a Hebrew stream to form the great river of Christianity which can carry all men to salvation. Nothing in history is a dead end since it is all part of God's scheme. In the *Inferno* Dante relies almost exclusively on pagan authority to find his way using the power of reason which is available to all men without the direct intervention of God. In the other two books of the *Comedy* he deals with biblical Christian authority which add divine grace to pagan reason.

We have now seen how Dante's intellectual universe is organized symbolically through the Chain of Being and the principles of plenitude, correspondence and authority. Now we must look at it in its physical aspect. The model of the physical universe in which Dante and his age believed is known as the Ptolemaic universe since it came to medieval astronomers in the work of Ptolemy of Alexandria who wrote in about 150 AD. Ptolemy said that in writing his book he drew upon the ancient Greek astronomers and for this reason, Ptolemy was taken to be an authority of a very important sort since the other stream of history, the Hebrew, contains very little astronomical information at all. Ptolemy's book was accordingly called the *Almagest* or "Great Work." (*Almagest* is an Arabic word and is the root of the English word "almanac.")

Much of what you need to know of the Ptolemaic universe can be seen by looking at the illustration of the universe in any modern edition of *Inferno*. The universe is explained in very common sense terms as would be agreed upon by peoples who did not possess any instruments of observation save their naked senses. The universe is geocentric, earth centered, with all the other heavenly bodies traveling about the earth in perfect circles. There are ten spheres, seven of them carrying one of the known planets (with the sun and the moon being counted as "planets"). Beyond the sphere of Saturn, the last planet, is the sphere of the fixed stars. That is, those heavenly bodies which travel in eternal fixed patterns (constellations) unlike the wandering paths of the planets. All of these spheres travel in perfect circles about the earth, but they are not perfectly concentric. For certain technical reasons certain eccentricities in their rotation had to be allowed, but since ancient philosophy held that the prime mover (the *Primum Mobile*, the outermost sphere, which imparted motion to all the others) has to be in essence the simplest, Ptolemy posited the existence of a tenth sphere, devoid of any bodies, which did rotate in a perfect circle with the earth exactly at the center. Beyond the last sphere is the empyrean or region of fire where God himself was said to have his being. Ptolemy's astronomical model is a system which serves to aid in keeping an accurate calendar and in navigation. It does these tasks perfectly well given periodic correction of errors in the position of the various celestial bodies. However, the principle of correspondence, in which all created things must point to God, will not let the matter rest there; further significances must be developed.

First, Aristotle's physics, authoritative at the time, held that there were different rules for motion in the heavens than for motion on Earth. "Proper" motion for celestial bodies was circular. Whereas on Earth proper motion was a straight line. The orbit of the moon was the dividing line between the two areas. Below the orbit of the moon, everything seems to be in constant flux. All things seem to be impermanent and undergoing change usually in the direction of decay. Above the orbit of the moon things seem to be permanent and changeless. The stars apparently repeat their endless dance unalterably for eternity. The Church, understandably enough given the operation of the principles above, proceeded to make a moral allegory of this appearance so that the heavens become a visible reminder of the unalterable, eternal state to which one aspires in contrast to the world of change and decay which one inhabits.

Other features of the Ptolemaic universe are laden with ethical significance. The Earth, motionless at the center of the universe, can be taken in two ways: First, its central location can be seen as a sign of its centrality in the concern of God, but, secondly, its remoteness from the Empyrean (the "location" of God) is a sign of the great gulf which exists between sinful man and the divine Creator. By allegorizing in this way, medieval people turned the model of the universe into a moral "map" (that is, a "place-memory system") with ethical values spatially located on it. Dante's Hell, Purgatory and Paradise are elaborations of this mapping process and learning the map and the significance of the moral locations upon it is one of the reader's tasks in understanding the poem.

It remains now to say a few words about some of Dante's other works. They are the *Vita Nuova*, the *Convivio*, the *Letter to Can Grande* and *De Monarchia*. The first of these, the *Vita Nuova* or "New Life," is a short collection of poems and their explanations, written according to an elaborate prescription of manners and custom, to and about a young woman, Beatrice whom Dante knew in Florence. This work will be discussed in more detail later, but for now you should know that, given the impulse to allegorize and explain the significance of things, Dante makes of this woman a symbol of divine grace and credits her appearance and example with the power of turning men's thoughts to God. After her death, with her immediate example no longer available to him, Dante turned to the study of philosophy which he characterized as another beautiful young woman to whom he addressed the same form of poetry he had addressed to Beatrice. This is the subject matter of the *Convivio* or "Banquet." Even though one of the most important conclusions of the entire *Divine Comedy* is that "My Lady Philosophy" cannot take the place of divine grace, the *Convivio* contains much information which is necessary to read the *Divine Comedy* including the theory of levels of meaning we have discussed, the principles of plenitude and authority with attention to the place of Artistotle whom Dante calls "the Philosopher," and his theory of history as a plan in the mind of God. The *Letter to Can Grande* is the dedicatory statement of *Paradiso* which Dante wrote to the Veronese nobleman who sheltered him in his exile from Florence. It restates some of the theory of allegory which is found is found in *Convivio* and tells of some specific principles of the organization and purposes of the *Divine Comedy*. *De Monarchia* (On Monarchy) advances Dante's theory that the world should be governed by an absolute ruler, an emperor, who would have everything and need nothing. In this regard he would be a human imitation of God. This ruler would have absolute control over all of man's secular business. The pope at Rome, on the other hand, would be poor and divorced from the material things of the world. He would attend to man's spiritual needs. Dante believed that this division of government would assure the peace of the world and allow mankind both to pursue the good things of this life and to achieve salvation in the life to come.

With this information the modern reader is ready to accompany Dante the Poet and Pilgrim on his great adventure. Nearly any edition of Dante's poem will include a biographical sketch detailing what is known about him and this should be read since *Inferno* is biographical as well as philosophical.

CHAPTER 2

Canto I

The Dark Wood: Failure and the Guide

While we can follow literal sequence of events in Canto I well enough, the reader should not expect to be able to penetrate the symbolic meaning of the events and images until a wider experience of Dante's universe and the art with which he expresses it has been gained. As we move through the narration, following the Pilgrim and his guide, the poem itself will teach us how to interpret it. In the beginning the poem is obscure, but its dim scenes are possessed of so much potential that they have excited the appetite of readers for understanding ever since the poem's appearance. The obscurity of the beginning is a part of Dante's plan; that later events will make things clearer is an explicit promise of the first few lines, "But, to treat of the good I found in it, I will tell of the other things I saw there" (Canto I, Lines 8—9). The dark wood is not further described than in the first seven lines, yet by the end of the *Inferno* we will well understand what place it was.

What will happen is that later events and allusions in the poem will cause the reader to reflect back on earlier parts and to constantly readjust his or her previous understanding. This is a vital component of Dante's method and an important element in the way he conceived that history itself worked. For instance, the Old Testament was taken to prefigure the New with figures and events "pointing" outside themselves to events that, in God's divine scheme of history, were to happen later. Abraham's attempted sacrifice of Isaac in Genesis 22 was thought to prefigure the crucifixion of Christ with Isaac symbolizing man doomed to death, who is spared by the alternate sacrifice of the ram, symbolizing Christ, which is offered in his place. This process demonstrates that all of human history has meaning in God's divine plan, that the present moment reveals the meaning of the past and vice versa. The experience of coming to understand earlier parts of the poem in the light of later experience is one of the major pleasures the *Divine Comedy* provides the reader.

The first two lines of the poem introduce two major figures of the *Comedy* and constitute an example of how carefully the poem must be read: "Midway in the journey of *our* life / found myself in a dark wood". The two figures are all of us collectively and Dante, a particular individual. Allegorically, all people undertake the journey of a life and Dante, in this role called "the Pilgrim," by commentators, stands in the allegory for the traveler on the journey from birth to death. This device is ordinary enough in medieval drama where "Everyman" is a frequent figure, but Dante enriches this commonplace by pointing out that it is he, Dante the Poet, a literal person, who finds himself in the dark wood. Everyman must sin, Everyman for the sake of his soul must seek the grace of salvation, but every man's story is unique. Dante intends to express both the common features of human experience and the uniqueness of the story of Dante Alighieri, this particular pilgrim. The tension between the roles Dante, both Everyman and individual traveler, has in the poem written by Dante Alighieri of Florence (The "Poet") is one of the major dramatic devices of the work. Dante tells us that he, the Pilgrim, lost *his* way midway in *our* life's journey. Psalm 90:10 tells us that the span of a life is 70 years. Dante is then 35. The year is 1300.

Dante the Pilgrim, then, is lost in a dark wood, which we, who share his humanity could very well find ourselves in also and in some sense, but not necessarily the same sense, do. Dante is in the "dark wood" because he has wandered from the "straight way." These images are clear enough being very usual in western literature. The straight road is righteousness and the dark wood error, confusion and sin. Dante makes no attempt to describe the straight road, but he does say that it is "hard to tell what the wood was" (4—5). On the journey, the Pilgrim's development will include an increase in his poetic ability His poetic power will develop as his understanding of the Divine Mystery increases. Later in the poem, possessed of his full powers by the grace of God, he will be able to approach describing the ineffable. Here, his inability to describe the dark wood indicates his confusion and his sinful state.

Still, Dante does say that the thought of the wood "renews the fear!" (6) which brings up yet another character in the poem. Readers will realize that the person speaking here must be the Poet who is writing the poem, remembering his experience. Sometimes the Poet will speak directly to the reader and it is important to distinguish between him and the Pilgrim who is the person *in* the poem. The fear, which the memory of the wood renews for the Poet, is (unknown to the Pilgrim yet) a positive factor, since his struggle towards the light is motivated by it. Had he not feared the dark wood, he might have stayed in it and been destroyed. The fear is a gift of God, which is not perceived as a good at the time it functions as a good (Spraycar 1978). Later, the Pilgrim will understand this, but he does not at the beginning of the poem.

The reason his perceptions are insufficient to the moment is revealed, allegorically, in the next lines (10—12). He is "full of sleep." To Dante, sleep is the symbol of an irrational condition of the mind. Reason itself, even without revelation, could prompt a healthy fear of damnation which would serve to keep one on the "straight road." Later we will learn that Hell is filled with the souls of those who have "lost the good of intellect" (III, 18) and that the easiest sins to fall into (and avoid) are those that involve a simple loss of rational control. Dante is lost, in both a literal and figurative sense, because of some sort of failure of reason. The one advantage left to him is that he is aware enough to be afraid, although he says the fear is "bitter." Nevertheless, it is his fear that prompts him to make an effort to save himself.

He sees a little hill bathed in sunlight, and the sight somewhat reassures him as well it might, laden as it is with powerful positive symbols. First, the hill itself, at the end of the valley, represents an upward direction and "up" in medieval cosmology is away from the center of the Earth, the site of Hell, and towards God, thus good. Secondly, the hill is bathed in the light of the sun and the sun is a common symbol of knowledge and reason in medieval literature. Thus light, which Dante, "full of sleep," needs, beckons him upward, the proper direction.

However, the Pilgrim's perceptions are incorrect as the Poet is careful to let the reader know. Stemming from the traditions of the Church is the idea that while knowledge exists in this world, certain forms of it are insufficient; knowledge can lead one to God, but cannot accomplish the salvation of the soul itself. Salvation, which man can neither deserve nor earn by any act of his own, including the effort to understand, can only come as a gift of God. To understand Dante's symbol of the hill, it is important to realize that he sees the light of the sun resting on the shoulders of the hill. He does not see the sun itself. Many scholars (Cassell 1976) think that the hill represents earthly philosophy which Dante, the Poet, was enthralled with during a significant portion of his life. The *Convivio* is a record of this involvement. For now, it is sufficient to note that Dante the Pilgrim's attempt to climb the hill of reason and philosophy is a failure.

The poem notes that the lake of Dante's heart is somewhat quieted and later the reader will learn that there is another "quiet" (and deadly) lake to be found in the depths of Hell (Spraycar 1978), but an even more powerful indication of the nature of the error is in the next few lines (22—26) which are the first of Dante's similes with which the poem is punctuated and which do much to create its atmosphere. The similes are among those places where Dante's powers as a poet are most evident (22—27):

> And as he who with laboring breath
> has escaped from the deep to the shore
> turns to look back on the dangerous waters,
> so my mind which was still fleeing
> turned to gaze upon the pass
> that never left anyone alive.

A swimmer who has escaped from the currents might feel too proud of his own prowess as a merely human philosopher might attribute too much wisdom to his own conclusions. The Pilgrim fails to realize that the fear he feels which motivates him to want to climb the hill comes from a source outside himself. Both St. Augustine and St. Thomas Aquinas wrote about the fear that leads to the search for salvation as a "gift of the Holy Spirit," a very special case of God's "graceful" behavior towards mankind.

A further symbolic significance here is that this is the first mention of the crossing of water, an action which will become a major symbol, associated (Demaray 1969, Wingell 1981) as it is with the sacrament of baptism, of the Pilgrim's true salvation. This present water reference, however, is only an apparent baptism since the Pilgrim is by no means saved by it. It is also, in the minds of many commentators, a reference to the crossing of the Red Sea which leads to the wandering in the desert of the Hebrew people as this action of Dante's leads to his crossing of the "desert strand" (29). A bit of thought here will reveal a good deal of the complexity of Dante's system of symbolic references: If the crossing of the Red Sea and the wilderness wandering represent a movement towards the partial (in the Christian view) salvation of the Hebrew people (they escape from Egypt, representing sin, and wander in the desert, a purification to reach the promised land, the earthly kingdom), then the coming of Christ completes that movement (it enables them now to reach the heavenly kingdom) not only for the Hebrews, but expands it to include all men. Dante's water passage leads him to a desert testing which is as partial for him personally as the wilderness wandering was for the Hebrew people collectively. In both cases, what is lacking is the saving grace of Christ. Dante's intent is to show that his partial movement towards philosophy, while not evil, is not an unqualified good either and needs to be fulfilled by the addition of grace. Likewise, his personal failure and his later salvation become part of the experience of all men and are available as an objective lesson as soon as we read the poem and understand it in the same way the escape of the Hebrews contained a lesson which was generalized to all men through Christ. Thus Dante's task is sacred and is a part of, and an illustration of, the divine scheme of history in which all things point to the Christian idea of salvation.

As Dante crosses the desert, "the firm foot was always the lower." The firm foot, the left, is associated with the appetite, the things a person desires. Desires, of course, can either be proper or improper and if Dante's error has been an appetite for worldly things rather than saving grace, then, allegorically, he can be said to be injured, or not properly functioning in the left foot which here always stays behind the right foot rather than taking its proper role in Dante's progress (Cassell 1976, Freccero 1959). The right foot, symbol of the intellect, in this case has to do all of the function of locomotion which properly should be shared between the appetite and the intellect. This picture of Dante, infirm in his appetite and yet requiring its proper function for his salvation, is to be elaborated in Canto XIV with the image of the Old Man of Crete and in the later cantos of the *Purgatorio*.

Dante meets the three beasts just as he begins to climb the hill. Various interpreters have offered explanations of the symbolic meaning of these animals and the debate still continues. It is apparent, though, that if Dante is to follow the multi-layered path of meaning (literal, allegorical, moral and anagogic) the beasts must begin to be understood as real beasts and as John Demaray (1969) has observed, they are of the kinds a literal pilgrim would have encountered on a real pilgrimage of the sort which were common during the Middle Ages when pilgrims reenacted the journey of the Hebrews across the Egyptian desert. On one level of meaning, the beasts are probably symbolic of the three levels of Hell which will be explained to the Pilgrim in Canto XI. Perhaps the wolf, of which Dante seems most afraid, symbolizes the category of sin to which he felt himself to be most susceptible, although all of them are fearsome.

Dante's fear of the leopard is tempered, somewhat, by the astrological significance of the time of day, the position of the heavenly bodies and the season of the year (For details of the astrology, see Singleton 1971). It is dawn, which is in itself a symbol of rebirth, and the stars are in the same arrangement that they had at the moment of creation which tradition had in Spring (a time of rebirth) near Easter. Dante's journey through Hell is a sign of the time Christ spent in the tomb and his exit from Hell will be a symbol of Christ's resurrection.

Even so, these good omens cannot completely defend him against fear of the beasts so that, at the sight of the wolf, Dante loses hope of climbing the hill. This despair, here, of even climbing the hill of philosophy, not to mention the mountain of grace, is most serious since despair of one's salvation is an aspect of the "sin against the Holy Spirit" and is rather like a negative version of the sin of pride since it is "prideful" to feel that one is so sinful that even the almighty God could not, if He wished, save one. The next few lines (54—58), the second simile of the poem, illustrate this moment. Dante's lack of confidence is as trivial as the despair of the gambler who is crushed by a temporary setback or is made overconfident by a temporary victory. In this allegory of salvation, either state is reproachful, but especially despair for, as Dante says, it pushes him back "to where the sun is silent" (60). The sun is the symbol of good, as noted above, and to be in a place where it stands silent is ominous, indeed. The rhetorical figure of speech, synesthesia, should be noted here. Synesthesia is perceiving something by a sense which is foreign to it. Here, the sun, which is usually seen, is heard to be silent. Dante uses such striking images to draw attention to important issues in the poem (Cambon 1970).

The next few lines use this technique. Dante perceives "one who seemed faint through long silence" (63), his sense of sight doing what hearing usually does. Here is the most momentous meeting in the *Inferno*. For this figure who appears to Dante in the desert of his despair reveals himself to be Virgil, the author of the *Aeneid* and Dante's artistic ideal. A part of Dante's veneration of Virgil can be attributed to the place of authority in the medieval world. All events and persons in history were thought to be a part of God's divine scheme. Virgil could have been venerated by Dante for that fact alone, but Virgil had a special value for Dante. First of all, he was a great poet. Dante is supremely conscious of his own powers as a poet and intends that we should understand him to be the successor of Virgil. That linkage is expressed by the Pilgrim when he calls Virgil "master and author." In that way, Virgil's authority is tied to Dante's own and authenticates it. Secondly, Virgil, as a poet, had written the *Aeneid* specifically to bring about a political goal in which Dante also passionately believed: the unification of Italy. In Virgil's time, the problem was to reunify the state after the civil war. In Dante's, the problem was the disunity of Italy brought about by the corruption of the Papacy, its acquisition of wealth, and the resultant political and military struggle with the Holy Roman Empire. Both Dante's role as poet and the destiny of Italy are central themes of the *Divine Comedy* and the figure of Virgil signifies both of them as well as Dante's literal admiration for the person and the poetry of Virgil himself (Davis 1975).

Virgil, after introducing himself by alluding to his birth, its time, place and his work, reveals something else of prime significance about himself when he asks the despairing Dante, "Why do you not climb the delectable mountain, the source and cause of every happiness?" (77—78). In the light of our discussion above, that the mountain represents earthly philosophy, Virgil's description of it as the "source of every happiness" is difficult to understand. The answer lies in the fact that despite Dante the Pilgrim's passionate veneration of the figure of the Roman poet, Virgil is one of the damned, and saving grace is not available to him. For him earthly philosophy is the source of the maximum happiness he can have, having lived, as he says, "in the time of the false and lying gods" (72). Later we will see that he understands, however, what the availability of grace means to someone like Dante, but he himself cannot have it. His recommendation to Dante that climbing the mountain would result in attaining the "source of every happiness" is a sign of his own limitations. However, the implication that philosophy could be good for Dante indicates that earthly philosophy, while not sufficient for salvation, is not in itself an evil.

At this moment Dante the Pilgrim is a failure (though Dante the Poet is most assuredly not) in that he has failed to see that his fear is divinely prompted, that he has mistaken his escape from the wood as the result of his own effort, that he has failed even to climb the hill of earthly philosophy and, most important, that he has despaired of his own salvation. Virgil is the agent which Divinity will use to turn that failure around (Cassell 1976).

Virgil's importance for Dante is shown in another way which would have been clear to those familiar with the *Aeneid*, as Robert Hollander (1968) has pointed out. Many of the features which the Poet has described and the failed Pilgrim has encountered are similar to details in the first book of the *Aeneid* including the figure of the castaway, the hill and the climb up it, the beasts, the despair of the sojourner, and the messenger, among others. Modeling his first canto on Virgil's first book is an obeisance which ties Dante into the continuity of the history of poetry which is, as much as anything else, a part of God's plan. Later (101—111) Virgil will utter the first of the historical prophecies which (in addition to the salvation message of the *Divine Comedy*) are a major message of the poem leading to a vision of a unified Italy. While scholars debate the identity of the figure who will come to kill the wolf and what is meant by the birth between "felt," it is nevertheless clear that the language used to speak of this figure (called the Veltro or Hound) is similar to the language used to speak of the second coming of Christ. If the Veltro is not taken to be Christ Himself, but an earthly leader who will unify the Italian state, he clearly prefigures in his person and what he will do for Italy, what Christ in his person will do for the world. Similarly, if Virgil's *Aeneid* contributed to the unification of Italy under Augustus (the salvation of the state), Dante's *Comedy* helps complete that action by contributing to a unification of modern Italy and adding a proper understanding of Christianity (the salvation of the soul). Thus one can see that Dante's use of Virgil and the figure of the Veltro is another elaborate example of his explication of history as the evidence and working of a divine scheme in which Dante himself has a significant role.

In any case, Virgil tells Dante "to go by another way if you would escape this wild place" (91—92). By this he can only mean the way of grace as the way out of the desert of error and despair rather than by earthly means. Virgil proposes to lead Dante through "an eternal place," Hell, where the damned are tormented, to Purgatory, where the blessed are purged of the stain of sin, and there to turn Dante over to "a soul worthier than I to guide you" (122) since Virgil is forbidden to enter into Heaven itself "because I was rebellious to His law." This last is a delicate point since Dante's praise of Virgil and his exemplary behavior in the trials to come will thoroughly convince the reader of Virgil's nobility of soul and "worthiness" even as we find the object of our admiration condemned to eternal suffering by the perfectly just God. Dante, and we, must learn a very hard lesson in relation to this issue about the nature of God's Justice and how it differs from earthly conceptions of "justice."

CHAPTER 3

Canto II

The Journey Begins: The Plan of History

A few lines from the beginning of Canto II, the Poet invokes the Muses. The muses are Greek goddesses, patronesses of the arts and symbols of poetic inspiration and creative power. An obvious question is why Dante, the most Christian of poets, begins his most Christian of poems with a prayer to pagan deities? One part of the answer is a further homage to Virgil who includes several such invocations in the *Aeneid*, notably in VI, 264–67, where he asks for aid in telling of his hero Aeneas's own trip to the underworld:

> Ye gods, who hold the domain of spirits! Ye
> voiceless shades! Thou, Chaos, and thou, Phlegethon,
> ye broad, silent tracts of night! Suffer me to tell
> what I have heard; suffer me of your grace to unfold
> secrets buried in the depths and darkness of the earth!

Dante says, in the *Letter to Can Grande*, that Canto II is the true beginning of the poem and that Canto I is introductory in nature. Therefore, the invocation goes here. That the forces that are invoked are pagan rather than Christian is due to his view of history as a plan in the mind of God (Davis 1975). The Muses, false Goddesses though they may be, do not lack a positive value and a place in the plan since God's history, being the product of perfection, does not have faults or dead ends. Therefore, it is proper for Dante to appropriate the figures of pagan religion in the service of the true religion. In this way, Christianity can be said to fulfill the incomplete pagan practices. There are many such invocations in the *Comedy* and the reader should note to whom they are addressed (Hollander 1973).

Considering then that the poem proper begins here, certain numerological significances can be established. In Dante's time, numbers were important symbols. Following the mystic tradition of the Greeks wherein music and mathematics underlay the operations of the cosmos, the power of number was an important part of the structure of medieval allegory. The number three, for instance, the number of the Holy Trinity, was taken to be the symbol of things spiritual in general, while the number four, the number of Aristotle's elements (Earth, Water, Air and Fire), was the number of material things. It followed from this that the number seven, the sum of three and four, was a number encompassing the totality of all things. In a similar vein, the special significance of the number three was emphasized in its square, nine, and the number one was important because of its perfect unity which has to be understood in order to contemplate the mystery of the Trinity wherein three Godheads exist as a single being. Nine, then, the number of the Trinity squared, plus one, the number of the mystic unity, yields ten as a symbol of perfection and unity. The square of ten gives us a specially significant number, one hundred, as a magnified symbol of perfection. Such considerations are exactly those which, for centuries, gave scholastic thinking a bad reputation and which, in the hands of a small talent, become trivial. But Dante is not a trivial artist and the use of number as symbol is an integral part of the design of the *Divine Comedy* (Singleton 1965).

Both the *Purgatorio* and the *Paradiso* contain thirty-three cantos. Thirty-three is a compound of three and also the age of Christ at the time of the crucifixion and therefore important. The *Inferno* contains thirty-four cantos, perhaps because the things of Hell are furthest removed from direct connection with Christ, but also so that the entire *Comedy* will consist of one hundred cantos.

The invocation continues by invoking genius, that is, the talent of the poet and then, memory. Dante's poem, as we read it, is that work which is produced by the Poet while he is seated at his desk remembering his journey through the afterlife which, as he says, "unerring memory shall retrace" (6). Memory is the particular aspect of the poet's genius which operates in creating the poem. This point has yet another level of significance. The invocation (7 — 9) says "O memory *that wrote down what I saw,* here shall your worthiness appear!" so that we must understand that memory, in some sense, functions separately from the personality of the poet as an autonomous power and wrote down what Dante saw. In this sense, Homer, the ancient rhapsodist, claimed not to be himself the author of the epic, but rather the mouthpiece of the god. And that is the function of the invocation: to invite the power, the god, to speak through the genius of the poet. In the Greek tradition, Memory (*Mnemosyne*) is the mother of the muses by the god Zeus. Dante by appealing to Memory is making an appeal to the very source of creativity. In an age when books and reading were rarer than now, a good memory was very much prized. St. Augustine, as had the Greeks, extolled memory and called it, along with understanding and will, one of the powers of the soul which comprise the image of the Trinity in man (Yates 1966).

Dante's personification of the external power, which writes the poem, as Memory can be also understood as a function of the ancient art of rhetoric. Rhetoric was far more than simply the skill necessary to speak in public, it was an important component of ethics itself. Descending to the Middle Ages from Aristotle, the concept of the art of rhetoric was connected with the art of government, with proper personal and civic action and hence with ethical action. The rhetorician, who spoke in the assembly, spoke, using the skills of rhetoric in order to move others to proper action. In the *Divine Comedy*, Dante, as he says in the *Letter to Can Grande*, wants to move his readers to a proper course, following his example, resulting in their salvation. To do this, he wishes to impress their memory with things seen, sounds heard, with all the evidence of the senses which his poetry can convey. Hence, the "worthiness" of his own memory and its special place, noted in the invocation, in the poem. To modern minds, the surprising nature of the practice of medieval rhetoric is that frequently, rhetoricians began the practice of their art by memorizing a structure, a large building say, and then mentally connecting their ideas with the architectural details. Therefore, remembering the building and remembering the ethical points of the discourse were the same act. We can see that this process is precisely that which Dante is following. The Dark Wood, the Desert, the Hill are structural details of Dante's universe upon which significant concepts, sin, the Exodus, philosophy, are "hung." The images are made to be vivid precisely so that they will catch in the memory of the reader (Yates 1966).

With this exposition we can now return to the beginning of the canto. It is nighttime, a time of rest, and Dante prepares himself, as he says, alone, since Everyman makes this journey "alone," for the "strife, both of the journey and of the pity" (5—6). The strife of the journey is a physical strife as Dante is a living man burdened by material flesh and all the problems thereof, while the strife of the pity is intellectual and emotion, the struggle of man to accept God's judgment as it is seen in Hell itself. It is necessary, for Dante as it is for Everyman, to be able to view the unspeakable torments of damned souls and still not doubt the perfect goodness of God. The reader has already experienced the "strife of the pity" when the worthy Virgil described himself as one of those banned from Paradise since he, who lived before Christ and therefore did not have saving Grace available to him, was one of those "rebellious" to Divine law (I, 25). The working out of this paradox is central to the resolution of the strife of the pity.

Dante's protest of unworthiness (10–33) can be understood as another explication of historical process as, in it, he ties himself to the tradition of visitors to the afterlife, reveals how the history of Rome is part of the Divine scheme as city and empire prefigure the seat of the Papacy (the "seat of Peter" 1.24), as well as how Virgil's *Aeneid* functions in the context. His protest, however, "I am not Aeneas, I am not Paul; of this neither I nor others think me worthy" refers back to his sin of pride in the first canto: thinking himself too sinful, he denies to God the power to save him. Here he says, "neither I nor others think me worthy" a false claim as Divine power itself has ordained him worthy as Virgil's subsequent reply explains. Allegorically, this passage refers to the Christian belief that God desires the salvation of all men even though none of them can be, in themselves, worthy of it, but that God bestows it as a gift. Dante's eventual grasp of truths such as these are the marks of his (and the reader's) intellectual and spiritual development.

Aeneas visits Hell in Book VI of the *Aeneid* and the story of St. Paul's visit to Heaven is in II Corinthians 12. It has been suggested several times that Dante was familiar with the *Vision of St. Paul*, an apocryphal account, which tells that Paul visited Hell also (Silverstein 1936). In any case, in this passage Dante has linked himself with a pagan traveler to the afterlife, Aeneas, and with a Christian. That the Christian visitor, Paul, fulfills the action of the pagan Aeneas should be expected. Singleton (1970) points out that Dante understands the pagan account to be fiction while taking the Christian version to be fact. How does Dante's own account, then, fit into this progression (fiction to fact, pagan to Christian, remote past to more recent)? Certainly Dante's journey is to be taken every bit as seriously as Virgil's tale of Aeneas's descent and, as those who follow the Poet all the way to the Divine Vision at the end of *Paradiso* will see, it is quite possible to believe that he saw his role as analogous to that of Paul's, given that his assertion that he is not Paul is associated with the Pilgrim's error about his own unworthiness.

The issue of the poem's truthfulness is an important one to which we will return later. For right now note that we have just encountered an important motif of the work. In literature, a motif is a feature or a theme which is repeated or developed throughout. In the *Comedy*, Dante likes to frame his issues, here the error of unworthiness of the Pilgrim and the question of the truthfulness of the story, with both a pagan and a Christian example. We will see it many more times.

Dante's request for reassurance is met by Virgil's narration which introduces the figure of Beatrice who is, along with Dante and Virgil, the third major human (or once human) figure of the *Divine Comedy*. Who she is and how she functions is an understanding central to the whole poem although this is her only appearance in *Inferno* and even though Dante only hears a report of her and does not see her.

Virgil, Dante's first guide, will accompany the Pilgrim through the circles of Hell where those souls who have lost all hope of ever achieving salvation are punished. During this phase of his three-fold journey, Dante will learn how to avoid and to hate sin and he will partially overcome the "strife of the Pity." Virgil then goes with Dante on his climb up to the top of the Mountain of Purgatory where those souls who are assured of their eventual redemption undergo hardships which remove the very last stain of their earthly sin (I, 112—129). Virgil, a resident of Hell, accompanies Dante until his powers are no longer sufficient, "there shall be a soul worthier than I to guide you; with her shall I leave you at my departing" (I, 121—124). The worthier figure is to be Beatrice. In this progression, most commentators agree, the reader is to understand Virgil to represent human reason and Beatrice, Divine Love.

Dante was a close student of the works of the great scholastic philosopher St. Thomas Aquinas (1225—1274) and, in many ways, the *Divine Comedy* relies on St. Thomas's work. To Dante, as a Thomist, reason was a particular human characteristic which men did not share with the lower animals, but which those higher in the Great Chain of Being, God and the Angels, possessed in even higher degree. Reason is a special gift of God to man since reason enables man to understand his own inadequacy and the need for Divine Grace to achieve salvation. Reason alone is sufficient to avoid most sin. Virgil, who is presented in the *Divine Comedy* as the highest type of pagan man, man whose entire power rests on reason, (Grace being denied to him) is an apt symbol of reason's power. Virgil is sufficient in himself to bring Dante to the point of assured salvation, but not to achieve that salvation either for himself or for Dante. Beatrice symbolizes the power of Grace which Virgil lacks.

Why, then, is Beatrice an appropriate symbol of the Divine? The answer lies in Dante's earlier work, the *Vita Nuova* or *New Life*, in his relationship with Beatrice when she was a living person and in Dante's Thomism. As a young man, Dante came in contact with certain elements of Provençal poetry known as the poetry of Courtly Love. Courtly Love poetry was written by noble gentlemen to noble ladies. Several volumes of rules for this practice have survived. The rules consisted of simple prescriptions for proper social relationships, demeanor, and sometimes delicately spoke of the sexual fulfillment of the relationship. Part of the practice included the composition of poems which were sometimes set to music. Dante's own work in this genre is found in *La Vita Nuova*, a volume of poems addressed to and about Beatrice along with a prose narration and explanation. All such poetry is "proper," in that it expresses correct relationships between the gentleman and the noble lady, but Dante's work, following the example of some earlier courtly poets, lifts the relationship completely out of the physical in that the beauty and character of Beatrice is made to be such that it calls attention to her spiritual properties which serve as a foretaste of heavenly perfection:

> **Ladies who know about love.**
>
> Lades who know about love,
> I wish to speak of my lady with you,
> not because I think I can encompass her praise,
> but in order to give my mind relief.
> I say that thinking upon her virtue,
> Love makes himself so felt within me
> that if I did not lose courage
> my speech would make gentle people fall in love.
> Moreover, I do not wish to speak so loftily,
> that by so doing I become timid;
> rather I will speak of her gentle state,
> lightly, in regard to her,
> with you, amourous ladies and maidens.
> as it is not a thing to speak of with others.

An angel calls out within the Divine intellect
and says, "Sire, in the world there are
miraculous acts made
by a soul whose glory reflects up to here."
Heaven, which does not have any other defect,
save having her, pleads with its Lord for her,
and every saint begs for this favor.
Only Pity defends our part.
for God speaks, knowing they mean my lady:
"Blessed of me, suffer now in peace,
that your hope pleases me there
where there is one who will lose her,
and who will say in Hell: ' O ill born,
I have seen the hope of the blessed.'"

My lady is desired in highest heaven:
to you, I would make her virtues known.
I say, that a lady who desires graciousness
should go about with her, for wherever she goes,
Love casts into vile hearts a chill,
which freezes and kills their every thought
and if such a one dares to look upon her,
he becomes a noble thing or else dies.
If she finds someone who is worthy
to look upon her, that makes him virtuous,
for when she grants to him her greeting,
he becomes humble and forgets every offense.
Also God has given her an even greater favor:
No one comes to a bad end who has ever spoken with her.

Love says of her, "This mortal thing,
How can it have such beauty and purity?"
Then looks again and swears to himself
that God intended to make of her something new.
She is almost the color of pearls, to the degree
proper to a lady, but not beyond measure;
she is the best that nature can provide;.
by her example beauty is defined.
From her eyes, wherever she looks,
come forth spirits radiant with love,
which enter the yes of those they encounter,
and penetrate until they find the heart
You will see Love drawn on her face,
there where no one dare let his gaze linger.

Canzone, I know you will speak
with many ladies, when I bid you go,
and since I have brought you up
as a child of Love, young and plain,
let me advise you to ask of anyone you meet:
"Help me to go where I am sent,
to her with whose praises I am adorned."
And so that you will not have gone in vain,
do not tarry with any vulgar people.
Try, if you can, to be open
only with ladies or with courteous men,
they will send you by the quickest path.
You will find Love with our lady.
Recommend me to him as is your duty.

This poem, one of the most justly famous in the *Vita Nuova*, is addressed to cultured people who know the nature of Courtly Love. The poet having said that he does not wish to speak so exaltedly as to "enamour all mankind" proceeds to, evenso, make the extravagant claim that the perfection of his lady is such that even Heaven itself feels itself incomplete and the saints ask God to bring her there. The request is denied and the lady is left with the poet who is, however, destined to lose her, but will carry her memory as "the hope of Heaven's blesses" to Hell itself. Her very presence, but not necessarily her physical beauty as she has color, "Pearl-like, not to excess" is enough to make those with whom she comes in contact virtuous.

Beatrice Portinari lived in Florence and was about the same age as Dante. Dante encountered her many times during her lifetime, but with especially significant encounters, sometimes accompanied by visions of Beatrice or of the Figure of Love himself, at the numerological significant ages of nine and eighteen (compounds of three). From the accounts, their interactions on these occasions were very slight; only once did Beatrice greet Dante even though she knew of his devotion since his poems about her, with her identity thinly veiled, were circulated to noble ladies by Dante himself. Beatrice died when Dante was twenty-five and Dante experienced a vision of her at the age of twenty-seven (another compound of three). Dante later married, apparently happily, although he had to leave his wife behind when he went into exile. Even so, Beatrice remained for Dante the symbol of what love implied and his continued devotion to her can be seen as a particular kind of Christian discipline which Dante exercised for the good of his own soul and which he exhibits in the *Divine Comedy* as an example to all. St. Thomas Aquinas says in the *Summa Contra Gentiles* (book one) that the subjects of sentences greatly affect the meanings of their predicates. Specifically, to say that "Socrates is wise" is one thing, but to say that "God is wise" is quite another, since God cannot be said to be "wise" in the same sense as is Socrates. Aquinas explains that the two uses of the term "wise" are only analogically equivalent. Earthly wisdom, while possessing some of the characteristics of heavenly wisdom does not possess all of them (Kenny 1980). Earthly wisdom is a pale reflection of the true glory of God's wisdom which, however, exists only in and of God. Similarly, earthly love and heavenly love are only analogically related. Earthly love, for instance, is constantly muddled by material concerns: lust, procreation and the demands of the flesh. Heavenly love, on the other hand, is purely spiritual. Dante's love for Beatrice, his Courtly Love, wherein he understands "court" as the court of Heaven, is a disciplined attempt to experience an earthly love as close to heavenly love as is humanly possible. Beatrice is a symbol, an analogy, of what love can be as it is experienced in the mind of God.

In Canto II of the *Inferno* this can be seen in the language of the conversation between Beatrice and Virgil (56 ff.). It is a conversation of great courtesy, all the more striking since it takes place between one of God's elect and one of the damned. It is filled with sincere compliments which note the virtues of each of the participants. This conversation is in the language of Courtly Love as Dante had developed it. In other places in the *Inferno* the reader will hear it again as well as language which contrasts strongly with it.

Beatrice asks Virgil, in the most courteous of terms, to aid Dante who is her friend, but not Fortune's (personified). Beatrice came "late" (65) to help Dante not in the sense that it is too late to save him, but rather in the sense that the memory of her example, which should have been enough foretaste of the glories of Heaven to keep Dante on the "straight path," has faded since he is "so full of sleep." The sleep of reason needs to be interrupted so that her transcendent example can function for Dante as it should. The full expression of this matter occurs in *Purgatorio* XXX.

Beatrice has come directly from Heaven and a particular part of Heaven, "that circles least" (78). Her presence at the mouth of Hell is difficult for even Virgil to understand. She says that she is not afraid of Hell

(87), that Virgil's suffering "does not touch" her. Yet earlier (71—72), that she longs to return from whence she came and that further, she is moved by love.

This passage, beginning "I am Beatrice" (70) through "no flame of this burning assails me" (93) needs careful attention in order to understand the workings of Dante's poem. The description of Beatrice presented here is significant because it points to Thomas Aquinas's interpretation of Aristotle's philosophy and the importance of Aristotle's physics. The reader should bear with the following explanation, as lengthy as it is, since Aquinas and Aristotle have so much to do with Dante's vision.

Thomas Aquinas believed that it was possible to unite reason and the act of faith. While faith, belief in things outside the evidence of the senses, and reason, that which we know or can deduce on the evidence of our senses, are clearly different ways of knowing, they can be, given the necessary perfection and unity of God's universe, in no way contradictory. Such contradictions as may be perceived are simply apparent and are caused by the failure of fallible human beings to see things from God's perspective. An example of such an apparent contradiction is the condemnation of the virtuous Virgil to an eternity in Hell as is the entire question of the "strife of the pity."

As faith and reason are united in the mind of God, so too are other seemingly contradictory things. We have already noted how Dante ties himself into a stream of history that flows through the ancients, the Roman Empire and Virgil, the establishment of the Papacy and the political woes of Italy to Dante himself. In Thomistic thought, far from being confused and muddled, history is two great streams, one Hebrew and the other Greek, which flow together, merge in the Roman Empire and reach their crest in the Papacy and the Church. To the Thomists, the contribution of the Greeks, reason and philosophy, were as necessary in God's scheme as the theological strand which came from the Hebrews. The two are joined when St. Paul brings Christianity to the Greeks. What this leads to is Thomas's conviction that it is never possible to sacrifice a reasonable truth on the altar of a truth of faith or *vice versa*. Given enough understanding, a reconciliation was always possible. All of history was a unity, so too was all that humans "knew" either by faith or reason.

Others in the Church disputed this and some, notably William of Ockham and the Franciscan order, were always willing to prefer faith over reason. If necessary, to deny validity to historical figures, especially Greek historical figures, whose reasonable "science" seemed sometimes to contradict the articles of faith. Beginning about 1200 much of what the West possesses of the works of Aristotle began to be recovered from Arab sources. Many in the church were suspicious of these since they immediately posed a challenge to orthodox thought. St. Thomas's success in his monumental defense of Aristotle in the *Summa Theologica* is the intellectual engine which drives the High Middle Ages when the great cathedrals were built and Dante's great poem written.

In the *Physics*, Aristotle has it that all matter in the universe consists of four elements: earth, water, air and fire and that each of these elements had its own proper place in the cosmos. Earth, being the heaviest element had its proper place at the "bottom" or center of the universe. Water lays on top of Earth surmounted by air. The proper place of fire is at the outermost circumference of air and this can be seen by the fact that fire flickers upward through air in a motion towards its proper place. In fact, the upward motion of fire is its "proper" motion. Similarly, water can be observed falling as rain in its proper motion or welling up from springs, another motion proper to it, to reach its proper place on top of Earth. Please notice that in these examples the proper motion of the elements is described as an up or down motion in relation to the center of the earth. Heavenly bodies, Aristotle thought, obeyed an entirely different set of rules so that their proper motion was not straight, but circular as the stars and planets appear to move in great circles about the earth.

To Aristotle, an element in motion (or an object, since all objects were made up of elements) was either moving properly, towards its proper place, or "violently," away from it. For instance, a stone ("earth") can be thrown upward, a violent motion against the natural tendency of the object, but its natural inclination will eventually assert itself and it will return to motion towards the center of the earth.

Beatrice's statement that she "comes from a place to which I long to return" is far more than a statement of nostalgia or preference, though certainly on one level of meaning she would rather be in Heaven than in Hell. She says, "I am made such by God, of his grace, that your suffering does not touch me, and no flame of this burning assails me" (91 — 93). That is, by the grace of God, her proper place is in Heaven, her visit to Hell is a "violent" motion against her God-given tendencies, and she will naturally return to "the Heaven which circles least." (At this point in this explanation the reader should know that the full truth here is more complex yet. Beatrice is *simultaneously*, both in Hell and in Heaven, contemplating the Divine Being of God, but this will not become understandable until the conclusion of the *Paradiso*). This, of course, is why she does not fear Hell and why she is not moved by Virgil's suffering. She is so made by God himself to know that she can never be made to suffer Hell and her enlightenment makes her understand the justice of Virgil's punishment.

One final point here. Beatrice, she says, is moved by love (72). Thomas's attempt to reconcile the physics of Aristotle with Christian Doctrine meant finding the theological significance of Aristotle's rationalizations. The bald fact of nature, say the falling stone, could not merely be a bald fact as it had, somehow, to point to the divine scheme. Here we have the root of Dante's assertion (in *Convivio*) that all things have a literal, allegorical, moral and anagogic meaning. God's love, to the Thomists, was the force in the universe which gave proper motion to all objects. All things in the universe felt the influence of love, but some things felt it more than others. A stone, being made of hard earth, feels the pull of God's love very little, thus it falls away towards the center of the earth. Beatrice, feeling the pull of God's love very much has a proper motion towards God, although love can move her on a "violent" expedition towards Dante. By connecting the theological notion of Divine Love, which can never be understood in purely rational terms. To Aristotle's theory of elements, which is based on sense perceptions, Thomism demonstrated the unity of faith and reason and the utility and place of pagan authorities in God's divine plan.

Beatrice's "violent" movement towards Dante is given her by the two ladies of Heaven: the "gracious lady" (94) and "Lucy, foe of every cruelty" (101). The "gracious lady" can be taken to be the Virgin Mary who intercedes with God for sinners and for whom "that stern judgment is broken thereabove" (96). That this interpretation is correct is indicated in *Paradiso* and also by the fact that the Virgin is spoken of in connection with Beatrice in the *Vita Nuova*. Lucy, to whom Dante is "your faithful one" (98) is a saint especially concerned with vision and vision is concerned with light which, as we have seen in the case of the light on the little hill of Canto I, is a symbol of knowledge. Here, it is that knowledge which Dante needs to begin his purification. Lucy is sent to Beatrice, seated with Rachel, symbol of wisdom, and Beatrice, as symbol of divine love is sent to Virgil, who comes to Dante. This whole movement is a progression from the highest status a purely human figure, Mary, has ever reached down through a chain of being and excellence to Dante. What is imparted through the chain is grace, that which (91) makes Beatrice untouched by the suffering of Virgil in Hell. Grace is a very technical concept in Roman Christianity and the reader will learn much more about it in *Purgatorio*. Here it is sufficient that grace is that free, unearned gift of God which permits a person to become better (sanctifying grace) and to achieve salvation (actual grace). Dante's sources of the doctrine of grace come from St. Thomas who demonstrates the categories of grace in *Summa Theologica* and St. Augustine who ties grace to the platonic notion of illumination in *De Magistro* or "the Teacher."

Dante, then, is changed by grace, a force outside himself with which he cooperates by choosing to undergo the strife of both the journey and the pity which he mistakenly thought himself to confront alone at the beginning of the canto.

CHAPTER 4

Canto III

The River Crossing: God's Justice and Aristotelian "Place"

The transition between Canto II and Canto III is abrupt and ambiguous. Dante enters "along the deep and savage way" concluding Canto II, and at the beginning of Canto III is confronted with the enigma of the inscription that we do not know is an inscription until he and we have finished reading it (Elwert 1971). In contrast, the transition between Cantos I and II is a smooth continuation broken only by Dante's meditation on the strife of the journey and the pity and the invocation to the Muses. It is well to notice how the Poet makes these transitions since through them he unites separate cantos into groups, leaves them disjunctive from their neighbors, or in other ways arranges things in order to influence the ways in which the reader experiences Hell. Here the fragmentary and confused nature of the experience which the Pilgrim (and the reader) is undergoing is both produced and symbolized by the way Dante moves from one canto to another.

The words of the inscription are striking and, indeed, they are some of the most memorable in the *Comedy*. A good deal of medieval theology lies behind them and they foreshadow some important messages of the poem. First of all, from the first line we can see that Hell is depicted as a city (called Dis, after the similar city in *Aeneid*). In structure it is like a medieval Italian city with a large outskirt. The outskirt itself is circumscribed by a high wall with towers at the gate upon which the inscription is written. "Through Me," continue the words, "You Enter Eternal Grief." There is a meaning here likely to be overlooked by anyone not familiar with the tradition which gives it birth. Dante's Hell is a state of the afterlife from which no condemned soul can hope to escape and which can be said in no way to improve or elevate the demeaned soul which finds itself in it. The God of Dante's Christianity will not relent, the souls will not be allowed to repent, and their state will only change to become even more horrible as time comes to an end. Dante the Poet fully recognizes this and Dante the Pilgrim will come both to understand it and to accept it as divine justice. Others in the course of western history have been unable to do so, notably certain seventeenth century theologians and preachers to whom the notion of a "useless" Hell (in the sense that it is static and does the souls of the damned no good) could not be made to square with the concept of infinite mercy (Walker 1964). This paradox lead them to doubt the concept of divine retribution altogether. Indeed, the doctrine of Hell has been one of Christianity's most cumbersome theological concepts. In Dante's time, the difficulty was avoided, at least in part, by linking the notion of a static punishment to the question of the existence of free will: "Justice Moved My High Maker" continues the inscription, justice, presumably, for the angels who rebelled with the highest Seraphim, Lucifer, and who were for that reason cast out of Heaven into the pit. This was before the creation of man and the sin of Adam, since before Hell nothing was created "if not eternal." (8). Even so, the certainty of the damnation of some portion of mankind would have been foreknown to God and the difficult question is how such foreknowledge can excuse God of the blame for the damnation of individual souls since foreknowledge aligned with infinite power implies the ability to change the fate of those who otherwise would be damned.

The solution of Dante's age to the problem of a "guilty God" begins with the assertion that the quality which we ordinarily call evil is not a thing in itself, but rather is simply a lack of good, a negative rather than a positive thing. The principle of plenitude requires that God create all possible things. It follows then that some men will possess less of the good than others, or, as we ordinarily speak, be more evil. To cause them not to be created, says St. Thomas, would create a defect in the Chain of Being and this cannot be since it would be a violation of the very essence of God. If men were created without the ability to sin (without free will) they would, in the words of St. Augustine, "be more like stones than angels." Hell is that aspect of the universe that makes man's choices significant. Furthermore, evil is necessary for the realization of some good. The zebra must die in agony to feed the lion and the unjust man must exist in order that the justice of the benevolent can express itself against him. Divine Providence does not operate in order to eliminate evil, but to see to it that such evil that exists functions to some good end. Hell, in one sense, exists so that Dante can see it and, having seen it and its horrors, can tell others and thereby move them towards good.

When Dante complains of difficulty in understanding the inscription, Virgil responds as a good teacher would, not by explanation, but by directing his pupil to the concept that is the key to understanding: "We have come to the place where I told you you will see the wretched people who have lost the good of intellect." The good of intellect is reason, a good that only the highest creatures, man, the Angels and God himself, have. Reason alone is enough to show man that he should seek God. Virgil's statement applies not only to the sinners Dante is about to encounter, but to all the souls in Hell although Dante the Pilgrim does not as yet know that. Allegorically, Virgil is human reason and his encouraging look and comforting touch symbolizes the sufficiency of the power of reason to avoid the damnation of the soul.

Dante is suddenly surrounded with a whirlwind of swirling souls whose motion echoes the nature of their sin and the confusion of Dante's mind (31). It is characteristic of Dante's vision of punishment that the sufferings of the damned should in some way mirror the nature of the sin that is the cause of the punishment. (The way in which the punishment mirrors the sin is called the *contrapasso*, Italian for "retribution.") Here, those individuals, the indifferent, whose lives stood for nothing, are punished by a meaningless pursuit of a banner and stinging insects. Their deeper punishment however, is that they have no place in Hell. They are denied conformity to the laws of nature which all other souls in Hell obey in that they cannot descend to their "proper" place as Aristotelian physics decreed that all substances must. This image will be made clear in Canto V where the pilgrim will see the souls of the damned examined and placed in the spot to which their sin has conditioned their soul. Briefly, the idea is an adaptation of Aristotelian physics to theological ends: as each element in the universe has a proper place, so each soul comes to conform to a proper station in the afterlife. These particular souls, since they were indeterminate in their lives, are punished by denial of any place at all—lest, says Virgil, "the wicked have some glory over them." This last is a fine point as the reader will see. In spite of the fact that the damned are without hope of the vision of God, nevertheless some of them, Farinata, Brunetto and Ulysses for instance, seem to be admirable figures (Glickman 1968). Sometimes because of their virtues in spite of their sins, sometimes because of their defiance or audacity. In any case, some of these souls are real individuals whereas the indifferent were nothing in their lives and must be kept away from those who are punished for definite actions so that their despicable status not lend comfort to other sinners.

Included in these forlorn ranks is "that base band of Angels neither rebellious nor faithful to God." Dante now taps a tradition which, while it is Christian, lies outside the scope of theology itself and is rather in the range of folk tale or legend. Dante is perfectly willing to use such material for his purposes as he similarly utilizes elements of pagan mythology. The reference here is to the story of the fall of Satan which, according to the story, took place in the very instance of the creation of the angels. Satan's sin was the sin of pride, which, being the first sin, is in some sense the origin of all sin implying the primacy of the sense of self rather than "other directedness" (towards God) which is the correct orientation of the personality.

That Satan, whose original name was Lucifer (Bright or Shining One, his name becomes an irony) could and would sin is necessary for the preservation of the notion of free will. In the war in Heaven some angels stood for God while others sided with Satan and fell with him. The indifferent angels are the ones Dante sees here. The others and Satan himself will be found later.

Virgil, in the spirit of ignoring those properly ignored, urges Dante to pass on (51). Dante does, but not before mentioning that he recognized the "shade of him who from cowardice made the great refusal" (60). With this line Dante again takes up the thread of the great historical and artistic synthesis which he began by linking himself to Virgil and the history of Christianity to the history of Rome. As Virgil's *Aeneid* was composed to heal the rifts left by the civil war, so too does Dante hope his poem will correct the disorganization of the Italian state. Dante's perception is that the ills of the state are caused by the Papacy's wealth and political ambition neither of which was the Papacy's proper concern. He who "made the great refusal" was Pope Celestine V who renounced the Papacy out of concern for his own soul (again a form of the sin of pride) and cleared the way for the election of Boniface VIII who was for Dante the personification of Papal corruption as the continued references to this Pope in *Inferno* show.

Next the Pilgrim's attention is caught by a crowd of people at the shore of the first of the three rivers of Hell, Acheron. The Acheron as a river of Hell or Hades is mentioned both in Book X of Homer's *Odyssey* and in Book VI of Virgil's *Aeneid*. Dante's careful use of Virgil as authority is particularly striking here as in the *Aeneid* (VI, 305 — 316) Virgil describes Aeneas' view of the same scene thus:

> Hither rushed all the throng, streaming to the banks; mothers and men and bodies of high-souled heroes, their life now done, boys and unwedded girls, and sons placed on the pyre before their fathers' eyes; thick as the leaves of the forest that at autumn's first frost dropping fall, and thick as the birds that from the seething deep flock shoreward, when the chill of the year drives them overseas and sends them into sunny lands. They stood, pleading to be the first ferried across, and stretched out hands in yearning for the farther shore. But the surly boatman takes now these, now those, while others he thrusts apart, back from the brink.

Dante appropriates both the river and the boatman who selects and directs the souls as well as the crowd driven by their desire to cross. He acknowledges his debt to Virgil by echoing the autumn and bird similes. However, certain features are his own and Christianize these pagan images. First of all, Dante makes it clear that his Hell is a place of punishment. To Virgil, the purpose of Hades is vague since nearly everyone, heroes and villains alike, go there though it is certainly an unpleasant place. Secondly, Dante makes the desire of the souls to cross the river conform to the Aristotelian ideas of proper place, since the souls are made, by Divine Justice, to desire their fate even as they fear it so much that they curse "God, their parents, the human race, the place, the time, the seed of their begetting and of their birth" (103 — 105). In Virgil, the unburied are rejected by Charon; in Dante, only Dante himself, since he is living, is unselected. Charon is overruled when Virgil rebukes him.

Readers should note that the whole Charon episode (a utilization of pagan myth to parallel the use of the Christian myth of the fallen angels) keeps alive the water motive associated with baptism which began in Canto I. As Charon says to Dante, "A lighter bark must carry you." A statement which is indeed prophetic of the boat image of the beginning of *Paradiso*.

One other issue remains. When Dante asks the reasonable question about the identity of the souls on the river bank in 72 — 75, Virgil's reply leads Dante to fear that he has been rebuked. The reader has no more insight into this matter than does the Pilgrim. Virgil's rebuke, if that's what it is, emphasizes the strangeness of the ground upon which we stand.

CHAPTER 5

Canto IV

Limbo: The Strife of the Pity
and Dante's Bibliography

The transition from Canto III is made when Dante suddenly awakes from his swoon. Dante twice faints during the first part of the *Inferno*, both times at moments of great intensity of feeling as here when he is startled by the sounds and strange sights of Hell. As his faint is violent, so is his awakening which is caused by a great thunderclap. On the literal level, the swoon serves to get the reader from one location, the ferry crossing over Acheron, to another, Limbo. One should always look for the allegory, however, and here it seems that Dante faints when he is not strong enough for that which he faces. Later, confronted by greater horrors and suffering, the Pilgrim does not faint and the fact that he does not do so should be taken as a sign of his increasing strength in the face of sin. In this case, we can see that the period of unconsciousness has done the Pilgrim good since, as he says, his eyes are rested (4). Again, the allegory is important as eyes are the organ of sense related to light, which signifies reason and knowledge. These are the two characteristics Dante's trip through Hell is intended to strengthen. His reason and analytic abilities restored, Dante is ready to face the next obstacle, but looking down, is unable to make out anything; a sign, presumably, that he is still very far from being able to cope with Hell by himself. Virgil suggests that he lead Dante onward and as he does, Dante sees Virgil's pallor of pity which he mistakes for fear. With this we take up once again the "strife of the pity" which we have already seen in connection with Virgil's fate, but now the issue becomes acute for this is Limbo, the location in the afterlife which is proper to the soul of Virgil.

The sources of the tradition of Limbo are found in the apocryphal Gospel of Nicodemus. (Apocryphal sources are works of doubtful authenticity which are not accepted as a part of the Bible. They can, however, be a source of Christian folklore as here.) Traditional thinking has it that there are two limbos, one for the souls of unbaptized children and the other for the virtuous pagans. Neither group is punished; their unhappiness, if there is any, caused only by their knowledge that they will eternally miss the supernatural joys of Heaven. St. Thomas Aquinas thought that the unbaptized children, unable to conceive of supernatural joy, would exist in a state of full natural joy. According to Nicodemus, at the time of Christ's crucifixion, Christ descended to Hell and there freed the souls of all those virtuous people who lived before the grace of baptism was made available. This event is known as the Harrowing of Hell. Dante's version is rather different in that he leaves some obviously virtuous people in Limbo in order to heighten the incomprehensibility of the fate of souls such as Virgil and the difficulty of the strife of the pity. (For a full discussion of the traditions of Limbo in relation to Dante's work see Iannucci 1980.)

Grace, in traditional Catholicism, is that essential goodness released into the world by Christ's crucifixion which was performed to atone for the sin of Adam which, up to the time of the Crucifixion, had damned all souls. Christ's sacrifice provides enough grace to save all of mankind although the acts of the martyr saints adds to the total amount of grace in the universe. Grace operates in two ways. First, since no one can ever of themselves be worthy of salvation, grace works to make them worthy by removing the guilt or original sin. This graceful action is understood as a free act of God Himself which is not merited in any sense by the individual. The other function of grace, broadly speaking, erases the penalty for sins other than original sin and moves the believer to participate in good works. It is the first sense which is most important here although in this whole process Dante is losing the stain of his own sin and is, by making his example available, participating in the salvation of others which is the most important type of good work. The question to be asked about those in Limbo is why God has not acted to make them worthy of salvation if they are truly virtuous.

How, if man is unworthy of grace, can he come to possess it? The answer is by the authority of the Church delegated, according to tradition, to the Apostle Peter by Christ himself. St. Peter was believed to be the first pope at Rome and the power of dispensing grace was passed by him, through the process of apostolic succession, to succeeding popes. The power of the papacy to dispense grace works through the agency of the sacraments which are imitations of acts which Christ himself performed. In the long history of the Church the exact number of sacraments has varied from time to time, but in general there are seven, many of which are important in the *Divine Comedy*. The traditional seven are: baptism, confirmation, the Eucharist (Lord's Supper), penance, holy orders, marriage and extreme unction (final blessing of the dying). Of these, the one at issue here is baptism in which the anointing of the (usually infant) individual with water removes the guilt which the individual bears as a consequence of the sin of Adam. The fact that the infant can neither understand nor will the sacrament is symbolic of the belief that the grace which is given by the action is a free, unmerited gift of God. Christ himself was baptized by St. John thus instituting this sacrament. The reader should remember that the sacrament of baptism has already been alluded to in the water simile of the first canto and in the crossing of Acheron, but that it has not been fulfilled, as yet, for Dante the Pilgrim. It will not be completed for the Pilgrim until he has exited Hell.

In the traditional version of the Harrowing of Hell, Christ descended, while his body was still in the tomb, and freed all the virtuous souls found in Limbo. In Dante's version many virtuous souls are left in Limbo and will remain there for eternity. Virgil is one of these and he explains (33−42) that the souls are there because they lacked baptism "the portal of the faith" because they lived before Christianity. "For no other fault, we are lost." Dante, caught by the paradox (46−50) asks if anyone has escaped and achieved Heaven. He asks, he says, "wishing to be assured of the faith that conquers every error." A reasonable interpretation of this is that the Pilgrim wishes to be reassured of the Justice of God, that is, that the real question which Dante is asking is, "How can a God who would arrange things so be considered good?" Virgil, "who understood my covert speech," replies with the story of the Harrowing of Hell, but in Dante's version in which only a select few of the virtuous pagans and prechristian Jews, the principle of selection being obscure, are removed. Only Hebrews are mentioned by name, but Virgil does indicate that "many others" were included, some of whom later information will reveal to be pagans. The purpose of this, of course, is to point up "the strife of the pity." One should also notice that Dante here has explicitly invited the reader to interpret the text deeply by his reference to "covert speech" which tells us that something is hidden here. Necessarily hidden, since an open suggestion that God is unjust is not only impossible, but blasphemous. Yet, this dangerous thought is exactly what must be faced. The open indication of hidden meaning is a technique to be used again at similarly critical points.

As Dante and Virgil proceed, through so many souls that they are like "a wood of thronging spirits," they come upon a place set off from the rest of Limbo and marked by a fire overcoming some of the darkness (68—69). Fire, of course, is knowledge and that it pushes back the darkness is significant. Dante knows the souls so separated are honorable and inquires of Virgil "who honors science and art" (74, science and art are those things which can be mastered by human reason without the aid of grace) why they are separated. The reply takes up again the issue of personal fame which the poem has touched before (notably in Canto I, 87—88 and in the description of the indecisive who are such nonentities that no one knows their names in Canto III). Here the fame which these souls possess in the world above earns them a special location in limbo. As we proceed we will see that the issue of fame is important to those souls in Hell who are not completely depraved and certainly important to Dante himself. The reoccurring references to fame make it one of the most important motifs of the *Inferno*. Dante is here interested in "honored fame" (76) equated with morality rather than the notoriety of villains.

Dante's acknowledgement of his reception into the company of great poets with no protestations of unworthiness like those of Canto II is seen by some scholars as further evidence of his sinful pride. I do not believe that this is the case, however, for while Dante protested that he was neither Aeneas nor Paul, he earlier claimed (I, 85—87) that his study of Virgil's poetry has done him honor. Dante is not "immodest" about his poetic powers, he is supremely confident in them. Indeed, as we will discover, the "truthfulness" of the poem is inextricably linked to the fact that Dante is a great poet and knows it. Dante specifically excludes the reader from the discussion which the company of poets share, yet the discussion takes them "onward to the light" (103). That the reader is excluded from the important conversations of *Inferno*, indicates, I presume, the secret and sacred nature of the art of poetry.

The "noble castle" which the poets now enter is surrounded by seven walls, indicative perhaps of the seven liberal arts (grammar, logic, rhetoric, arithmetic, geometry, astronomy, music) which are capable of being understood by reason alone, and by a stream which Dante and Virgil nevertheless manage to cross somehow on "solid ground" (110). Whatever the allegory may be here, the literal sense is again that this division of Limbo is set off from the rest as the abode of those ancient people whose fame reflects their virtue (Guzzardo 1979). The list of individuals in the meadow are a summary, mixing mythology with fact, of Dante's view of history. The movement from Electra (mother of the founder of Troy) through "falcon-eyed Caesar armed" (Julius) to Cornelia summarizes the history of Rome. Next he mentions Saladin the "good Muslim" who stands for the world outside Greece and Rome, Hebrews having been mentioned already in the list of those released by the Harrowing of Hell.

So far Dante has listed Hebrew patriarchs, great poets, warriors (all Trojan or Roman, no Greeks). He now notes all the philosophers, Greeks, Romans and Arab, beginning with "Master of those who know" (131), that is Aristotle, through Averroes who wrote the Arabic commentaries on Aristotle. The importance of all these lists of names goes beyond the requirements of the narrative of the poem. The individuals listed in Limbo are those pagan and prechristian figures most important in Dante's vision of the past. In a way, the names here, especially those of poets and philosophers and other writers, function much like the bibliography of a modern work. As we will repeatedly see as we accompany the Pilgrim on his quest, knowing the works of these figures will help us to unlock *Inferno's* meanings. Here Dante has given us a list of sources of which we should be aware as we approach his poem.

From this separate place, set off by honor and wisdom and lit by the flame of knowledge, Dante and Virgil now turn to "a part where there is naught that shines."

CHAPTER 6

Canto V

Francesca: The Sin of Love
and the Pilgrim's Failure

Canto V of *Inferno* is one of the very most important cantos of the entire *Divine Comedy*. It has at least four functions: First, the story of Paolo and Francesca continues the problem of the strife of the pity which began with the question of Virgil's fate earlier in the poem. It is typical of Dante to put important issues in both a pagan (that is Virgil) and a Christian (Francesca) frame. The device both appeals to the medieval sense of completeness (related to plenitude) and emphasizes Dante's theory of history which mandates the necessary existence of both the Christian era and its pagan past. Second, the canto raises two new motives (issues which will occur again in the poem). One is the entire question of the corruption of language and its contribution to human sinfulness and misery. Dante was critically aware of the destructive potential that exists in the misuse of language and raises the issue several times in *Inferno*. Each time he does so there is some sort of reference that refers the reader's memory back to Francesca's narration. The other is the issue of figures who, in a sense, can be thought of as enemies of God's plan of history, people who either act against the Children of God, the Hebrews, or Christ or who can be seen as opponents of the Roman Empire or the Trojans whom the Romans considered to be their ancestors. Third, the structure of the incident concerning Paolo and Francesca corresponds to certain parallel structures which are used later in the poem to define the stages of the Pilgrim's progress through Hell. Fourth, the canto, concerned with lust as the sin most similar to love, alludes to the practice of courtly love, Dante's involvement in it, and his relationship to Beatrice. Thus the canto carries a heavy structural and conceptual burden. Moreover, it is one of the most appealingly human stories in all of *Inferno* and that emphasizes its importance.

The movement of the opening of the canto, to "a smaller circle of so much greater pain," is a part of the gravity and weight motif of the poem. As the Pilgrim descends, the spirits he encounters become more and more substantial; things, so to speak, become concentrated. Spiritual substance becomes more like matter (Paolo and Francesca are light and blown by the wind, but there is far more "substance" to them than to the indecisive of Canto III) and the space of Hell becomes crowded. The nature of the sins becomes worse and the punishments harsher. Thus circle two is "a smaller circle of much greater pain." It should be noted that Hell is dark and noisy (25—30) as darkness is the opposite of Heaven's light and the noise contrasts with the divine melodies of Paradise (Musa 1974).

Dante's weight metaphor ultimately derives from Aristotle's theory of proper place in the universe which was discussed in Chapter I. The "weight" of the sinner's soul pulls it downward to its proper location in Hell. Dante symbolizes this action by the figure of Minos who assigns the soul to its place after each one's eager confession. The willingness of the confession suggests, as did the similar crowding around Charon's ferry, that sinners will their own punishment and place in Hell. Like all of Dante's monsters, Minos is depicted in such a way as to make his figure memorable. Monsters and demons are an important element of the place memory system of the *Inferno* (which Dante borrowed from the art of rhetoric) functioning in their extreme individuality as signposts in the development of the structure of the whole poem. Like many of the other demons Minos is part human, part beast which symbolizes that human sinfulness has its roots in the bestial part of our nature. Minos' birth was unnatural; Father Zeus in the form of a bull raped Mother Europa. In classical mythology Minos was the wise judge and king of Crete. Virgil employs him as the judge of the dead in *Aeneid*. Here, Minos does not seem to be evil rather he is a kind of functionary who carries out the will of God (in concord with his classical role as a "wise judge"). In fact, Minos' advice to the Pilgrim (16—20) is absolutely accurate and it is difficult to read any intent to deceive in it: "Watch where you go once you have entered here, and to whom you turn," says Minos. Considering that Dante is about to turn to Francesca such could well be considered good advice since she will certainly be one of Dante's (and our) most difficult obstacles. Note that Virgil's rebuke of Minos does not imply that Minos' statement is untrue, merely that such affairs are not his business. "It is his fate to enter every door (22)," which might be understood that it is the Pilgrim's fate to make every error.

The souls of the carnal swirl subject to the winds of Hell as they were subject to the winds of their passion while alive. (The *contrapasso* of the sin.) The two bird images of 39 — 48 which describe the movement of the souls in general are augmented by those in 82 — 84 which describe the movement of the particular souls of Paolo and Francesca. The three birds which are mentioned, starlings, cranes and doves, have particular, if sometimes contradictory, meanings in the system of medieval symbols. Starlings, then as today, were considered unattractive. They are boisterous, they foul whatever they approach and they were thought to steal into other birds' nests (as in an allegorical sense adulterers do). Cranes, while admired for their discipline were said, in their old age, to lament their past sins. Some varieties of dove (the turtle dove) were symbols of faithfulness, others (the pigeon) were symbols of lust. Here Dante refers to *coloumbe* or pigeons (Ryan 1977).

The guide Virgil points out some of the notable figures of this circle. The sequence of identifications is important: Semiramis, Dido, Cleopatra, Helen, Achilles, Paris and Tristan. Of these, Semiramis (Ryan 1977, Shapiro 1975) indicates that as well as being about lust, this canto is about the willful corruption of language. Semiramis "was Empress of many tongues," that is, she was Empress of Babylon. Babylon was an ancient empire made up of many peoples who spoke diverse languages. Its very name conjures up corruption and license since that is the way it was consistently portrayed in the Bible and in Christian symbolism. The name Babylon is related to the word "babel," meaningless speech, and the name of the spot where the Tower of Babel, the immediate cause of incomprehensible language, was built. Semiramis is supposed to have wanted to marry one of her own children. Reasonably such acts were illicit even in Babylon. Semiramis changed the laws so that relations between parent and child were legal. Hence, "She made lust licit in her law" (57). This last turns on a pun. The line in the original reads "che libito fe' licito in sua legge". The word "licit" *(licito)* differs in only one letter from the word "lust" *(libito)*. Semiramis twists language in an attempt to make her own desires legal. Of course, Semiramis' saying that abominable practices were right does not make them so anymore than anyone who corrupts language in such a way really avoids the issue of morality. In addition to her associations with the sin of lust and the corruption of language, Semiramis can logically be considered a symbol of the enemies of the Children of God, the Hebrews, since in the Old Testament Babylon is the place of captivity for the Children of God. It is this role as nemesis of God's plan that ties Semiramis to the next figure and into Dante's structural concerns.

The next figure is not named directly, but referred to as "she who broke faith to the ashes of Sichaeus" which identifies her as Dido of Carthage from Virgil's *Aeneid*. If Semiramis is a Babylonian and opposed to the Children of God and thus, in a sense, an Old Testament figure, then Dido is a female figure opposed to Aeneas and thus to the Roman Empire. This coupling of images is similar to the linking of the figures of Paolo and Francesca (Christian) with Virgil (pagan) in the symbolism of the war of the pity and other such pagan-Christian frames. Dido was the mythological queen of Carthage who, out of her lust, tried to delay Aeneas on his holy mission to found Rome. She was in this way "faithless to the ashes of Sichaeus," her dead husband, to whom she had vowed to be true. She falls by her own curse which Virgil has her speak in *Aeneid* (Book IV, 24−29):

> "may earth yawn for me to its depths, or may
> the Almighty Father hurl me with his bolt to the
> shades-the pale shades and abysmal night of
> Erebus-before, O Shame, I violate thee or break
> thy laws! He, [Sichaeus] who first linked me to himself, has
> taken away my heart; may he keep it with him, and
> guard it in the grave!"

Cleopatra's successive affairs with Caesar and Mark Anthony lead to the civil war that split apart the Empire. Therefore, she is guilty not only of lust, but also of opposing God's plan in history which calls for a unified Roman Empire to be in place to receive Christianity. Helen, the female cause of the Trojan war, moves the scene back to the beginning of Virgil's tale and Aeneas' quest as do Achilles and Paris. The great Greek warrior Achilles was the greatest foe of the Trojans and Paris was the Trojan whose lust for Helen led to the war and the fall of Troy. The list of those named is completed by Tristan, seemingly an anomaly, since his love for Isolde has nothing to do with Troy, Rome, Classical antiquity and only marginally with Christianity. In the version of the legend of Tristan and Isolde that Dante probably knew, Tristan the knight and Isolde the Queen, in spite of an intense struggle not to do so, commit adultery and betray King Mark who is Tristan's Uncle and Isolde's husband. In the story of Paolo and Francesca which is to follow, Paolo is the brother of Francesca's husband (Musa 1974).

All of the figures in the list are there because (with the exception of Achilles) they are common figures of lust in medieval literature and because they illustrate issues important to Dante: corruption of language, opposition to the people of God or the Trojan or Roman cause and hence God's scheme of history, or the corruption of a pure love gone wrong. Achilles, not a common figure of lust, earns his place in Dante's vision because of his political role as an enemy of the Trojans. In the versions of the Achilles story which Dante most likely knew, Achilles was killed by Paris at a tryst with Polyxena with whom he was in love. Hence, he "fought at the last with love" (66 Singleton 1974).

No figure mentioned by Dante in the whole of the *Comedy* should be taken for granted as the poet does not name names just to fill space. The *Comedy* is always urging its readers to see resemblances and to make associations which unfold the poetry. Here, certain suggestions might be made. In some ways, both Tristan and Dido brush against issues in Dante's own life and against the lives of the next important group in this canto, Paolo and Francesca. Tristan's chaste love for Isolde resembles Dante's chaste love for Beatrice. The story of Tristan and Isolde is a type of arthurian romance similar in several ways to the story of Lancelot which figures within Francesca's tale which is to follow (Popolizio 1980). Romances are a literary form, long narrations about chivalry, and chivalry is important in the courtly love tradition in which Dante's poems about Beatrice are written. Dido's story has certain parallels to Dante's life also. She vowed to be faithful to the ashes of Sichaeus and failed for which failure she died. Dante vowed to be faithful to the memory of Beatrice and failed with the lady Philosophy and was for that reason in danger of the "second death of souls." Paolo and Francesca are figures related to the courtly love tradition (in that their illegitimate relationship is a perversion of courtly love) and faithlessness is an important element of their story. Dido (who alone of those in the list is mentioned again in 85) and Tristan form an appropriate bridge to Francesca's narration with the added purpose of joining the whole to Dante's own autobiography.

The narration of Francesca which now follows has been the subject of many diverse interpretations in the centuries following the composition of the *Comedy* (Della Terza 1981). Some early commentators, impressed with the human quality of the sin of Paolo and Francesca, were moved by the pitiful narration of Francesca to see in the important lessons of this episode an indication that human love can survive even Hell. They concluded that Dante, as poet, sympathized with the lovers in their plight. More modern scholars tend to think that, far from being a sympathetic figure, Francesca represents a trap for both the Pilgrim and the reader. Surely the story of Paolo and Francesca, as told, was intended to evoke pity. The tale of a beautiful young girl, forced into a political marriage with a coarse man many years her senior, and turning to her husband's handsome, younger brother, is a sympathetic story. Never mind that it is not accurate in this form as the folk-tale like shape of the story precluded the necessity of its invention in any case. Dante has taken the basic story and by the use of imagery and suggestion made it even more sympathetic. There was a historical Francesca who was a relative of the nobleman who sheltered Dante at Ravenna during his exile. There is no historical evidence that she was adulterous with her husband's brother or that she died as Dante reports the story.

There are a number of elements which might incline a reader to sympathize with Paolo and Francesca. First, Dante the Pilgrim enters the Francesca episode in a state of pity (72) for the "more than a thousand shades whom love had parted from our life" (67 – 69) and his pity predisposes the reader to pity also. Secondly, he expresses a desire to speak "with those two who go so light upon the wind." This is the only time that the lustful are spoken of as a pair (a common condition for the sin itself). In the list above, only Paris and Helen form a couple and they are not spoken of in conjunction. The suggestion that Paolo and Francesca travel lightly implies that they are somehow above their surroundings. That they are in the company of their past lover implies that they are somehow special. We are told that they are lead by love and that they will respond to requests in its name. That they are wearied (80) while being lead by love implies unjustness. Dante's vibrant dove simile, "lead by desire...to their sweet nest," does little to dispel the reader's positive impressions. Francesca's gracious response to the Pilgrim's summons, like the language of courtly love which is its model, confirms the first impression. She would even have God's peace given Dante since he has pity on her "perverse ill" (93). Indeed, Love had an easy time with Paolo since he is of a gentle nature (100) and Francesca, being loved, was powerless but to reciprocate (103). The delight she had in Paolo "does not leave me even now" (105). Their murderer is clearly evil since he will some day find himself in Caina (a lower section of Hell).

At this point (106), there is a division of the narrative. Dante bows his head and must be prompted by Virgil to continue. The implication of context and language is that the Pilgrim is overcome by the pathetic nature of Francesca's story and, for a moment, unable to speak. When Francesca does continue, she again, she says, responds to Dante's desire to know how they fell. The facts are simple and poignant. For a pastime they read about Lancelot and Guinevere. The story of that fabled passion led Paolo to kiss Francesca and she, prisoner of love's impulse, reciprocated. The innocent kiss led to other things: "that day we read no farther." Francesca calls the book a Gallehault, that is to say a panderer. Gallehault was the figure in the story of Lancelot who set up the fatal encounter between the knight and the queen which led to their downfall.

It is easy to perceive these sympathetic issues since Dante the Poet has allowed the reader to experience the episode through the perceptions and feelings of his Pilgrim. Modern analysts, however, point out that the Pilgrim is not a very reliable guide. He is, in fact, on the journey because his perceptions are clouded and one of his misperceptions has to do with the issue of pity. Fundamentally, since Hell is the final state of some souls, it represents both the result of the tendency of those souls and the conclusion of God's judgement. To doubt the justness of Francesca's punishment is to deny any real significance to her actions in life or worse, to suggest that one's human judgement is superior to that of God. Dante the Poet has learned that lesson but his Pilgrim is still in the process of assimilating it. The story of Paolo and Francesca is one of the climaxes in the struggle for understanding. Recent critics point out the following among the clues which indicate that Francesca's story is to be taken with caution: First, Dante does indeed call to the lovers in the name of love, but it is, as Virgil says (78), "*that* love which leads them" There are different kinds of love, not all of them good (Lust, for instance is clearly not a good form of love). Dante, when he calls, is still bewildered and in the grip of Pity for the figures whose names he has just heard and he speaks to them in pitiful, emotional tones, "O wearied souls! come speak with us, if Another forbid it not" (80—81). The suggestion here might be that emotion and pity are poor guides in a situation which reason and detachment might serve the Pilgrim better. True, the souls of Paolo and Francesca come like doves, but they are driven by *desire*. The question is the nature of that desire and whether it is spiritual or merely physical. Francesca later provides the answer. The doves (really pigeons symbolizing lust, Ryan 1977) come through the air "borne by their will" as indeed all the sinners in Hell are borne by perversion of their will to their ultimate destiny. Here the poet reminds the reader that Paolo and Francesca come from where Dido and the rest of the list of the lustful are found (85).

Francesca's blessing of Dante is at best conditional: "*if* the King of the universe were friendly to us we would pray him for your peace, since you have pity" (92–93). At worst, the blessing is meaningless since God is manifestedly not her friend. Without waiting for any questions from the Pilgrim, Francesca impulsively begins her narration. She tells us she is from Ravenna ("where the Po descends"), that Paolo was of a gentle nature and was seized with passion for "the fair form that was taken from me" (101–102), that is to say, her physical body. She goes on to say that being loved, she could only love in return. By this time in her story, Francesca has strongly implied that she is a victim of Paolo's appetite and of the power of love which left her helpless and even (104) seized her "with delight in him that, as you see, it does not leave me even now." At the same time she confesses to a love affair which was physical, not spiritual, in nature she attempts to absolve herself of responsibility for it. She even implies that there is something noble in it all since "it does not leave me even now." This last requires some scrutiny. *What* does not leave her even now? Surely not love for Paolo since what she felt for him was not love, but lust. A state of lustfulness, impossible to satisfy in an incorporeal state such as Francesca's would be a horrible punishment. Paolo's shade which accompanies her, far from a comfort, eternally arouses her to a passion which can never be released. In any case, it seems that Francesca's words imply things which might not be wholly the truth of the issue. Whether Francesca herself is aware of this is another question since a misdirected will and self-deception are so closely related. Perhaps Francesca, never having known love, cannot distinguish it from lust.

What does Francesca receive for her story? Possibly a respite in her eternal punishment; possibly she is temporarily refreshed by the Pilgrim's pity. If the latter, Dante's bowed head at this point shows she is well paid. Of course, to desire pity is not a particularly ennobling thing. When she resumes her speech (121) she (inadvertently?) sheds a bit of light on the question of the nature of her punishment: "There is no greater sorrow than to recall in wretchedness, the happy time." Is being forced by the call of love to recall her happiness in fact part of her punishment? So she "weeps and tells" of the occasion for sin. How reading a book, "suspecting nothing," led Paolo to kiss Francesca as Guinivere was kissed by Lancelot and "that day we read no farther." Again, she has made of herself the victim this time of Paolo and the book.

The list of those damned for lust began with the name of Semiramis who "made lust licit in her decree." Semiramis' crude attempt to subvert language is easy to see through. Francesca is much more subtle. She appeals to the passion in all of us, she invites us to "understand" her, she suggests that it was really someone else's fault. She deceives the Pilgrim and she may deceive herself. Paolo, whom Francesca presents as the leading character in the drama, never speaks. He merely weeps speechlessly. The reader is invited to speculate about who was the tempter and who was truly the tempted (Musa 1974).

In one of the most interesting suggestions made about the *Divine Comedy* in recent years, Anna Hatcher and Mark Musa (1968), in an article entitled "The Kiss: Inferno V and the Old French Prose Lancelot," report that in the versions of the Lancelot tale known to Dante's time, Lancelot is kissed by Guinevere. That is, that the female figure in the story takes the lead in beginning the adulterous relationship. Hatcher and Musa believe that Dante knew this and deliberately allowed Francesca to distort the story to imply that Lancelot kissed first, "how the longed-for smile was kissed by so great a lover" (134) and to continue to claim that it was Paolo who kissed her. Hatcher and Musa think that knowledgeable readers in Dante's time would note this distortion and understand that it was Francesca, as it was Guinevere, who was the leading person in the affair as, indeed, her leading role in the conversation suggests. If so, this interpretation further strengthens the assertion that the mention of the corruption of language by Semiramis foreshadows the less obvious, and therefore more dangerous, example of Francesca. The fact that we gain so much by knowing something of the work to which Francesca refers, as well as the example of how useful knowledge of Semiramis is, points out to us how much Dante expects us to bring to the text in order to understand it.

At the conclusion of Canto V, the Pilgrim swoons as he did at the end of Canto III. There it was for terror, here for pity. In both cases the swoon is a sign of the Pilgrim's inability to cope with sin and the fact of Hell. As the *Comedy* was intended by Dante to mirror human spiritual development or lack of it, the difficulties readers have in recognizing Francesca's lack of self-discipline or her refusal to take responsibility for her own actions form an active demonstration of the human struggle with sin.

CHAPTER 7

Cantos V through IX

Form in *Inferno*

In this chapter I will discuss Cantos V through IX in general terms. These cantos are alike in that they share a particular sort of organization which we can come to understand and recognize. Several times in *Inferno*, Dante ties groups of cantos together with recurring motifs. Such groups of cantos I call "movements." I think Cantos V — IX are a movement and the first part of the discussion will tell you why. In the second part of the chapter I want to talk about the political history of Dante's time since complex issues are raised by Ciacco in Canto VI. The last section will be concerned with the explanations of various things offered by Virgil to the Pilgrim. Readers will need to have their copies of *Inferno* close at hand since I will make many references to it.

To this point, we have considered the *Inferno* in terms of its symbolism, underlying philosophical concepts, literary and historical associations and the like. We have now reached a point from which we can begin to consider the poem in its formal or structural aspects as well. Great works of art such as the works of Michelangelo, the plays of Shakespeare, the symphonies of Beethoven, as well as the *Divine Comedy* of Dante Alighieri owe their effectiveness in large part to the principles of construction and organization which the artist devised for them. An awareness of these will help the reader's appreciation and understanding. In this regard, Canto V, the canto of the lustful, can serve as a structural model to which Cantos VI through IX, as well as others, (notably III) can profitably be compared. If you look at the sequence of events in Canto V, you will see that they occur as follows (the line numbers refer to the line numbers in the Singleton translation of the *Inferno* and might differ slightly in other translations):

Lines 1 — 3: A transition passage which moves the Pilgrim from the first circle to the second.

Lines 4 — 24: A description of the demon (Minos) and of his rebuke by Virgil.

Lines 25—49: A description of the area, identification of the
sin punished here and an explanation of the punishment and
its *contrapasso*.

Lines 50—51: The Pilgrim makes a request of Virgil.

Lines 52—68: Virgil replies to the request.

Lines 70—75: The Pilgrim makes a further request.

Lines 76—78: Virgil again replies.

Lines 79—138: The Pilgrim interacts with some of the souls
in this location.

Lines 139—142: The Pilgrim reacts to his experience and
this reaction, a swoon, forms a transition to the next Canto.

If you now read Cantos VI through IX as well as reread Canto III, you will
see that they share these elements:

1. There is always a description of a demon or demons and
these demons are always rebuked.

2. There is always a description of the area and its
contrapasso which Virgil explains in response to a request or
requests by the Pilgrim.

3. The Pilgrim is given the opportunity to interact in some
way with the sinners or, if he is not, the omission is strongly
noted (as in Canto VII).

In addition to these common elements, Cantos VIII and IX each have a
passage wherein Dante the Poet speaks directly to the reader. The reader
is addressed many times in the *Inferno*. In most cases, as in I, 4—6, the
address is indirect. In a few, the Poet is more forceful and asserts his
presence (distinguishing himself from the Pilgrim) by saying "Reader!" or
"You!" or by making a command such as "Consider!" As you would expect,
these instances are especially important moments in the poem (Beall 1979).
There are also in some of the cantos occasions when Virgil gives philosophical explanations which are generally based on the works of Aristotle as they

were merged with Christian doctrine by St. Thomas Aquinas. These elements generally have to do with the workings of the universe in some sense and tend to confirm the emotional elements of the Pilgrim's education by relating them to theological or philosophical issues.

There are other actions which are unique; they do not form part of reoccurring patterns. Examples include:

1. Questions the Pilgrim asks about issues other than philosophy or punishment. (See IX, 16 — 33, where he asks how it is that Virgil knows the way to go.)

2. Certain interludes such as the moment the Pilgrim is overcome by pity in the midst of his interaction with Paolo and Francesca (Canto V, 108 — 115) or when he is praised by Virgil for his reactions (Canto VIII, 43 — 51).

If we take Canto V to be the archetypical version of this form, we can summarize it as listed above as transition; the demon and its rebuke; description of area, sinners and punishment; interaction with sinners; and transition to the next canto. It is easy to imagine that once having invented such a formal arrangement for a canto, Dante might, for a time at least, have simply repeated it until he had completed dealing with sins of the type with which he is here concerned. Dante, however, does not do this, but, in a manner which is consistent with the structural practices of other great western artists, varies the formal structure over a very broad range while at the same time preserving its essential characteristics (the four mentioned above) so that in spite of the variations in structure, we always can perceive the underlying unity of the form. In this way, it seems to me, Dante's procedure resembles the theme and variations forms produced by the classical composers Haydn, Mozart and Beethoven.

We can examine cantos V through IX now to see how this works to develop Dante's theme in one regard. Careful examination of the text will reveal other examples. In Canto V, clearly, the drama, the art of Dante's language and the reader's interest are dominated by Francesca's narration. Minos, his function and rebuke take up only 20 lines, the description of the area and the *contrapasso* only 24 lines. Virgil offers no explanations as such, merely information (who is who, how to proceed). Indeed, it is not even clear (37—39) that Virgil is the source of the identification of the nature of the sin punished here. In contrast to this, 92 lines are given over to either direct or indirect interaction with the sinners themselves. Canto VI is quite similar, but the form begins to alter. Again, the demon and the description of the area are very succinct while the interaction with Ciacco takes up most of the canto. What is new in Canto VI is the appearance of the motif of Virgil's philosophic explanations with reference to Aristotelian concepts in lines 91−99 and 106−111. In addition, the demon Plutus, who is really a part of the next canto, appears at the end of Canto VI as a part of the transition.

Look now at Canto VII. The passage concerned with Plutus and his rebuke takes no more space than the similar passages in V or VI, yet here, Virgil makes it a point to assure the Pilgrim that the demon is no real obstacle. Virgil has spoken *to* the demons before, but not *about* them. As we will see, this is part of the particular movement within the general form which will eventually result in the demons replacing the sinners as the objects of our (and the Pilgrim's) greatest concern. This shift in focus is emphasized by the denial of the Pilgrim's request to speak to the hoarders and wasters of this circle. Yet the shift to concern with demons over concern with sinners is not complete in this canto since the major lesson learned here by the Pilgrim has to do with the role of Fortune in the lives of men which is explained by Virgil (in another discourse based on Artistotle) in lines 70−96. The canto's formal arrangement is further developed by the inclusion of yet a different group of sinners and their *contrapasso* (still with no interaction with the Pilgrim) before the transition which brings us to the Tower of Dis.

In Canto VIII, the imbalance in the formal structure (differences with the organization of Canto V) which we began to perceive in Canto VII increases even though there are still enough familiar elements to make us feel we are still dealing with the same formal structure the artist demonstrated in the circle of the lustful. The familiar elements are the transition to the new area which (as the text indicates in the first line of the canto) continues from the end of Canto VII. The demon, Phylegas, is encountered and rebuked in the economical manner of earlier cantos. The incident with the sinner, Filippo Argenti, is familiar in that the Pilgrim does speak to him, but there are important variations in this scene. First, Dante expresses no pity, but rather a desire that the sinner's punishment be increased. Second, Virgil takes an active role in the conversation speaking directly both to Dante and to Argenti. He has not done this before, either speaking only to the Pilgrim or only to the sinner. This further develops the motive which began with the conversation with Plutus when Virgil begins to include the Pilgrim in his conversations with the denizens of Hell. Third, Virgil fulsomely praises the Pilgrim for his sentiments, the first time that he has done so. That he does so at the moment when Virgil (human reason) and Dante (the Pilgrim) cooperate in excoriating a sinner marks this as an important moment in the strife of the pity and the formal variation in what we have come to expect becomes the means by which that meaning is communicated; that is to say that at this moment, all the elements of the poem coincide in such a way as to make a very strong point.

These variations of familiar elements precede another transition (64—69) to yet another area, this outside the city of Dis, where the major formal alteration of this canto occurs: Here we find not one, but many demons (the rebellious angels themselves) and the now customary rebuke is not offered. Virgil tries another technique, a private parley with the demons (86—87), but the poets are refused entry into the city. While Virgil continues to reassure the Pilgrim (as he did when they confronted Plutus), it is clear that he is perplexed. Equally so is the Pilgrim, but his perplexity is articulated by the Poet who expresses it in the first of the direct "Addresses to the Reader" (94—96). Here, clearly, the emphasis has shifted. What was, in a sense, secondary, dealing with demons, has now become of equal importance with that which was primary, interacting with sinners. If the interaction with Argenti in this canto has an important allegorical significance, the Pilgrim's growing strength in the strife of the pity, it is reasonable to think that Virgil's failure with the demons must have a meaning also. Of course it does, and that allegorical point becomes clearer in Canto IX. We can already see how it is that the poem's form and its variations are the vehicles for meaning.

Canto IX is the climax of this section of *Inferno*, one of the major climaxes of the entire *Divine Comedy*. Everything is suspended. The journey, in spite of being divinely ordained, is halted. At the beginning of the canto Virgil's confusion fuels the Pilgrim's fear. The interaction with the demons, which by now has completely taken over the role formerly occupied by the theme of the interaction with sinners, continues with a second set of demons, furies, even more horrible and threatening than the fallen angels. At the climax of their threats ("Let Medusa come and we'll turn him to stone."). (For information on the furies and Medusa, see Freccero 1972, Mansfield 1970 and Suther and Giffin 1979.) Virgil moves to protect the Pilgrim and, at the climax of fear and despair, Dante the Poet again speaks directly to the reader, emerging from the page not as the character in the poem, but as the mind behind the vision inviting us to unravel the allegory (61–63). By this device, the Poet forces the reader to go beyond the narrative and consider the imagery.

Part of that allegorical meaning, of course, is contained in what happens next, the long delayed rebuke of the demons done not, as in previous versions of the form by Virgil, but by a messenger direct from Heaven itself. The messenger easily accomplishes that which was beyond the powers of Virgil in his role as human reason. The canto concludes with a description of the area within the city and the *contrapasso* of the next group of sinners.

This discussion of some of the formal arrangements of this group of cantos demonstrates how the artist invents the structural elements of his own art work and then manipulates them to join form to meaning. Such discussions about the *Divine Comedy* can never be anything other than partial since it is apparently never given to anyone other than the creative genius himself to perceive all of the structural elements in the work of art. Whether the artist himself knows all the elements on a conscious level of his mind is a question which is of great interest, but unfortunately unknowable. It is safe to assume, however, that the artist, by his very nature as artist, sees more than anyone else. In any case, having considered these arrangements of elements, we are in position to begin to draw some tentative conclusions about the meaning of this section of the poem.

As we have seen, Cantos I through V contain a good deal of conceptual information central to the *Comedy*. Cantos III and IV describe some sinners, but in both cases, the indecisive and the virtuous pagans, they are in some sense exceptions to the general run of Hell, one group kept eternally outside, the other punished in a seemingly ambiguous manner. It is only when the Pilgrim encounters the lustful, gluttonous and the wrathful (though the inclusion of "hoarders and wasters" here is confusing) that we feel ourselves to be witnessing a systematic discussion of the categories of sin. Indeed, if you are acquainted with some of the aspects of traditional Christianity, you might recognize lust, gluttony and wrath to be three of the traditional categories of "deadly sins" of which there are usually seven; the remaining sins being avarice, sloth, envy and pride. Having seen lust, gluttony and wrath systematically treated, many readers are surprised not to find the rest. In fact, Dante does not treat the Seven Deadly Sins in systematic order until the Pilgrim reaches Purgatory. Commentators, over the years, have suggested many reasons why Dante does not carry out such an obvious formal scheme. Some, for instance, think that after the first few cantos of *Inferno* were written there was a gap of some years before Dante was able to take it up again and that, in the meantime, he changed his mind about his organizational principle. This is reasonable and it may be so. However, other scholars note that for Dante, and for Medieval Christianity in general, the root of all sin was the sin of pride. This is inherent in the story of Satan who is lead to envy (the sin of avarice) through his pride and thus rebels (the sin of wrath) against God. This suggests that Francesca, Ciacco and Argenti are, in the final analysis, all prideful types and that one of the intents of this section is to demonstrate the role of pride in all other sins. Still others, yet, suggest that sins other than lust, gluttony and wrath are punished here. For instance, Ciacco's gluttony is also an example of sloth since it represents a slowness to take up the things of the spirit (man's proper concerns) and a concentration on the concerns of the flesh (Wenzel 1967). Likewise, examining Canto VII, one notes that there is more than one group of apparently wrathful types punished there and it is certainly true that medieval thought recognized many subdivisions of the major types of sin (Atchity 1969).

There are many levels of meaning which can be extracted from these five cantos. In general, most critics agree that the progress is from a sin which, while deadly, is the least to be censured of all to a really horrible sin. While lust is the sin closest to love, wrath, far worst, is somewhat its opposite. Perhaps the domination of the form by demons at the conclusion of this section represents this movement from "undemonic" lust to "demonic" wrath.

We should now turn to historical concerns. The political prophecies of Ciacco in Canto VI, are the first of several such predictions by sinners in *Inferno*. The "Veltro" prediction in Canto I was made by Virgil. An important motif of the *Comedy* is Italian unification as part of God's divine scheme (expressed in Canto II) and Florentine politics are the point where Dante is personally concerned. The issues are very complex and interact with universal concerns.

In the period from about 800 AD until well into the nineteenth century, there existed in Europe a ruler (In concept, at least. There were times when no one held the office.) known as the Holy Roman Emperor who was presumed to represent and replace the central authority of the old Roman Empire which had finally collapsed about the year 476. The ruler who took the title of Holy Roman Emperor was "Holy" because he was Christian in contrast to the pagan emperors of the old empire. Even though the Holy Roman Empire replaced the Roman Empire, its seat was not at Rome, but was at Aachen in what is now Germany. The Holy Roman Emperor was, in fact, the head of a rather loose confederation of Germanic states where his authority was only rarely more than titular. In practical terms, the existence of the emperor served to symbolize the supposed unity of the Christian world which was itself more idealistic than real.

Another power in Europe was the Pope at Rome. The Pope was the head of the Church and traced his authority back to St. Peter, the apostle whom Christians believed to have been delegated head of the Church by Christ himself (Matthew 16:18 — 19). While the Popes represented sacred authority, they frequently made claims to secular authority as well. These claims were based on a document called the "Donation of Constantine" which was believed to have been written by Constantine the Great, the last emperor of the Unified Roman Empire, and given to Sylvester I who was then Pope. Legend has it that Sylvester had cured Constantine's leprosy and converted him to Christianity. (We will read about this incident in Canto XXVII.) Constantine's gratitude and the fact that he moved the capital of the Empire to Constantinople, moved him to give The Donation to Sylvester. This action delegated to the Pope secular authority in Rome and in the Western lands generally. Thus both the Holy Roman Emperor and the Pope made claims to domains of authority which inevitably conflicted. Dante in *De Monarchia* and in the *Comedy* advocates the existence of a universal monarch who would wield all secular authority and a Pope whose concerns would be completely sacred. The fault of the Papacy was that it had allowed itself to become immersed in worldly affairs and the pursuit of wealth. Dante's political feelings were rooted in his political experience in Florence.

In the year 1250, Florence was an independent city-state already beginning to feel the economic and intellectual stirrings of the Renaissance. Politically, the city had two parties which reflected the larger divisions of power in all of Italy. On the one hand were the Ghibellines who supported the claims of the Holy Roman Emperor to universal secular authority. Generally, the Ghibellines were the newly wealthy classes who had the most to gain by breaking with the traditional Florentine relationship with the Papacy. On the other hand, the conservatives, the Guelphs, supported the Pope and were allied with the powerful guilds which organized the work force of the city. The Holy Roman Emperor, Frederick II, died in 1250 and the resulting confusion in Ghibelline ranks (since the election of a new emperor was always a process fraught with uncertainty) provided the opportunity for the Guelphs to establish the First Florentine Republic, a remarkable political experiment since it provided for a legislative body, the Signory, elected by some portion of the populace, including members of the guilds.

The Republic lasted until 1260 when the forces of the Guelphs were defeated by a Ghibelline army at Montaperti. The resulting antirepublican government itself was overthrown in 1266 when the heir presumptive to the imperial throne, Manfred, son of Frederick II, was killed at the battle of Benevento. The victorious Guelphs exiled the Ghibelline leadership and administered further defeats to them at the battles of Compaldino and Caprona in 1289. The 24 year old Dante participated in these battles on the Guelph side. The Second Republic which was now established lasted until the fifteenth century, but the strife characteristic of Florentine political life continued in new forms. The Guelphs split into two factions called the Black and the Whites. The White party, which included Dante, was the faction most like the old Ghibellines since it was the party of new wealth and was opposed to any extension of Papal authority within the city. The Blacks were pro-Papal in their sympathies and represented the old aristocracy.

Between 1295 and 1300, Dante became increasingly active in politics. In 1300 he was elected Prior, a legislator of the city. Terms of office were only two months long in order to keep power from falling into the hands of any clique. So strong was the desire for relief from internal dissent that during Dante's term of office the leaders of both the Black and the White parties were exiled. It may have been that the resulting power vacuum was noted by the Pope and influenced his next move.

The Pope in 1300 was Boniface VIII an elderly man who had obtained the holy office by, in Dante's opinion at least, unscrupulous means. (The reader should remember the mention of Celestine V, "who made the great refusal," in Canto III.) Politically very ambitious, Boniface constantly sought means to secure secular power in central and northern Italy and to increase his own wealth. Boniface sent Cardinal Matteo d'Acquasparta to Florence to maneuver the Black party into power. The Florentines, however, resisted this meddling in their affairs and Boniface in retaliation excommunicated all the magistrates of the city at the end of the year. Fortunately Dante was out of office by that time and so escaped the ban which effectively forbade those excommunicated from participating in the sacraments, tantamount to condemning them to Hell. Such excommunications for political purposes were understood by theologians to be invalid and so would Dante have understood any such "punishment."

Boniface's next move was to send Charles of Valois, a brother of the King of France, Philip IV, to help the Blacks gain power. The French crown cooperated in this since it promised them gain and because the French usually resisted the interests of the Holy Roman Emperor and were, in this regard, natural allies of the Papacy. Dante was one of a number of prominent Florentine citizens who went to Rome to see Boniface to try and reconcile the situation. When the other ambassadors returned to Florence Dante was kept in Rome by Boniface. He never saw Florence again.

All else failing, Charles of Valois invaded the city with an army. Neither the Blacks nor the Whites offered any resistance. The Blacks, now in power, proceeded to plunder the holdings of the Whites by any means at hand. In Dante's case, he was tried *in absentia* on charges of corruption while in office (probably false) and of opposition to the Pope and to Charles (certainly true). He was sentenced to exile and later to death, but that part of the sentence could not be carried out as he remained away from the city for the rest of his life. Not, of course, that Dante didn't try to come back. Between 1303 and 1304 the exiled Whites, now joined with the remnants of the old Ghibelline party, made several military attempts on the city which all failed. Dante was disgusted with the internal dissension in the alliance and finally withdrew to concentrate on his work of political theory *de Monarchia* and to work on his *Comedy*.

It was not only Florence, but all of northern Italy which was corrupt and rent by conflict. The throne of the Holy Roman Empire was vacant since no ruler had come to Italy to be crowned by the Pope, as was the custom, since the death of Frederick II in 1250. The Papacy itself soon fell into abject subjugation. In 1303 Philip IV, king of France, took Boniface VIII captive in Italy. The corrupt old Pope died very soon after this. His successor, Benedict XI, tried to make peace between supporters and enemies of the Papal throne, but failed in part because his pontificate only lasted until 1305. Benedict was followed by Clement V who was himself French and who, in 1309, moved the seat of the Papacy from Rome to Avignon in France, the beginning of that long period called the Avignon Captivity which made the Papacy a tool of the French crown.

Still, there was a bright spot in this gloomy scene, at least for a time. Surprisingly, Clement V supported the arrival of the new Emperor, Henry VII, in Italy in 1310. Dante, full of enthusiasm, wrote a series of political statements supporting the Emperor's claims to secular authority and had them circulated. Henry was crowned in the traditional manner at Rome in 1312 and immediately turned to a siege of Florence which remained under the control of the Black party still loyal to the Pope even though he was now a French vassal to all intents and purposes. Henry's siege was halfhearted, however, and he quickly withdrew. Clement, not mollified, declared against him and the throne of the Empire was declared vacant and all power, sacred and secular, transferred to the Pope. In 1313, Henry died and no new emperor was to make any serious claims in Italy for many years.

Dante's *Monarchia* expresses the view that there ought to be an absolute separation of power between the sacred and secular rulers. The emperor should be supreme in all worldly affairs and possess everything so that his rule might not be tainted by jealousy or greed. (That is, he should be like God in the scholastic definition, "beyond envy.") As the Emperor should rule in his sphere, so should the Pope rule in his, but the Pope, whose attention should be turned towards spiritual concerns should renounce wealth and power. The Emperor and Pope, said Dante, should be like twin suns, equally bright and equally illuminated by the light of God.

Ciacco's prophecies in Canto VI are about the circumstances and events we have just reviewed. They are stated as prophetic utterances although the events they refer to had already occurred by the time Dante wrote *Inferno*. Specifically, Ciacco refers to the short domination of the Whites over the Blacks and the return to power of the Blacks, aided by Boniface ("through the power of one who presently is temporizing"), and the resulting exile of Dante and the Whites. Dante inquires if any are just in Florence (the question echoes the story of Abraham and the fall of Sodom and Gomorrah in Genesis. Corrupt Florence is the modern Sodom or

Gomorrah. Kay 1978.) and is told there are two, but they are not named. Here the issues become mixed as the Pilgrim inquires of some individuals whom he presumes to have "set their minds upon doing good" (81) and finds that they are to be found in yet more horrible reaches of Hell. Thus the pilgrim learns that God's perception of good might differ from that of man, an issue related to the still ongoing strife of the pity.

Ciacco falls back into the slime at the conclusion of his speech with his eyes asquint. This is one of the many memorable expressions and gestures of the *Inferno*. Italian speakers utilize many such visible aids to meaning when they converse and sometimes the meanings conveyed are quite specific. Here, the squinting expression signifies a weakness of the senses and was discussed as such by Thomas Aquinas (Singleton 1970). Virgil's discourse, which concludes the canto, concerns the future of the damned and with it, we will turn our attention to the nature of Virgil's explanations. In this case he first explains that at the last judgement, the souls will resume their bodies and be resentenced to Hell in accord with the Christian doctrine which promises a resurrection "of the flesh." The Pilgrim asks if the punishments will be lessened, worse, or just the same. Virgil's statement that the damned will be more perfect when they again are a unity of spirit and body is Aristotelian as the reference to "your science" indicates. The import of the answer is that as a thing which is more perfect can feel more of both pleasure and pain, the "improved" sinners will be able to suffer even more. Clearly, this brings to mind once again the strife of the pity.

The next and more elaborate explanatory passage in this group is the famous discussion of Fortune in Canto VII, 70—96, a superb example of Dante's ability to condense several meanings in a single figure. Here Aristotelianism, the Principle of Plenitude, the *contrapasso* of the hoarders and wasters of Canto VII and moral teaching all combine.

First, Fortune is a figure of motion, and as such, she is related to the *contrapasso* of the hoarders and wasters and to the Aristotelian theory of the dynamics of the universe. Fortune is involved in ceaselessly turning her sphere (96) most commonly depicted as a gambling wheel (like a roulette wheel) in medieval manuscripts. As such, her motions are perfect, which is to say complete circles, whereas the hoarders and wasters, imperfect, go halfway around and then return (35—35, Atchity 1969). As Fortune's distributions are divinely perfect, the hoarders and wasters try to resist divine equity and behave unnaturally. At the same time, Fortune is only one "minister" among several, one for each heaven (72−75). In Chapter One, we saw how Aristotle, on the basis of what he could observe, believed that there were two types of "proper" motion in the universe. In the heavens things moved in circles, on Earth, in straight lines. To Christians, obsessed with discovering the signs of divinity in creation, the circles of heaven were evidence of heavenly perfection, the straight line, generally downward direction of earthly motion signified the "fallen" nature of this existence. Every motion must have an impetus and this impetus was provided by a divine being, an angel, on each sphere of the heavens who moved it. The movement of the spheres was, further, in response to the natural attraction of everything in the universe to God. God's attractiveness, and knowledge of him, was symbolized by light. It is light that the beings of the spheres distribute (73−76). Fortune is simply the angel assigned to the sphere of earth. However, as earth is an exception to the orderly laws of the universe, she does not turn the earth, which is stationary in the center of the universe, but turns the goods of the earth in inscrutable ways from one hand to the other. This complicated image further agrees with the accepted view of the sphere of the earth as the only sphere of change, the heavens being changeless and thus "perfect."

The image thus "explains" the punishment of the hoarders and wasters and provides the Pilgrim with more information about the workings of the universe. There is also a moral point here which reflection will reveal. Fortune works in unknowable ways to do the will of God and yet both those who benefit and those who lose curse her. She, however, is like Beatrice (II, 91 − 93), untouched by things which are not of Heaven (94, Remember, too, that the messenger who rebuked the furies was annoyed by Hell only to the extent of waving away the "gross air" with his left hand, IX, 82 − 83). This relationship is strengthened by the fact that Beatrice referred to Dante as being "not the friend of Fortune (II, 58 − 60)." How then should man value earthly goods and what moral status should we attribute to those who are rich or poor?

CHAPTER 8

Canto X

Farinata: Virgil's Quarrel with Dante

Canto V presented the Pilgrim and the reader with the powerful challenge of Francesca. Farinata, five cantos later in X, is the next of the great sinners of Hell, those who are serious obstacles to both the Pilgrim and the reader.

That we are at an important division in the plan of Hell is clear to everyone. The wall of the city of Dis, like the gate of Hell and the noble castle of Limbo (all physical structures), is a locus in the place memory system of the *Inferno* in which important ideas are associated with memorable images. However, the passing of the wall of Dis, while clearly marking a stage in the journey, does not clarify things greatly. Neither the Pilgrim nor the reader knows why the wall is where it is or why the sinners so far are outside it. The ordering of those sins has not been made plain. The Pilgrim, of course, has been confused at all of the structural locations, confused about the fate of the virtuous pagans and about the meaning of the inscription over the gate. Here, at the circle of the heretics, the uncertainty is caused by the lack, so far, of a principle of organization and by the fact that there is a growing rift between the Pilgrim and his guide. Merle E. Brown (1971) points out that over the course of the preceding cantos, Virgil has become overconfident and, as a result, becomes stuck before Dis. Worse, he has attempted to hide his lack of competence from the Pilgrim in his care. Virgil's growth of confidence is traced in his speech and actions. First, when he rebukes Phylegas (VIII, 19−21), he does so with no reference to the divine power which he has invoked in all other rebukes, acting as if dominion over the power of Hell is in his own hands. Similarly, the rending of Argenti (VIII, 59−63) is promised by Virgil himself with no reference to heavenly power. When the wayfarers are refused entry into the city, Virgil, though frustrated, assumes his own personal triumph, assuring the Pilgrim that, "I shall prevail in this" (VIII, 122). In spite of his confidence, Virgil is clearly shaken as his unsuccessful attempts to cover up his fear show (IX, 7−15):

> "Yet we must win this fight," he began,
> "or else...such did she offer herself to us!
> Oh, how long to me it seems till someone
> come!" I saw well how he covered up the
> beginning with the rest that came after,
> which were words different from the first;
> but none the less his speech gave me fear,
> because I drew his broken phrase perhaps to
> a worse meaning than it held.

Virgil is so demoralized by the threat of the Gorgon that he even raises the possibility of the failure of their mission, a mission which, as Virgil well knows, is divinely ordained. Virgil's overconfidence and his failure have now lead him to impiety, as pride, the mother of sins, leads as always, to other errors (IX, 55–57);

> "Turn your back, and keep your eyes shut;
> for should the Gorgon show herself and you
> see her, there would be no returning above."

None of this is lost on the Pilgrim, of course, who at the beginning of Canto X, tries to bolster Virgil's confidence by speaking with elaborate courtesy—but the attempt sounds like sarcasm (X, 4–6):

> "O supreme virtue," I began, "who lead
> me round as you will through the impious circles,
> speak to me"

This speech follows the collapse of Virgil's attempts to enter Dis and the rescue of the pair by the messenger. Dante's speech may be courteous and it may have been well intentioned, but in its own way it is as dishonest as Virgil's attempts at hiding his uncertainty have been. Virgil's response (9–18) is civil, but barely, and includes the charge that Dante is unsuccessfully hiding HIS thoughts (16–18):

> "Therefore to the question which
> you ask me you shall soon have satisfaction
> here within, and also to the wish which you
> hold from me."

Now the pot has called the kettle black and the Pilgrim's response is rich in elaborate courtesy and sarcasm (19—21):

> And I, "Good leader, I do not keep my
> heart hidden from you except in order to
> speak little, and to this you have before now
> disposed me."

This little goad brings to mind the passage in Canto III (70—81) where Virgil does indeed admonish the Pilgrim to wait for explanations, much to his confusion or, in contrast, to the moment in IV (31—32) when Virgil seems to criticize Dante for NOT asking questions about his surroundings. Neither Dante nor Virgil are being honest with the other and the language they use is as designed to conceal truth as any speech of Francesca's which we heard in Canto V. As Brown points out, something must occur to restore a proper relationship between master and pupil if the educational enterprise is to continue. Now Farinata speaks into the midst of this incipient quarrel. Francesca was the challenge to understanding and judgement in Canto V and Farinata is the challenge here.

Farinata is a heretic, or worse, a heresiarch (IX, 127) a leader of heretics, in this case a follower of the doctrines of Epicureas (died 270 B.C.) who taught as a part of an elaborate atomic theory of matter that the soul must die with the body. Apparently, Epicureanism was a common heresy in Dante's time and safe enough, for powerful people at least, to be openly acknowledged in spite of the penalty of live cremation (burning at the stake) which was technically possible. Virgil identifies the sin, but its nature is not discussed in Dante's dialog with the sinner as was Francesca's lust. What we learn about the sin and its *contrapasso* must be gleaned from what we observe. The damned are in fiery tombs with the lids ajar although we are told the tombs will be closed after the souls rejoin their bodies. Cassel (1971) notes that the open tomb is reminiscent of the tomb which was opened when Christ escaped death. These sinners who denied death any importance by denying life after death reverse the action and are trapped in that which they should have escaped. Brown observes evidence of God's sense of humor here. Beyond this, we must look to the person and speech of Farinata. Farinata rises from his tomb (35—36):

> "upright with chest and brow thrown
> back as if he had great scorn of Hell"

The prominence of Farinata's chest is itself a motif of the poem and will be seen in the presence of other prideful figures (Cassell 1977 is a superb guide to this canto).

Later he tells the Pilgrim that the earthly fate of his descendants "torments me more than this bed (78)." In the face of God's justice he is as unbending to death as he was unbending to God's word in life. As the open tomb recalls the resurrection, this characteristic stubbornness (in another of *Inferno's* references to the wilderness wandering) recalls that when the Hebrew people were waiting for Moses to descend from the mountain with the tables of commandments, they began the heresy of the worship of the golden calf. God says to Moses (Deuteronomy 9:13−14):

> I have seen this
> people, and, behold, it is a stiff-
> necked people:
>
> Let me alone, that I may destroy
> them, and blot out their name from
> under heaven.

Farinata is "stiff-necked" both intellectually and in demeanor and he is destroyed by it. As he despised Hell in life, he must continue to despise it in death as Francesca must persist in her lust, repentance being forbidden to the damned as the essence of their damnation. Here, it seems to me, is further evidence to answer those who wish to see in challenging figures such as Francesca and Farinata examples of human dignity in the face of damnation. In Dante's conception even the dignity of acknowledging one's errors is destroyed by sin. Further evidence is in Farinata's conversation with Dante and involves Virgil and Cavalcanti.

Farinata's conversation with Dante is about Florentine history and politics. Its formal arrangements reflect political contentiousness and Farinata's unbending, aggressive sinfulness. The Pilgrim is led by the sinner into a dialog which, veiled as it is by formal courtesy, is a combat. It consists of a verbal infighting which is a continuation of the incipient quarrel we have seen developing between Dante and Virgil. The Pilgrim is dangerously close to allowing his admirable patriotism to degenerate into political factionalism (Cassell 1977). In Canto V the Pilgrim's concept of love was challenged by a description of lust in a similar manner.

Farinata's sin is basically a kind of contentiousness. Heresy is contending with authority, the church, and it was considered a mortal sin. Political contentiousness is not a mortal sin, but it springs from the same aggressive spirit that leads to heresy. Thus, the political conversation illuminates the nature of heresy.

Farinata died in 1264 (Dante was born in 1265) and was an important leader of the Ghibellines (the imperial party opposed to Dante's Papal or Guelph faction). Farinata enters the conversation immediately after the Pilgrim's courteous (but cutting) speech remarked above. His address is abrupt to the point of imperiousness as he begins his speech with the clear intent of dominating the conversation. (Francesca's speech was also "impetuous" in an analogous manner. She begins her explanation without waiting for a question, although she invites one.) He acknowledges Dante's "modest" tone and speaks himself in that mode. A modest suggestion that "perhaps" (27) he had too much harmed the fatherland implies reasonable-ness of discourse. Since Farinata was a leader of the Ghibelline forces at the bloody battle of Montaperti, a major action in Florence's civil war, her "perhaps" is far too mild a term. Still, Virgil is certainly impressed, and in a way which seems undignified, upbraids the Pilgrim and physically pushes him into the correct attitude. Virgil is still shaken by his recent failure and his near quarrel with Dante and this unseemly behavior is evidence of it. His admonition to Dante to make his speech appropriate is good advice however Virgil, in his agitated state, might have meant it. What is the proper way to speak to a heretic damned by the justice of God who is also a violent man of war? The Pilgrim's eager obedience to the peremptory challenge "who were your ancestors?" is one answer, but is it the right one? It certainly leaves the Pilgrim vulnerable to Farinata's thrust at Dante's family line "twice over I scattered them" (48) and the combat is joined. Thrust and counterthrust are most courteous, even beautiful as Dante's attack on Farinata's descendants, "but yours have not learned that art well." (51), but designed to injure. Cassell (1977) says that Farinata's impulse is to dominate everyone and the Pilgrim joins him here in a degraded use of language to see who can prove himself superior. It is as easy to overlook the viciousness that underlies this conversation as it was to overlook the lust which underlay Francesca's romantic story. Even the "blessings" the adversaries pronounce for each other are precisely timed to be bitterly ironic: Farinata's "And, so may you return some time to the sweet world" (82) immediately follows his prediction of Dante's coming exile which will make the world much less than "sweet" for the Pilgrim, and Dante's "may your seed sometime find peace" (94) follows his explanation of why the descendants of Farinata are treated fiercely rather than peacefully by the Florentines.

The conversation with Farinata is interrupted after its first exchange by Cavalcanti. As the challenging figure of Francesca was joined to another soul, Paolo, Farinata shares his tomb with Cavalcanti. If we take Francesca and Farinata to be special challenges (in ways that, say, Ciacco is not) for the Pilgrim, the poet's linkage of them, having them both share their punishment with another, creates a motif which encourages the reader to see them, as the poet intended, as related cases.

Cavalcanti, like Farinata, has his entire focus on earthly things and thus his question is about his son whose state is unknown to him. Guido Cavalcanti was a poet and early friend of Dante. He is the first of the many poets mentioned in the *Divine Comedy* outside Limbo. He is the only Italian poet other than Dante mentioned in Hell, although there is an allusion to an earlier poet in Canto XXXIV. Guido was among those leaders of the Black and White factions who were exiled by the Signory while Dante was a Prior. At the supposed time of the poem, Spring of 1300, Guido was indeed alive. He died in August of that year of a disease he caught in exile. Much has been written about whom Guido is supposed to have "disdained." in the Pilgrim's comment of 61 − 63:

> "I come not of myself.
> He who waits yonder, whom perhaps your
> Guido had in disdain, is leading me through here."

The obvious assumption based on a reading of the poem in English, is certainly that Virgil (Reason, ancient poetic authority, etc.) is meant. In the Italian manuscripts upon which modern English translations are based, however, the issue is not quite so clear because of the ambiguity of the pronoun "cui" and variations in the punctuation of the passage. This has enabled various scholars to suggest that it is Beatrice or even God to whom the reference refers. Most authorities, however, stick with Virgil and I agree for reasons of context. By the end of Canto X, and certainly by the beginning of Canto XI, the Pilgrim and his guide are no longer in discord. It seems to me that the healing process which must occur starts here in Dante's response to Cavalcanti. The reference to Virgil as Dante's aid and worthy leader is spoken simply and is, in contrast with the other conversations of the canto, directly honest. Virgil, hearing it with ears attuned to any sarcasm, must be soothed and calmed by the assurance that the Pilgrim considers him worthy of his office.

If Virgil understands the Pilgrim's speech, Cavalcanti does not and falls, still anguished for fear of Guido's fate, back into the tomb. Farinata, of course, ignores the whole episode and simply continues his conversation where it had been interrupted even though the Guido of whom the others were speaking was his son-in-law. (There are other interesting interconnections here. Farinata is a Ghibelline, Cavalcanti a Guelph. One of Cavalcanti's forbearers was responsible for instituting the penalty of burning for heresy (Cassell 1977).

Dante's conversation with Farinata includes the passage about the knowledge of the damned. In Canto VI the future, "more perfect," of the damned is spoken of. The suggestion that "perfection" might permit more pain is delicately implied. Here a further refinement of the final state is explained. The end of judgement is the end of time. After that, there can be no "future," no change, as the afterlife of the damned becomes static. They will be left only with memory of their past which, because it was given over to sin, can only be a source of regret for them. It is, however, unclear whether the future state of knowledge discussed here applies to all the damned or merely to those of this circle.

The conversation concludes with a final egocentric gesture by Farinata as he names only those souls with him in the circle of the Epicureans who were important to the Ghibelline cause. Dante is left troubled by Farinata's hostile words (123). Virgil inquires as to the cause of Dante's distress. This inquiry, the answer to which must have been obvious to Virgil, is another example of returning balance to the relationship of the pair. The inquiry is solicitous, the answer is satisfactory (126). Virgil does not denigrate Dante's fear, but commends the prediction to Dante's memory and suggests that real understanding will come from Beatrice. Brown thinks Virgil's acknowledgement of the greater role of Beatrice, in contrast with his own earlier egocentricism, is another step in healing the rift which so threatened the journey at the beginning of the canto. There is more evidence that this is so at the beginning of Canto XI to which we shall now turn, but there is a different but interesting issue also lurking in this last exchange between the Pilgrim and Virgil.

Older commentators usually took Virgil's inquiry here, "Why are you so disturbed?" (125) as evidence that Virgil has the power to read Dante's mind. Indeed he does seem carefully attuned to Dante and very quick to note his state of mind in several instances. Mark Musa (1977), however, argues that if you read all the instances of "mind reading" carefully, you can explain them satisfactorily simply on the basis of Virgil's prior information or careful observation. Here, Dante's distress could easily have been visible in his demeanor. The crown of Musa's argument, to me, is his simple observation that, if Virgil is to represent human reason and the peak of human achievement without grace, it simply will not do to grant him superhuman powers. In fact, as the last few cantos have shown us, Virgil is a superb example of human fallibility, a fallibility which will be revealed to us in many more ways in the poem.

CHAPTER 9

Canto XI

Virgil's Lecture on Hell:
A Review of Landmarks

In contrast to the vibrant tensions of the preceding canto, Canto XI is characterized by unity of purpose on the part of the travelers and even a sense of real comradeship. It is as if the struggle with Farinata, Virgil's admission of his limitations (the limitations of human reason), and Dante's recognition of Virgil's proper leadership has focused everyone's attention on the real goal of the journey, the salvation of the Pilgrim, rather than the gratification of various egos. Canto XI is a kind of interlude in the progress of the poem, static in terms of physical progress, but dynamic in the growth of intellectual understanding. It has few of the elements (the rebuke of demons, interaction with sinners, etc.) seen in previous cantos, as it is given almost entirely to an elaborate explanation by Virgil of the organization of Hell. As we have come to expect, the explanation contains several references to the authority of Aristotle. It resolves many of the uncertainties which the Pilgrim, and through him, the reader have found in the journey to this point and presents the plan of what is to follow.

The beginning of the canto continues the motives with which the previous canto concluded: the walk into the valley, the increasing stench of the "more cruel pen" (XI, 3) and the open tombs of the heretics. At the tomb of Pope Anastasius the travelers are in an area where the heresy that is punished is not that of Epicureanism, but Acacianism which claims that Christ was conceived and born as are other men. This heresy, as a consequence, denies to the Virgin any divine significance and through that any special symbolic significance to womankind, specifically to Beatrice as a symbol of divine love. This fact might explain why Dante, from all the vast catalog of medieval heresies, chose to allude to Acacianism at this point. In addition to his heresy, however, Anastasius (Pope from 496—498) was notable since it was he who decreed that no priest was to neglect his duty for any reason whatever. The issue of priestly duty is an important one for

Dante and has already been alluded to in III, 58—60 where, among the opportunists, the Pilgrim says:

> After I
> had recognized some among them, I saw and
> knew the shade of him who from cowardice
> made the great refusal.

Commentators identify this figure, already mentioned in Chapter 4, as Celestine V who renounced the Papacy in 1294 after only five months on the throne. Rumor current in Dante's time had it that Celestine was convinced to renounce his seat in order to attend to the salvation of his own soul (Singleton, 1970) thus violating the decree of Anastasius. The argument to do so, said the rumors, was presented by Cardinal Caetani who promptly became Pope upon Celestine's resignation and took the name Boniface VIII, Dante's political and spiritual nemesis. The reference here in Canto XI serves to keep the issue of Papal responsibility alive. It climaxes elsewhere in the poem.

The lid of Anastasius' tomb acts as a shelter for the poets who delay their journey to become accustomed to the stench of Hell. To become accustomed to the stench, that is, to become used to dealing with sin, is important to the Pilgrim's journey and therefore this pause is another marker of his educational progress. This positive sign is reinforced by the fact that the student and the teacher find themselves in absolute agreement about the productive use of time (10—15) in contrast to their quarrelsome state in Canto X.

Essentially, the dialog which takes place in the shadow of the tomb is the Poet's explanation, put into the mouth of Virgil, of certain elements of Aristotelian ethics which St. Thomas Aquinas attempted to absorb into Christianity. The explanations of this canto owe more to Aristotle (and to Cicero's *De Officis*) than they do to Thomas. This is appropriate as they are spoken by the pagan Virgil. The language, the frequent references to God, do give the discussion a Christian flavor.

Aristotle's work was secular in that what Dante (and Aquinas) label "sin," the philosopher called "dispositions to be avoided" more for civic than for metaphysical reasons. One of the major purposes of Aquinas' work was to give Aristotle's definitions and classifications a proper Christian application so that they might be an aid to the Church rather than a powerful secular challenge. Therefore, although in this canto the classifications of sin are, for the most part, properly credited to Aristotle, their Christian context does derive from St. Thomas. This is a very good example of the synthetic nature of Dante's philosophy which attempted to see all of creation and its history as a supernatural unity in service of the Christian story of redemption. Aristotle's secular work existed, in this view of things, in order to be Christianized. Dante's view of history in Canto II is another example of this same process as is the use of pagan figures to illustrate Christian moral points throughout the poem.

If the reader follows Virgil's explanation carefully, the basic classification of sin into the types of incontinence, violence and fraud are clear enough. The principle of distinction is, however, rather removed from modern conceptions of justice although there are interesting points of similarity. The sins of incontinence (67—87) are like personal failings which are outside the legal code in most modern countries. Sloth, lust, wrath and the like are faults which are inconvenient, but not ordinarily liable to judicial correction. In the system expounded here, such dispositions of the soul likewise most often lack a secular penalty, but they can require serious sacred retribution, that is, eternal damnation. The scholastic understanding of this is found in the definition of the term (incontinence) which designates this class. Incontinence, of whatever type, implies a failure of will. The sins of incontinence are sins of self-control. The sinner's will fails to control a natural passion such as lust or gluttony. Dante's theology held that no particular metaphysical insight was needed to know the necessity to avoid such sins since human reason, the special quality which distinguishes mankind from lower beings on the Great Chain, suffices for one to not only avoid sin, but to seek salvation. A failure here (such as the failure of Ciacco) is a failure of man's most basic resource, his God given will to salvation prompted by his reason. In the *Inferno*, this failure is symbolized by sleep as when the Pilgrim explains his confusion at the beginning of the journey as the results of being "full of sleep" (I, 11) or when Ciacco, having been temporarily aroused, slips back into vacuity at the conclusion of his conversation with the Pilgrim (VI, 91—99). In sleep, one's will power does not function and the necessary struggle for salvation does not take place.

The sins of incontinence the Pilgrim is told (67—90), incur the least of God's wrath. Violence and fraud are the classifications of the sins of lower Hell within the City of Dis which are punished more harshly since they require for their commission, not so much a neglect of reason in favor of natural passion, as a more or less active use of reason to unnatural ends. In modern conceptions of justice, distinctions are made between sins of violence committed while reason is impaired (manslaughter committed while intoxicated) and those where reason is called upon in commission (crimes of intent such as first degree murder). Dante's concept seems to agree in that he acknowledges that passion (impairment of the will) frequently has a hand in violent crimes. Murderers, suicides, usurers and the like are in fact driven by passion; but their crimes also require the active use of the will to be accomplished.

The bottom of Hell is reserved for those guilty of fraud ranging from seducers and fortune tellers to those most guilty of all, the traitors. Dante's reasoning is perfectly consistent as no one can behave in a fraudulent manner unless reason and will cooperate. No one is a fraud by accident nor can one be successful in the commission of fraud if passion clouds reason. However, Dante here clearly departs from modern conceptions of justice since, for instance, he sees murder as less serious than seduction or hypocrisy (hardly "crimes" at all to us). Lansing (1981) notes that the sins of violence against God, Nature and Art are unnatural acts against life. Francesca's lust, while excessive and uncontrolled, is natural and could, if controlled, be good. Sodomy is unnatural and could never be good. Nor could war making or violence against one's neighbors. Lansing perceives that all the sins punished in lowest Hell are sins against the fabric of society, in that they are denials of the bonds of trust which hold our relationships together. Presumably a sin which destroys human trust can disrupt culture and can interfere with the important work of salvation. Such a thing would be worse to Dante than a sin, such as murder, primarily directed against individuals.

Considering then, the plan of Hell to depend on a scale which measures the involvement of the will in sinful acts and considering the worst misuses of reason and the will to be a malicious denial of God's plan, certain subdivisions in Virgil's catalog can be noted: First, violent sins are ordered in three sections, from the least bad to the worst. These are, one, the violent against neighbors (murderers and warriors), two, the violent against themselves (suicides and destroyers of themselves), and three, those who are violent towards God, Art (man's proper activity, but not meaning just the fine arts here), and Nature (the divine ordering of the universe). These last classes include blasphemers, sodomites and usurers. In each of these classes, it can be argued, the scale moves from the most passionate subdivision (i.e. blasphemy) to that which is most willful and demands the most involvement of the rational aspect (i.e. usury). In a similar manner, the area of fraud is divided into an area devoted to fraudulent acts directed against people in general, that is, with indiscriminate targets, and the lowest area given to the punishment of sinners whose victims are people to whom are owed special obligations. The sinners punished here are guilty of forms of treason. It is notable that the least form of fraud is seduction, the form of fraud most like love, which should remind the reader that in the scholastic conception, sin is not so much a positive thing as it is the manifestation of a lack or a perversion of the primary force in the universe, divine love. This observation illustrates once again the central importance of the Francesca episode in the formal and intellectual ordering of the *Inferno* since it is there that the Pilgrim is confronted by a perversion of love in a vibrant image and by a test, the comprehension of Francesca's error, which he fails.

When Virgil recites the catalog of the divisions of lower Hell he first identifies violence and fraud as the divisions of the lowest areas. In lines 22—24 Virgil classifies these subdivisions under the general heading of malice which has for its end "injustice." It is only after Dante's question (67—75), that he returns to an explanation of the upper areas, outside the walls of Dis, and names incontinence. Many readers and commentators have noted that in this explanation the areas are called not incontinence, violence and fraud, but "incontinence, malice and mad bestiality" (83—84) and some have been led by this to search for a sin of bestiality in the list of the sins punished in *Inferno*. Hatcher and Musa (1970) argue that the reference to bestiality at this point is merely a device used by Virgil to remind the Pilgrim of the passage in Aristotle's *Ethics* where the distinction between incontinence and sins of intent is made and that the reader should not be thereby distracted from the primary categories of violence and fraud which are the actual divisions of the *Inferno*. In other words, incontinence, violence and fraud are the scholastic divisions of sin, but the process of categorizing began with Aristotle's incontinence, malice and bestiality. Musa and Hatcher's suggestion is a good one since the efforts to specifically identify bestiality have not been very successful. However, in Dante things rarely, if ever, have only one significance and considering the nature of bestiality might be of some profit here. In Book Seven of Aristotle's

Nicomachean Ethics referred to here, incontinence, malice and bestiality are defined in terms of their opposites: incontinence as the opposite of continence, and malice as the opposite of virtue. Of bestiality, however, the philosopher implies that there are some difficulties of conception:

> But the opposite of bestiality? One may with propriety call it 'superhuman virtue' - moral goodness or virtue on the heroic or godlike scale. One thinks of the words which Homer has put into the mouth of Priam respecting Hector, of whom, because Hector was preeminently brave, he says:
>
> > Nor seemed he to be
> > Son of a mortal sire, but of a god.

Bestiality, then, is the opposite of godliness, a conception amenable to Dante's view of the universe as a chain of existence stretching from the Most High to the most ignoble thing in existence. And where to find the ignoble but in Hell? Humans, because they are the only mortal beings with reason, are the only beings capable of misusing it. No matter how bestial a beast might be it cannot suffer guilt because of its nature. Aristotle comments "the badness of a beast is different in kind from our vice". It follows that if the depths of ignobility are to be reached, they must be reached by something possessing reason and that being must be found in Hell.

Dante's symbolism includes this concept by depicting evil in images which mix the images of beasts with the form of rational man. Minos is a man with a serpent-like tail. Cerebus is dog-like, but he has hands and a beard. Plutus, in classical mythology the offspring of a god and a mortal woman, is nevertheless called "wolf"; the furies are human in form with snakes for hair. The reader will discover other examples of man-animal admixtures which show the evil which results when man's primary attribute of reason is abandoned or perverted for beast like appetites or behavior. It stands to reason that while the reference to incontinence, malice and bestiality might be primarily an index to the classifications of Aristotle, the reference to bestiality also serves to illuminate the meaning of some of the poem's symbolic allusions.

Whether the preceding suggestion is of much help or not the reader will have to decide. It should be noted, though, that even after Virgil's explanation, many elements of the classification of sin remain obscure. Notable issues include the logic of the place of the opportunists, the heretics, those in limbo, along with the obscure nature of violence and its punishment. There are other difficulties with Virgil's catalog which will become important later in Hell.

The section of Canto XI which is introduced by the Pilgrim's question (67—75) about the upper regions of Hell also contains several other notable issues. The first of these concerns language. We have already noticed that the canto begins on a note of harmony and cooperation when the poets agree that their delay in the journey must be filled with some profitable occupation (10—15). The sense of courteous attention and respect continues throughout Dante's questioning of Virgil even though occasionally the teacher implies a mild rebuke of his student (76—84, 100—105) in referring him to the authority of Aristotle whose works, presumably, he should have known well. The Pilgrim's elaborate courtesy (67—69, 91—93) in complimenting his teacher for the clarity of explanation is intended to be taken seriously although the latter case, where the student says that he is grateful for his confusion so that he might experience the joy of explanation, might sound overdrawn and lead an edgy Virgil to suspect sarcasm if his feelings of fellowship with his pupil were not running high.

In any case, the second question, about usury (94—96), is important, not only because it relates to the nature of sin, but also because the answer includes further information about Dante's view of the ordering of the universe. Usury, the lending of money for interest, is one of the pillars of modern capitalistic economies. It is probably as difficult for modern readers to understand it as a sin as it is for Dante's pilgrim. Dante the Poet, however, understood usury as a sin very well and the introduction of the issue here is an important point in his political polemic. Dante considered the pursuit of wealth, to the neglect of spiritual affairs, to be one of the most important sources of sin in the world, especially when wealth was pursued by the Church itself. The decline of the Papacy was caused by popes such as Boniface VIII whose taste for wealth and luxury exceeded their spiritual calling. (It is of historical interest as an indication of Dante's perceptiveness that Leo X's usurious loan to Albert of Hohenzollern in the sixteenth century was one of the immediate causes of Martin Luther's break with the papacy and the beginning of yet another serious decline in papal authority and prestige.) Dante's age was witnessing the beginnings of modern banking practices and Dante, a conservative in this regard, was very opposed to it. Traditionally, lending money for interest was prohibited and that prohibition was based on numerous biblical injunctions (Deuteronomy 23:19, Exodus 22:25, Ezekial 18:8 among others. See Diorio 1978). The early stages of Italian capitalism in the Thirteenth Century were marked by many abuses so that Dante's objection to interest banking was practical as well as theological. Even so, the argument put forth here is in terms of a violation of God's scheme. Nature (personified) is a reflection of divine intellect (God) and of God's art. Art here, as noted above, is not used in a restricted, modern sense, but means all of God's activity. Nature working, imitates God working. Man's art imitates Nature's, "so that your art is as it were grandchild of God." (105). Here is the Great Chain of Being in operation: God works, Nature imitates God, man imitates Nature. In this view of things every individual activity takes on a sacred connotation and nothing is exempt from consideration in terms of the light of the divine. God's "labor" in the act of creation (from which He rested on the seventh day) is the prototype of all human labor. The ultimate problem with usury is that it provides increase without labor and is therefore a perversion and a direct violation of God's command in Genesis 3:19 where, as a part of God's curse on Adam and Eve, He says:

> In the sweat of thy face shalt
> thou eat bread till thou return unto
> the ground: for out of it wast thou
> taken: for dust thou art, and unto
> dust shalt thou return.

Labor is as fundamental as death itself.

Virgil's amazing ability to tell time by the stars where there are no stars (a supernatural ability?) functions again and the teacher and his student resume their interrupted journey.

At this point, now that the Pilgrim (and the reader) has heard Virgil's explanation of the ordering of Hell, it is a good idea to review the journey so far in order to see it in terms of our new knowledge of the nature of sin and in terms of our physical location. We already understand that the *Inferno* is a place memory system in which ideas are linked to places, the impressive features of the landscape serving to anchor the ideas in memory. The purpose of the Pilgrim's journey is not only his own salvation, but also the salvation of others. The lessons the Pilgrim learns and remembers are passed on through the medium of the poem. What of this shared experience is actually recalled by individual readers varies, of course, but certain issues are certainly shared by most and these are generally the concepts linked to features of the landscape and the beings in it.

At this moment we are resting with Virgil and his charge just after the encounter with Farinata among the tombstones. We are now at the edge of a high cliff rimmed with broken boulders (XI, 1 −2). Thinking back over the journey so far we remember (at least) the little wood, the gate of Hell, the strange, insubstantial spirits of the undecided, the demon Charon, poignant Limbo with its seven towered castle, Minos with his warning, seductive Francesca, Cerebus, Ciacco and Plutus, the dead swamp and vicious Argenti, the city of Dis, the messenger and the tombs. Each of these elements has its value in the memory: the little wood with its sense of fear and irrationality, Limbo where fatalism and a sense of hopeless injustice reigns. Each reader's own experiences color the interpretation, but all tend towards Dante's purposes. Who can forget how eagerly the damned crowd towards frightful Charon and what that crowding means about the nature of sin?

The reader will have discerned without much direct instruction that Hell is a vast, funnel shaped pit and that the journey follows around ridges on the inside of the chasm. Alert readers will have noticed that at the descent from circle to circle the travelers have always turned to the left with one exception when, as they enter Dis, they turn right (IX, 132). There is certainly a meaning to this exception as well as to the general direction of the spiral the travelers make in their journey, but it is likely that the allegory is bound up with the highest meanings of the poem, not to be understood until the reader has gone with the Pilgrim to the peak of Paradise (Freccero 1961).

So we know the general shape of our journey and the important episodes within it. Dante's poetic genius ties the elements of it all into a seamless experience very much like life itself. The very reality of the experience and the literalness of the narration has lead "many," says Uberto Limentani, "including Galileo 300 years after the poem was written, to attempt to gauge with mathematical and architectural detail the size and shape of Hell" (Limentani 1985). Indeed, it is an essential part of the work that Dante requires of his readers that everyone should labor to make an adequate mental image of the place where we are. Over the centuries a kind of consensus has come about concerning the geography of Hell and most maps of the pit included in all editions of the poem look much alike. These maps repay careful study.

One useful way into the map is to observe the many times the Pilgrim has come through places associated with water. Dante's vocabulary is rich in words denoting water. To this point he has used the Italian words for water, river, little river, bog, marsh, stream, pond, slough, fount, and waves, at lest. In many cases the nouns are modified by adjectives to emphasize their infernal nature (the "dismal little stream" of VII, 107, for instance). In Chapter Two, I mentioned the first simile of the poem and pointed out there its relationship to both the historical crossing of the Red Sea and the sacrament of baptism. In Dante's sacramental system of salvation baptism was absolutely essential as we learned from Virgil's despair in Limbo. The Pilgrim must complete a true baptism at some point which will remove from him the traces of sin. This "true" baptism cannot occur in Hell, however. Nevertheless, the continual references to water and its crossing keep this very important allegory alive for the reader.

Dante, then, had a poetic reason for providing Hell with wet places (not all of the liquids are water) and literary references to water (Virgil is called "that fount which pours forth so broad a stream of speech" in I, 79—80 and he will allegorically save the Pilgrim from Hell as Baptism can do in actuality) so that the developing baptism motive could continue. He did this by creating a system of rivers as an integral part of the geography of the *Inferno*. As the Pilgrim and his guide have progressed to this point, they have several times crossed water: the Acheron in Canto III, the "Fair Stream" of Canto IV, the "dismal little stream" of Canto VII, the Styx in Canto VIII. Donno (1977) observes that the vertical relationship of the various waters ties the essentially horizontal circles together thus providing a structural as well as an allegorical motif. For these reasons, tracing the course of the waters and noting the relationships to the ethical structure Virgil has just explained will be a useful way for us to get our mental bearings.

In Canto I, to repeat what I have already said, there is no literal water, but there are several allusions to it: Dante speaks of the "lake of his heart", there is the simile of the crossing of water, and Dante's savior, Virgil, is compared to a fountain. All this is just outside the dark wood, before the entry into the pit of Hell. Canto II, which is also preliminary to the poets' entry into the "deep and savage way (II, 142)", has only a single reference to water and its crossing, but that one, as we shall see, is a pregnant one. Beatrice, in her address to Virgil, asks (107), "Do you not see the death that assails him on that flood over which the sea has no vaunt?" The significance of comparing Dante's struggle to a watery storm is a motif which is born here in *Inferno* and climaxes in *Paradiso*.

It was in Canto III that Dante came actually into the presence of water, when he crossed Acheron in Charon's boat. There he moved from the Vestibule of Hell with its souls of the undecided and joined the stream of the damned. In terms of Virgil's explanation, he entered then the area of incontinence which physically consists of the five circles between Acheron and Styx. Each of these circles either has some form of water in it or there is some reference to water in the text. Canto IV, the first circle, has its "fair stream" (108). In V, Circle II, we are told that Hell "bellows like the sea in tempest when it is assailed by warring winds" (29−30 which brings to mind Beatrice's characterization of Dante's plight in II) and Francesca is identified by the relationship of her birthplace to the river Po (V, 98). In the third circle of the gluttons, foul water falls as rain.

In Canto VII, fourth circle, the water references are particularly rich as we approach the limits of the sins of incontinence. Plutus, when rebuked, falls like a mainmast in a storm at sea (13−15), the hoarders and wasters are compared to waves clashing together (23−24) and the "dismal little stream" flows (99−108). This last is an important point, since it is by this stream that the water, first seen in Acheron, flows into the marsh of the Styx. One should note that only rarely do the waters of Hell actually flow; the Acheron, like the Styx, resembles a lake conforming to the shape of the circle of which it is a part. Styx is, like Acheron, a major landmark denoting the end of incontinence with its sullen and wrathful sinners and its crossing marking the entry into the area of violence. In VIII, Circle 5, the Styx is actually crossed and Virgil is referred to as the "sea of all wisdom" (7).

All during Canto IX while Dante and Virgil are delayed outside Dis the marsh of the Styx is the scene of the drama and when Dante, now inside the city, wants the reader to picture the cemetery he finds there he compares it to the cemetery of Aries on the Rhone river and the cemetery at Pola on the bay of Quarnero "which shuts Italy in and bathes her borders" even as the Styx bathes the borders of Dis. All of these markers make this location especially memorable and it is fitting that we have now entered into Hell proper. The canto of the heretics, X, is almost free of water references, although Dante does comment that the battle of Montaperti dyed the river Arbia red with blood (86). We are told at the beginning of Virgil's explanation in Canto XI of the three further circles reserved for the violent and when the descent is made to the first of these in Canto XII, we again find ourselves by a river, this time Phlegethon, the River of Blood, and much of the imagery of the poem has to do with crossing that stream.

CHAPTER 10

Canto XII

The Minotaur: Dante's Elaborate Relationships

Canto XII resumes the variations on the formal pattern we have been observing since Canto III, variations which serve, as always, to advance important themes of the poem. One important motif is embedded in the description of the area at the beginning of the Canto. It is one of many places in *Inferno* where Dante makes an explicit comparison between the landscape of Hell and the landscape of Italy as in Canto IX in the reference to the cemetery of Pola just mentioned. Here the way down the cliff to the circles of the violent is by way of a landslide like one near Trent. Later (31) Virgil offers an explanation of the ruin which links it to the Harrowing of Hell, another major theme of the *Inferno*, which we have already seen accounting for the broken gates in Canto VIII, 125—6:

> a less secret gate
> which still stands without a bolt.

The earthquake that accompanied Christ's challenge at the gate of Hell broke open the gate forever, caused this landslide here and, as Virgil says (45), other damage elsewhere.

Dante's description of the fall of rocks as similar to the one near Trent is intended to make the scene real to his readers, some of whom would have been to Trent. There is also the implication, however, that there is something hellish about Italy and that is precisely the point. Italy's corruption and divisiveness make it a place whose inhabitants suffer. One of the purposes of the *Comedy* is to seek the renewal of Italy.

This description of the area is also the transition between Cantos XI and XII since by the end of it in line 10 we have made our way down the cliff to the seventh circle where we find another familiar element of the form, the rebuke of the demon. Now here the plot immediately thickens. Dante, the supreme intellectual, certainly enjoyed playing with ideas and relationships. The whole exegetical exercise of providing literal, allegorical, moral and anagogic meanings for the poem and its elements is itself an elaborate game of relationships. At certain places in the poem, probably more than we suspect, there are explosions of relationships. One such "explosion" we have already seen was the elaborate set of connections between the crossing of the Red Sea, Dante's trip to Hell and the coming of Christ in Canto I. The present moment is similar in its complexity, but now the reader, more practised, will probably be able to make more of it out. One of the wonders of the poem is that it succeeds in teaching its readers how to read it.

The demon in this case is "the infamy of Crete," the Minotaur. Certainly, his nature, half human, half bull, fits the "bestial" theme discussed in Chapter Eight. The consensus of the commentators seems to be that Dante's version of the Minotaur has the body of a bull and the head of a man (Singleton 1970). Although to my mind there is precious little direct evidence for that in the text, there is some contextual support for it. One of the ways Dante structures his poem is by the process of prefiguration in which events mirror in advance things that are to happen later in the poem. For instance, Dante's attempted ascent of the little hill of Canto I "prefigures" his later ascent of the Mountain of Purgatory. This example is typical in that the earlier "small" event comes before a "large" one. Similarly, the arrival of the "Veltro" of Canto I prefigures the second coming of Christ. In this regard, the successful rebuke of the Minotaur, as all rebukes of demons do, prefigures the ultimate rebuke of Satan which is to come and also is closely related to the overcoming of Geryon which we will see in Cantos XVI and XVII. Since both Geryon and Satan have (more or less) human heads, the context suggests that the Minotaur does also. The supposition gains added strength because it allows us to detect a wonderful allusion in the simile of lines 22−25:

> As a bull that breaks loose in the moment
> when it has received the mortal blow, and
> cannot go, but plunges this way and that, so
> I saw the Minotaur do.

Singleton says that this simile refers to the traditional way of slaughtering cattle. First they are stunned by a sledgehammer blow to the head. In this instance the blow would fall in the center of the Minotaur's human forehead, an allusion, I think, to God's own rebuke of the Serpent (identified by Medieval Christianity with Satan) in the third chapter of the book of Genesis. Dante's encyclopedic knowledge even includes the reference to cattle:

> 14 And the Lord God said unto the
> serpent, because thou hast done this
> thou art cursed above all cattle, and
> above every beast of the field; upon
> thy belly shalt thou go, and dust
> shalt thou eat all the days of thy life:
>
> 15 And I will put enmity between
> thee and the woman, and between thy
> seed and her seed; it shall bruise thy
> head, and thou shall bruise his heel.

It will help to recall here that the Pilgrim is depicted in Canto I as being injured in his left foot, symbol of the appetite or desire.

The series of relationships through the Minotaur is further elaborated by the words of Virgil's rebuke (15 – 21):

> My sage cried out toward him, "Perhaps
> you believe that here is the Duke of Athens,
> who dealt you your death up in the world.
> Get you gone beast, for this man does not
> come tutored by your sister, but journeys
> here to see your punishments."

The Duke of Athens (Theseus) finds the Minotaur, a devourer of men, at the center of a labyrinth in Crete by following clues left by Ariadne and thereby saves the youth of Athens. Dante will find Satan, devouring souls, at the center of the labyrinth of Hell by following clues provided by Beatrice and will thereby participate in saving humanity.

Finally, all these relationships refer to the Harrowing of Hell which caused the rock slide referred to at the beginning of the canto. Theseus' trip through the labyrinth results in the freeing of the captives as Dante's trip metaphorically frees men, both "types" (actions which mirror a primary event) of the trip Christ made to free those in Limbo. Readers should remember that Beatrice's trip to Virgil to free Dante is another type of the harrowing. Again, it is an important characteristic of Dante's formal apparatus that such images should be given in both a pagan (Theseus) and a Christian (Dante) context. In a similar way in Canto II, Dante links himself to both a pagan and Christian visitor to the afterlife, Aeneas and St. Paul. There are many other such pairings.

The complex set of meanings so far discussed are linked to the next part of the canto by the figures of the centaurs who, the reader can see, carry the bestial image further as man-animal combinations. Two relatively recent commentators, Robert Hollander and Richard Lansing, shed some light on how the linkage is accomplished. Hollander (1984a), deals with a very old problem in this canto. When Virgil explains his mission to Charon, he makes three requests of the centaur chief (L. 93–6):

> "give us one of your band
> whom we may keep beside, that he may show
> us where the ford is, and carry this one on
> his back, who is not a spirit that can go
> through the air."

Virgil wants a centaur to go with them, this centaur must show them the way and, he must carry Dante on his back. The problem is that the poem never tells us that the poet mounts or dismounts. That he does so depends on a very close reading of the text. Hollander comments that "Few pre-modern poets make as many such demands on their readers and perhaps none is as precise in his importunity." Indeed, the complex interweaving of images which we saw marking the first part of this canto is another example of the kind of work Dante expects of his readers. Hollander's article, as he says, "reflects poetic taste rather than pertaining to 'allegory' or doctrine." Here we are primarily concerned with both allegory and doctrine, but Hollander's poetic analysis can help us with them.

Hollander's poetic analysis consists in paying close attention to a few important verses. First, to paraphrase Virgil, we will walk beside our guide, who will then show us where the ford is and then carry Dante on his back. This seems close to what happens. In line 100 we read that we move WITH the trusty escort. In line 114, Virgil orders Dante to mount, "Let him be first guide to you now and I second." After that, locomotion is spoken of in terms of the centaur (115):

> A little farther on the centaur stopped.

Or in terms of the centaur, Dante combination (126):

> and here was our passage of the ditch.

If this does not convince the reader that Dante mounts the centaur, Hollander adduces a contextual argument similar to the contextual point made above about the shape of the Minotaur. Hollander points out that Dante is carried over the river Acheron by the demon Charon, over the Styx by Phylegas and that he will be placed on the frozen Cocytus by Antaeus later in the poem. While Hollander does not mention that it is on the back of Geyron that Dante spirals down the waterfall in Cantos XVII and XVIII, he does establish that the fact that the Pilgrim is always carried across, around or onto water is an important motif of the poem. I might mention here that these "real" crossings, assisted, contrast strongly with the first, "imaginary" and unassisted crossing of water in Canto I, where the Pilgrim mistakenly attributes his success to his own powers (22−25):

> And as he
> who with laboring breath has escaped from
> the deep to the shore turns to look back on
> the dangerous waters.

These observations lead our discussion back to allegory and doctrine.

Dante mounts the centaur, that is, he comes directly into contact with it. By the power of Virgil's authority (that is reason) he surmounts the agent of Hell. So much does he command the situation that the poem refers to the demonic centaur as a "trusty escort" (100). Here the allegory of the Pilgrim's increasing growth and power over Hell surfaces as it did in the case of the treatment of Argenti in Canto VIII. The mounting motif, always associated with passage over water, begins with Charon, proceeds through the centaur, Geyron and Antaeus and culminates in the "mounting," and thus overcoming, of Satan himself. At the same time this allegory is developing, the Pilgrim is observing those "violent against neighbors" punished in Round I of Circle VII.

Richard H. Lansing (1981) thinks that the punishment of these, as well as the punishment of those in the next two rounds, violent against self and violent against God, are an example of Dante's use of the image of the Great Chain of Being. According to Aristotle and emphasized by the Thomists, soul consists of three aspects. There is a mineral soul, a vegetative soul and an animal soul which combine to form the rational soul of man and all must be present for man to be whole. In this way, in a sense, man contains within himself all of the lower orders of creation, an expression of plenitude. Lansing's point is that the rounds of the violent show a successive descent to the lower orders of soul. The violent against neighbor have descended to the level of animals symbolized by the bestial nature of their centaur guardians and by the fact that the sinners do not speak, as animals characteristically have no speech. Lansing speaks of the sinner's silence, but in fact they utter "piercing screams" (102), mere animal expressions of grief and pain. The violent against themselves in the next round have become trees, expressive of their descent to the level of the vegetable soul and those guilty of violence against God are trapped on a desert plain expressive of their sterile mineral nature. Lansing's insight has the advantage of providing a reason for the puzzling placement of the heretics at the beginning of the circles of violence. It is that their irrational rejection of the immortality of the soul is the first step in depriving man of his special place in the Great Chain and the descent to a level lower than the animal.

That the violent against others are punished in a river of blood is appropriate. Phlegethon is apparently fed by some stream like the little stream that feeds the Styx, continuing the image of all the waters of Hell as part of a single hydraulic system. Like the others, Phlegethon is more like a lake than a flowing river and it varies in depth allowing for fuller immersion of the more guilty. Dante crosses on the back of Nessus at the shallow ford and enters a wood.

CHAPTER 11

Canto XIII

Pier della Vigne: The Sin of Despair

Like the Canto of lust, Canto XIII is much analyzed and written about. My view is that critics are attracted to it not only because suicide is a touching subject, but because, to some degree, they all recognize the canto's structural relationship to Canto V, which, as I have already suggested, is central in establishing some of the formal orderings of the entire canticle. With Canto X, Farinata and the heretics, XIII joins with V as elements in one of the major architectural supports of the poem.

The canto of Pier della Vigne repeats variations of many of the motives established in Canto V. As in V, part of its subject matter is the use and misuse of language. Remember that Francesca spoke beautifully in the language of the *dolce stil nuove*, (the sweet new style), that is courtly love, and that her speech was desperately misleading. Courtly love and its elevated language is, of course, a subject important to Dante's own story as are the issues of faithfulness and adultery which Francesca's story raises. In the case of Pier's narration (54 — 78), we have another example of elevated speech. This time the style is that of Ciceronian rhetoric. Rhetoric is a subject already mentioned in this analysis since the place memory system is an element in the whole rhetorical process. The style of rhetoric utilized by Pier is the language of the courts, of diplomatic missions and of government bureaucracies. Pier della Vigne spent his whole life in such arenas. The known facts and usual suppositions about his life are these. Most think he was of humble birth; his name, della Vigne, of the vine, seems to indicate that his father was something like a grape grower or a vine tender. We do know that he attended the University of Bologna which was, in the early thirteenth century, the most important center of legal studies in the western world. Then, as now, the law degree was the passport into government service and Pier began his career as a notary at the court of Frederick II, the Holy Roman Emperor. He was apparently very competent since in a very few years he became a judge of the highest court and engaged in the most important government work, revising the legal code and organizing the curriculum at the university. During the same period, he established his reputation as a supreme master of the rhetorical style to the extent that his documents were collected and used as textbook examples for the teaching of rhetoric. About 1247 he was named chief minister of the court. Two years later he was disgraced, imprisoned and dead by suicide. It is said that he killed himself by bashing his brains out against a stone wall, an act which, if possible for a human being at all, speaks to a high degree of desperation. The reasons for his sudden downfall are unknown, although stories current in Dante's time speak of bribes, embezzlement and papal plots.

You can see that there are several parallels in the life of Pier with the life of Dante. Both were masters of language who had a part in the government, Pier at the court of Frederick II and Dante in the Signory of Florence. Both were partisans of the Empire and both were condemned by their own government on charges of corruption. As in the case of Francesca, the poet has chosen a figure who can be related to himself both in terms of the details of biography and in master of language. It is on these points, as well as the nature of suicide, that the moral issue of the canto rests.

As the canto begins, we again find ourselves in a trackless wood. Doubtless, we are at this point to remember the trackless wood of Canto I (Sheehan 1972). There, the poet tells us how hard the wood is to describe; here we are given a description of a dark, gnarled, trackless and fruitless place and the description is emphasized with another comparison of the landscape of Hell with that of Italy. The description of the area includes the identification of the local demons who are the Harpies (part human, part bird) from Virgil's *Aeneid*. Significantly, in this variation of the formal structure, there is no need to rebuke these demons. A sign, I think, that the Pilgrim is not threatened by Pier's particular sins. The poem identifies the Harpies (10–11) as those "who drove the Trojans from the Strophades with dismal announcement of future ill" William A. Stephany (1985) points out that "the dismal announcement of future ill" which the Harpies pronounce upon the Trojans is false. Their evil prediction is that the Trojans will be driven by hunger to eat their very tables (*Aeneid* III, 257–258). In the event, the prophesy is benign as the "tables" turn out to be the pieces of bread the Trojans eat after having dined from the other foods piled on them (*Aeneid* VII, 107–118). The moral seems clear. If the Trojans had been overcome by this vision of a bleak future they would not have fulfilled their divine mission to found Rome and would have been denied the joy of discovering the hollow nature of the false prediction. Suicide involves evaluating the future as so bleak as to be unendurable, in short, to despair.

With Stephany's insight, we can now appreciate the relationship of this wood to the wood of Canto I. In that first wood, recall, the Pilgrim sought to escape by climbing a little hill which seemed, on its sun-lit slopes to offer refuge. His access to that seeming place of safety, however, was denied him by the beasts which so oppressed him (I, 54) "that I lost hope of the height." In short, the Pilgrim despaired. This movement of Canto I is very close to the story of the Trojan's expulsion from the Strophades. Like the little hill, the Strophades are a false goal. At that point in the *Aeneid*, Aeneas and his followers know that their real goal is Italy as the Pilgrim must know that his true goal is salvation. Both the Pilgrim and the Trojans are, however, lost, the Pilgrim in a wood, the Trojans in a storm. The Pilgrim finds the hill as the Trojans find the islands. The hill seems lit with light, the islands are abundant with food. But as the light of the hill cannot be reached, the food of the Strophades cannot be eaten as it is despoiled and fouled by the bestial Harpies. Both goals are false and unreachable, but to despair at not being able to reach a false goal would be a terrible failure, similar to the terrible failure of the suicide who, evaluating the possible future woes of this life, neglects the more important nature of the life to come. The pertinence of the Harpies as a warning against mere earthly despair due to false expectations is underlined by the Pilgrim's experience in Canto X where Farinata's prophesy causes Dante grief and moves Virgil to caution him that it is only Heaven (in the person of Beatrice) which knows the true course of his future life (X, 120—132).

In a parallel to the conversation with Francesca, the Pilgrim is so overcome by the midpoint of Pier's narration that he asks Virgil to continue the conversation. Virgil's request, "tell us further how the soul is bound in these knots; and tell us, if you can, whether from such members any soul is ever loosed," (87—90) leads to a straightforward explanation by Pier of some of the elements of the punishment of the sin of suicide and indirectly of the *contrapasso* (94—108):

> "When the fierce
> soul quits the body from which it has up-
> rooted itself, Minos sends it to the seventh

> gullet. It falls into the woods and no part is
> chosen for it, but wherever fortune flings it,
> there it sprouts like a grain of spelt; it shoots
> up to a sapling, and to a wild growth; the
> Harpies, feeding then upon its leaves, give
> pain and to the paid an outlet. Like the
> rest, we shall come, each for his cast-off
> body, but not, however, that any may inhabit
> it again; for it is not just that a man have
> what he robs himself of. Hither shall we
> drag them, and through the mournful wood
> our bodies will be hung, each on the thorn-
> bush of its nocuous shade."

That it is the "fierce" soul which uproots "itself" points to both the bestial (ferocity being a characteristic of beasts) and the selfish nature of this sin. Both pagan and Christian authorities condemn suicide in terms of duties one owes to higher things; Aristotle points to society and Augustine and Aquinas to God (Rolfs 1974). Minos conveys the soul to the seventh circle, but chooses no place for it; that is left to Fortune over whom, as we learned in Canto VII there is no control. As we will see when we examine the first part of Pier's speech, the suicide always considers himself to be the victim of outside forces, beyond his control, and the chance distribution of the souls in the woods is an admirably apt retribution. Similarly, the pain of broken branches comes by chance as the Harpies seem to have no goal in breaking one or another of the plants other than to satisfy their hunger. (The dogs of the next part of the canto break the trees merely by blundering into them.) The Harpies, the "false vision of future ills," who tortured the suicides in life continue to do so after death. The sinners fail to escape as they had hoped.

The central point of the *contrapasso*, that the Harpies "feeding then upon [the] leaves give pain and to the pain an outlet" is both poetically appropriate and consistent, I think, with modern characterizations of suicide: that the suicide's last desperate act is an attempt to communicate their distress. The image of the broken stick, sputtering blood, in order to speak conveys the same message.

The next point is elucidated by Pier himself. After the final judgement, the bodies of the sinners will be hung on the "tree" of the soul in a grim parody of the crucifixion (Cassell 1984). The souls will not enter their bodies "since it is not just that a man have what he robs himself of." I take this strange estrangement in unity to be the parallel of the unity of Francesca with her lover/tormentor in Canto V and the eternal unity of Farinata with his old enemy in Canto X.

The second part of Pier's narration in which he explains the general conditions of the suicides is very clear both in its description and in its implications; it is not so with the first part where Pier exercises his formidable powers of rhetoric (L. 55−78):

> And the stub said, "You so allure me with
> your sweet words that I cannot keep silent;
> and may it not burden you that I am enticed
> to talk a little. I am he who held both the
> keys of Frederick's heart, and turned them,
> locking and unlocking, so softly that from
> his secrets I kept almost every one. So faith-
> ful was I to the glorious office that for it I
> lost both sleep and life. The harlot that never
> turned her whorish eyes from Caesar's house-
> hold-the common death and vice of courts-
> inflamed all minds against me; and they, in-
> flamed, did so inflame Augustus that my glad
> honors were changed to dismal woes. My
> mind, in scornful temper, thinking by dying
> to escape from scorn, made me unjust against
> my just self. By the new roots of this tree
> I swear to you that I never broke faith with
> my lord, who was so worthy of honor. And if
> one of you returns to the world, let him com-
> fort my memory which still lies prostrate
> from the blow that envy gave it."

Commentators have frequently read this speech and emerged from the experience with a verdict of sympathy for the "maligned" Pier della Vigne in much the same way that they were lured into sympathy for the "inno- cent" Francesca or struck with admiration for the "noble" Farinata. Recent scholars have approached the poem, for the most part, in a less romantic attitude and taken it as a matter of course that to properly read Dante's poem, one has to side, temporarily at least, with Dante's God who has made the judgement (and since He is who He is, He cannot be mistaken) that those in Hell are not innocent or noble and that "maligned" in some sense or not, suicide is a sin worthy of damnation. I think that we have been able to see the sinful nature of Francesca and Farinata and that we can see through Pier, too. Later we must confront figures such as Bruno Latini and Ulysses, equally complex problems. (Even if we are successful in determining the justice of God's judgement in all these cases, we will still be left with the case of Virgil who is likewise condemned to an eternity in Hell. Virgil represents the central battle in the "Struggle of the Pity.")

Virgil's invitation to the bush (never identified by name, Pier della Vigne was very famous in Dante's age and the Poet evidently expected his readers to identify Pier from context) is in terms of fame and his response to the invitation is eager. Please note that what Pier lacks is honorable fame, infamy he already has. In his taste for earthly fame with honor Pier is not different from several of the souls we have already encountered and some we shall meet shortly. Indeed, this taste even fails to distinguish Pier from Dante himself whose "fair style has done me honor" (I, 87) and who admits to being one of the six greatest poets of all time (IV, 93−102). The difference is, of course, that Pier's taste for fame and honor overrides his concern for the spiritual; a threat to his merely temporal reputation causes him to lose his eternal soul. As he says, "my honors were changed to dismal woes" and that it was an attempt to escape from scorn that moved him to suicide.

Whence came this fatal blow to his pride? The harlot, he says, the "common death and vice of courts" who never turns her eyes from Caesar's household. The sin of the eyes is envy (Singleton, 1970), indeed a common vice in bureaucracies. It is Envy who sets the events in chain that are to ruin Pier. This is the inexorable outside force referred to above. The suicide can ascribe no chance to the world, no possible escape from "fate" and succumbs to the Harpy by despairing of the future (a crucial observation about Pier made by William Stephany 1982, 1985). In this way the suicide comes to see his suicide as the inevitable outcome of a course of events which he cannot control. In exactly the same way, Francesca attributed her sin variously to Paolo's lust, to "Love" itself (personified there as Envy is here) or to the book which she was reading. In neither case is there the slightest acceptance of personal responsibility, a denial of free will itself.

Examining Pier's speech further, we see that the issue of control has a large part in it as several recent commentators have noted (Levenson

1972; Sheehan 1974; Baird 1967). He emphasizes his control of Frederick; he held the keys and used them so skillfully that everyone else is excluded from his confidence. Baird says that to Pier (and suicides in general, in Dante's analysis) everyone is either controlling or controlled. A fact reinforced by the anonymous suicide, concluding the canto, who denies his own control, "What blame have I for your sinful life?" (135) and in turn blames Mars for the woes of Florence (143—145). Pier swears "that I never broke faith with my lord who was so worthy of honor." He probably didn't, in the Poet's view, since those punished for treachery are further down the pit. Treachery is not the issue, suicide is. What we should think of Pier's characterization of Frederick as "honorable" is revealed by Frederick's presence in the circle of Heresy (X, 1119).

Pier's speech, when analyzed, makes a bad case for him. Why then is it so persuasive that we have to be so critical in understanding it? The answer is the same as in the case of Francesca's speech. It is persuasive because it is beautiful and designed to appeal to our emotions. Even Farinata shows a pretty turn of phrase and is a master of the empty compliment that turns out to be an insult, but Pier della Vigne is a master of technical rhetoric with a reputation so grand that even Dante himself profitably studied his works. Some commentators (Sheehan 1974, Higgins 1975) have subjected Pier's speech to a technical analysis using the principles and procedures of classical rhetoric. Higgins finds the parts of an oration, *Exordium, Narratio, Partitio* etc. Sheehan analyses it profitably in terms of *notatio, ethos, and pathos*. On a very pragmatic level, Ciceronian rhetoric works. The techniques put the reader in a receptive frame of mind and he believes, if he isn't careful, what it is wanted of him to believe. Dante thought any such use of the arts of language to deceive to be evil.

There is evidence that Dante had reason to despise all of Pier's motives in using the art of rhetoric whatever he may have thought of his technical skill. William A. Stephany (1982) again helps us, through a study of documents "not readily available to the modern reader," discover the reason for Dante's distaste for Pier. The fact is that the Holy Roman Emperor, Frederick II, apparently was a heretic as Dante claims and at his court in Sicily where Pier was chief minister and sycophant, revived the pagan practice of emperor worship, seeing himself very much as a "Roman" emperor. This fact explains the references that Pier makes in his speech to "Augustus" and "Caesar." Both references clearly refer hyperbolically to

Frederick. Stephany has studied one of Pier's most famous examples of rhetorical style, an *Eulogy* written in praise of the emperor (written while the emperor was alive, not as a funeral oration). This eulogy borrows freely phrases and images from ancient sources and from the Bible itself, notably from Jeremiah, Ezekiel and Isaiah. The point of the document is to identify Frederick as both Caesar and Augustus and even as a new Messiah. The Biblical citations are ripped from their context and freely rearranged by Pier to suit his purposes. It is all rather like using Holy Scripture as a box of old spare parts to be fitted in as convenient. Dante was properly horrified at this sacrilege and took his revenge by placing Pier where we see him. Many of the details of the *contrapasso* are arrived at by the Poet reexamining Pier's misappropriated passages and deriving the punishment from the proper context. These details include such as Pier's rejection by the "Eagle" (the emperor) and his betrayal by his fellow courtiers. As Stephany points out, the depths of Dante's meaning can only be discovered by examining the entire context of the issues the Poet raises. That this should require us to consult works outside the *Comedy* should not come as a surprise by now as we have already seen that Dante expects us to know the details of Virgil's *Aeneid* and, as we learned in Canto V, to know what really happened in the tale of Lancelot and Guinevere.

I think this all helps to explain why there is no necessity to rebuke the demon Harpies in this canto. The Pilgrim, so to speak, met his Harpies in Canto I. With Virgil's help and by virtue of his continued growth in confronting sin, he is no longer in any danger of despair. In the rest of the *Inferno*, he will sometimes express his fear, but he will never despair. Unlike Pier, the Pilgrim understands his fate in terms of free will, his freedom to bend himself to the will of a benevolent God. Pier can only think in terms of malevolent fate and his response is to try to control everything, the emperor, the other courtiers, even the text of the Bible which he "controls" by ripping segments out of context for a blasphemous praise of his heretical master. Underlining the distance of Pier from the figure of Dante is this issue of language. Pier della Vigne joins the list of those in Hell, Francesca, Farinata and others yet to come, who utilize language only to conceal truth or to cause harm in marked contrast to the Poet whose attempt is to speak the truth convincingly.

The association of Lano of Siena and Jacopo da Santo Andrea with the suicides of this canto is due to a peculiarity of Dante's Italy that is the fad for wealthy young men to deliberately and quite self-consciously to spend themselves into penury, even organizing themselves in clubs for the purpose of doing so (Singleton, 1970). The great Jacob Burckhardt in *Civilization of the Renaissance in Italy* (and he counts Dante's time as "Renaissance") credits the Italians with such a high degree of self-consciousness that they turned all human activities into works of art or artistic "games" such as the "game" of chivalry or the "game" of courtly love. Though he does not treat of prodigality, I think he would see it too as such a game. The stories about it are stunning (again, see Singleton) from Jacopo passing time on a voyage by tossing coins in the water to the "Spendthrift Club" of which Lano was a member tossing their gold plates and utensils out the window when they were soiled. It is hard to account for such tastes. Perhaps the strain of possessing the great amounts of wealth generated by Italy's changing economy at the time (note Dante's difficulty with usury) was simply more than some pre-modern consciousnesses could stand. In any case, Dante thought it horrid, equating the wasting of substance, wealth, with the taking of one's own life. Already the Pilgrim has encountered a version of this sin in Canto VII, but those were the merely incontinent. These are individuals who deliberately willed their own financial ruin. Perhaps the symbolism is that these squanderers by their sinful "control" of their wealth lose all control, becoming finally helpless, sustained only by charity. The suicides similarly lose control when they reduce themselves to the single option of death.

The last sinner, the "anonymous Florentine," as we noted above denies his responsibility for others and blames Mars for the woes of Florence. He pitifully asks for his broken members to be gathered around him and relates his own meaningless end, hanging from the timbers of his own house.

CHAPTER 12

Canto XIV

Capaneus: Blasphemy and the Fall of Man

This canto contains two obviously difficult problems: the problem of the river which cuts across the burning plain ("The most notable thing seen in Hell so far," says Virgil.), and the problem of the interpretation of the figure of the *gran veglio*, the "Old Man," which Virgil's explanation (XIV, 94–120) places inside Mt. Ida on Crete. What is the relevance of the Old Man here? In his poem, Dante has taught us to look for unity and so therefore we look for a connection between the figure and other things in the poem. Why, we also must ask, is this river so special? Can it really be more marvelous than *anything* so far seen? That the figure of the Old Man allows Virgil to complete the description of the river system of Hell is indeed useful, but the careful detail of the figure leads readers to suspect that there is much more than that. The river is useful too, in that in the next canto the travelers are able to walk along it protected from the falling flames, but again we expect more.

I think we should begin with Capaneus, the only sinner with whom the travelers interact (although we are told there are others experiencing differing degrees of pain) and through his sin and the *contrapasso*, come to the Old Man and the river. Capaneus's sin is among the most easily understood in the entire *Inferno*. He blasphemes and defies God. This simple fact is explained, with ever increasing clarity, three times in the canto, once by each of the actors. First Dante explains it in his question to Virgil (46–48):

> "who is the great one who seems not to heed
> the fire, and lies disdainful and scowling, so
> that the rain seems not to ripen him?"

Capaneus's interruption (51–60) furthers the same point, that Capaneus is pridefully disdainful:

> "What I was living, that I am dead.
> Though Jove weary out his smith, from
> whom in anger he took the sharp bolt by
> which on my last day I was smitten; and
> though he weary out the others, turn by turn,
> in Mongibello at the black forge, crying,
> 'Good Vulcan, help, help!' even as he did
> at the fight of Phlegra, and hurl at me with
> all his might, he would not have thereby
> glad vengeance."

Both Virgil's rebuke of Capaneus and his aside to Dante reemphasizes the point (63–70):

> "O Capaneus!
> in that your pride remains unquenched you
> are punished the more: no torment save your
> own raging would be pain to match your
> fury." Then he turned round to me with
> gentler look saying, "That was one of the
> seven kings who besieged Thebes, and held,
> and seems to hold, God in disdain and prize
> Him little; but as I said to him, his revilings
> are quite fitting adornments to his breast."

All of the sinners of Hell blaspheme from the moment they find themselves on the banks of the Acheron (Cassell 1984), and others such as Farinata seem as if "he had great scorn of Hell" (X, 36). Filippo Argenti in Canto VIII was similarly rebuked for his fury. But blasphemous pride is Capaneus's principle sin and his persistence in defying God even while undergoing punishment for it is a clear illustration of the principle we have so far consistently found: Argenti persisting in range, Francesca in lust, Farinata in Heresy, and that persistence being, in fact, part of the *contrapasso*. Capaneus says it himself, "What I was living, that I am dead."

Blasphemy, violence against God, is similar to all other sins in that it comes from pride. It was pride giving rise to envy which caused Satan to offer violence to God in the primordial act of sin, just as it was pride, the desire to be the "equal of the Gods" (Genesis 3:5), that led to the fall of man. The sin of blasphemy was thought of as symbolically defeated by the sacrament of baptism; a sacrament of particular importance to the *Inferno*.

In the typology of medieval Christianity the sacrament of Baptism leads people from blasphemous idolatry to the true worship of God. The sacrament is prefigured by the crossing of the Red Sea and the drowning of the Egyptians (idolaters, the old life, sin) and the entry into the new way. Perhaps the fact that Dante and Virgil cross this burning desert of blasphemy protected by the banks of a river whose "redness" is reminiscent of blood (of redemption?) and the Red Sea, and which so impresses the pilgrim (76–78), is intended to bring this image to mind. Blasphemy can be not only defying God, as in the example of Capaneus, but also denying Him worship by replacing Him with false gods. Cassell (1984) uses the term "perfect" blasphemy for this last sort and equates it with acts such as that of Alexander of Macedon (significantly mentioned in the simile of 31–36) who set up himself as a god.

Many critics have understood the Old Man as a symbol of the decline of man. The ideas of symbolizing the "ages" of human history by different materials apparently comes from Ovid and the Old Testament. Here is Ovid's image from the *Metamorphoses* as cited by Singleton (1970):

> Golden was that first age, which, with no one to compel, without a law, of its own will, kept faith and did the right. There was no fear of punishment, no threatening words were to be read on brazen tablets; no suppliant throng gazed fearfully upon its judge's face, but without judges lived secure.

The church fathers, to whom the idea of history as a decline was in accord with their beliefs, variously interpreted the significance of the different materials. The whole idea is really an application of the image of the Great Chain to history, since gold has more "value" than silver or iron. St. Jerome saw the various materials symbolizing successive civilization: gold was the Babylonian, silver meant the Medes and Persians, the bronze was the Greeks and iron, Roman (Cassell 1984). To Dante, the frail pottery foot on which the figure bears its weight has an obvious meaning and is related to the image of the lame pilgrim in Canto I. It is important here that the issue of the "lame foot," the injury caused man by Satan, was brought up as recently as Canto XII and there in connection with the Minotaur of Crete. We need to examine this Cretan connection and I will return to it in a moment.

The image of the Old Man is then an application of the traditional symbols applied to a statue. Dante's source of inspiration, in addition to Ovid, is three-fold. One source is Pliny's *Natural History* which Dante would have known well. In it, Pliny reports that, after an earthquake, the body of a giant sixty-nine feet tall was found inside a mountain in Crete. His second source is the story in Daniel 2 of the dream of Nebuchadnezzar and its interpretation by Daniel. The dream, as it was recalled to the King by Daniel, is as follows:

> 31 Thou, O king, sawest and
> behold a great image. This great
> image, whose brightness was excel-
> lent, stood before thee: and the form
> there of was terrible.
>
> 32 This image's head was of fine
> gold, his breast and his arms of silver,
> his belly and his thighs of brass.
>
> 33 His legs of iron, his feet part of
> iron and part of clay.
>
> 34 Thou sawest till that a stone was
> cut out without hands which smote
> the image upon his feet that were of
> iron and clay, and brake them to
> pieces.
>
> 35 Then was the iron, the clay, the
> brass, the silver, and the gold, broken
> to pieces together, and became like
> the chaff of the summer threshing-
> floors; and the wind carried them
> away, that no place was found for
> them: and the stone that smote the
> image became a great mountain,
> and filled the whole earth.

Daniel then interprets the dream for Nebuchadnezzar in a way similar to St. Jerome's adaptation cited above. Nebuchadnezzar's is the kingdom denominated by the gold, successively later and lesser kingdoms are meant by the metals declining to the clay foot. The stone signifies the coming of a kingdom which will last forever. In Dante's time theologians interpreted the stone, of course, to be the kingdom of Christ. For the poet, Nebuchadnezzar's image could then stand for all of sinful human history as it is before the kingdom of God is established. It is unknown what direct connection might exist between Ovid's metaphor and the story told in the Old Testament, but as we have seen, Dante likes to frame his points with both a pagan and a Christian image and this occurrence of a similar image in the literature of both cultures was fortunate for him.

The third source, pagan legend, brings us again to Crete. (In fact, Pliny has already brought us back to Crete.) According to the stories, Saturn, the father of the gods, had reigned on Crete. This is the reference Dante makes in lines 94–96:

> "in the middle of the sea there lies a wasted
> country," he then said, "which is named
> Crete, under whose king the world once was chaste."

"Chaste" because there was only one God and all creation worshiped him. This is the pagan "type" analogous to the period after the Judao-Christian creation and before the flood when the God of the Old Testament received the homage of all men. It was said, however, that Saturn was destined to be overthrown by one of his own children. As they were born, in order to avoid this, he ate them. This is the reason Rhea hid the birth of Jove in Mt. Ida and had her Curetes conceal his cries with their shouts (97–102):

> A mountain is there called Ida, which
> once was glad with waters and with foli-
> age; now it is deserted like a thing outworn.
> Rhea chose it of old for the faithful cradle
> of her son and, the better to conceal him
> when he cried, made them raise shouts
> there.

Jove does survive and succeeds in banishing his father, but in doing so ushers in the age of polytheism and idolatry (the age of silver). The Cretans' own legend though is that Jove himself died and was buried on Crete (Cassell 1984). Significantly, the Cretans worshiped Jove in the form of a bull. This aspect of Cretan religious belief was considered very important by the very early Christians, the point being that the pagan god dies and is dead, while the Christian God rises again. This image of a dead god (a blasphemy) is what St. Paul in 1 Corinthians 1, 23 calls a "stumbling block to the Jews and to the Greeks a foolishness" since it is the major difficulty in the face of the conversion of these peoples, that in order to be saved they must believe (an act of faith, not reason) in the resurrected Christ. The stumbling block to the Jews is an issue to which Dante returns in the last canto of *Inferno*.

To Dante, of course, Jove is merely the pagan word for God, reflecting a pagan level of understanding and a blasphemous statement about Jove amounts to a blasphemy about God himself. To say that God is dead and buried is surely such a blasphemy. After all, Capaneus is in Hell for blaspheming against Jove, not God. So it is that the false image of the dead God, Pliny's giant in the mountain, the ages of Ovid and Nebuchadnezzar's dream are combined to create the image of decadent and blasphemous mankind concealed in the mountain on Crete. The statue faces Rome, symbolizing Dante's time and the contemporary stage of history, but seeing only itself in a mirror. Its back is to Damietta in Egypt, symbolizing the past. Dante's contribution to the syncretic image is the fissure through which its tears flow. These are the tears of sorrow and hopeless ignorance, for as we see, the image of the Old Man is the image of man without a true vision of God; the old man of history unredeemed by the new man, Christ.

Why does this complex of images revolve around the island of Crete? Because, as many commentators know, Crete, in the geographical scheme of the time, was the center of the hemisphere of land and it was appropriate to Dante that the tears of man's sorrow flow from the center of man's habitation down into the pit of Hell. The tears, says Virgil, flow (115–120):

> "from rock to rock into this valley: they
> form Acheron, Styx and Phlegethon; then
> their way down is by this narrow channel
> until, there where there is no more descend-
> ing, they form Cocytus - and what that pool
> is, you shall see; here therefore I do not de-
> scribe it."

What perhaps many critics have not seen is how carefully Dante has prepared his Cretan connection by the Minotaur episode in Canto XII where we are reminded of Theseus, a type of Dante the Pilgrim, who descends into the labyrinth, a type of Hell, to overcome the Minotaur, a type of Satan. Crete is a major symbol of all that is sinful, past and outworn about mankind. Its central location emphasizes the centrality of man's sinfulness.

Now, what about the river? Its significance seems to lie in the *contrapasso* of the blasphemers. They, the violent against God, are the most severely punished on the plain since they must lie on their back on the burning sand. The fact that they suffer the most is indicated by Dante's statement that they "...gave more tongue to their pain" (27). I think the nature of this punishment could come, in part, from the Nebuchadnezzar story which is so prominent in the figure of the Old Man. In Daniel 3 is told the story of Shadrach, Meshach and Abednego cast into the fiery furnace precisely because they would not participate in an act of "perfect" blasphemy and fall down and worship the golden image which Nebuchadnezzar had set up on the plain of Dura. It is therefore fitting that the blasphemers should suffer the pain of flame with which the blasphemer Nebuchadnezzar tried to destroy the righteous. I think Donno (1977) is convincing when he argues that the notability of Phlegethon is precisely that it offers a way through the falling flames protecting the travelers by the rising vapors which quench the flames above it (85–90). Donno points out that all else in Hell is designed for pain, but that this is a mitigation. The *contrapasso* is that as the blasphemers scorned the mercy of God in life, they now must suffer by seeing that mercy present eternally before them, but not be able to participate in it. No sinners are protected by the river; truly, their punishment is horrible as the poet so calls it in line 6 and implies in the direct address to the reader (13–16):

> O vengeance of God, how much should
> you be feared by all who read what was re-
> vealed to my eyes!

Now, all the punishments in Hell are "horrible." Most readers notice in fact, that in terms of severity, it is difficult to distinguish among them. For instance, it is hard to see how Farinata's bath in a tomb of flames is any less than Capaneus's experience of fire. The particular horribleness of this "mode of justice" (Cassell's term) must be so because it takes place directly contrasted with the river which is a reminder of God's capacity for mercy. When the Pilgrim reaches the mountain of Purgatory, he finds there, as Virgil

anticipated in Canto I (118–120), souls likewise punished in the presence
of the capacity for mercy and who, because they know that they will experience it, are joyful:

> Then you shall see those who
> are content in the fire because they hope
> to come among the blessed, whensoever that
> may be.

Dante and Virgil are ushered into Purgatory by Cato the Younger of
Utica, a pagan suicide whose beloved wife is found in Limbo (see Purgatorio
I). It has always been a problem for Dante scholars why a pagan and a
suicide to boot is given such an honorable position as the gate-keeper of
Purgatory (rather an analogy to St. Peter as the gate-keeper of Heaven).
The problem, is, in fact, part of the whole issue of the treatment of the sin
of suicide as no pagans at all are condemned for suicide itself, but instead
are punished for their motives in committing the act. The best explanation
seems to be that Dante was moved by his respect for the great minds of
antiquity as necessary parts of God's plan of history and by the fact that he
understood that many pagans viewed suicide to be sometimes a duty one
owed the state or a higher ideal (Rolfs 1974). Cato was a philosopher and
a statesman who fought against the usurpation of the Republic by Julius
Caesar and, when the cause was hopeless and Pompey defeated, killed
himself by falling on his own sword. Cato's campaign in North Africa is part
of the subject of Lucan's *Pharsalia* which recounts Cato's visit to the shrine
of Jove in Libya where, in spite of the fact that he was urged to do so, he
refused to tempt the god. Cato's devotion to opposing tyranny and his piety
probably account for his special position in *Purgatorio*. Alexander of
Macedon (31) visited the same shrine in Libya and blasphemously used the
oracle there for his own deification (Cassell 1984). The present canto, line
15, is the only place in the *Divine Comedy* that Cato is mentioned by name,
only a few lines removed from the canto of the suicides where we might
expect to find him. Rolfs (1974) thinks that the Poet expected his readers
to notice this juxtaposition and to reflect as to the reason why Cato was not
found in the trees.

One final point. While the Pilgrim begins this canto with an act of
sympathy after hearing the anonymous suicide of Canto XIII, his gesture is
not for the sinner, but as he says (1–2), "Because the love of my native

place constrained me" The Pilgrim "properly" understands suicide, although the rhetorical skills of Vigne posed a challenge for him. Blasphemy is no such ordeal. He expresses no pity and easily recognizes the arrogance of Capaneus. Virgil severely castigates Capaneus for that fault in much the same way he participated in the Pilgrim's interaction with Argenti. There, we took this cooperation to be a sign of the Pilgrim's development and so we should here too. If we understand the Pilgrim's progress to be indicated by his use of reason (allegorically the quality of his relationship with Virgil), it is notable that it is in this canto that once again the issues that divided the two at the walls of Dis are openly spoken of (43–44):

> "Master, you who overcome all
> things except the obdurate demons that came
> out against us at the entrance of the gate."

Like a wound that is healed over, the quarrel can now be mentioned without arousing rancor. Virgil in turn indicates his pleasure in his pupil by approvingly commenting, "Truly you please me in all your question" (133). The Pilgrim's hard won understanding will now again be brutally tested.

CHAPTER 13

Canto XV

Brunetto Latini: Sins Against Nature

There is certainly as much hellish commotion among Dante scholars over whatever the sin of Brunetto Latini is as about any other issue in the *Divine Comedy*. It ranks as a subject of controversy with the identity of the Veltro, the case of Ulysses, Ugolino's feast, and the DXV.

The first issue that confronts the reader in this canto is a question of fact, the problem of Brunetto's homosexuality. We are here in the third round where are punished those guilty of violence against God, nature and her goodness. In Canto XI, Virgil described it thus (46–51):

> "Violence may be done against the Deity,
> by denying and blaspheming Him in the
> heart, and despising Nature and her good-
> ness; and therefore the smallest ring seals
> with its mark both Sodom and Cahors, and
> all who speak contemning God in their
> heart."

Already we have seen Capaneus prone on the burning sand still emptily blaspheming. He is the representative of the violent against God. Now we have come to those violent against Nature. Nature is, of course, a "thing" of God since He created it (or her in Dante's characterization). The important intimacy between God and Nature is explained by Virgil in XI, 97–105 where he said that Nature in its working imitates God and is in turn imitated by man in his work. In the wood of suicides we saw that those who did violence to themselves were punished along with those who did violence to their "things" or goods. The same principle operates here: violence to Nature is as direct an assault upon God as is blasphemy.

The problem with this understanding is in the question of how, exactly, Brunetto and the other runners on the burning sand were violent against Nature. The answer seems simple since Virgil has told us that this ring "seals with its mark both Sodom and Cahors." Cahors was a French city noted for usury and as the Pilgrim will soon meet several usurers, Cahors clearly designates that sin. Likewise, it should be with Sodom, a city identified with homosexuality. Unfortunately for such an easy understanding, none of the individuals met here, either Brunetto, those he names, (Priscian, Francesco d'Accorso or the scruffy transferee of 110–114) or the "three noble Florentines" of the next canto have the slightest reputation for sodomy. The contemporary figures in the list were so well known that it is impossible that only Dante would have known of their unnatural vice and would have chosen to accuse them in the verses of his poem. Priscian lived about 500 A.D. and there is no tradition of his being a homosexual and we possess the same information about him Dante did. True, the earliest commentators, such as Boccaccio, simply took it for granted that Dante was revealing his own secret knowledge and accepted the sin of the runners as homosexuality. Modern scholars cannot be so uncritical, however, and have attempted to look as deeply into the matter as the distance of time allows.

The best place to begin is with the work of Richard Kay (1978). Dr. Kay's work is far too complex to adequately summarize here (he devotes over 400 pages to this question), but we can seize on some of his conclusions. The most important of these is, I think, exactly what a man of Dante's time, place and education would have understood by a sin sealed with the mark of Sodom. First, Professor Kay notes that such a sin is said to be "sealed with the mark" of Sodomy, not necessarily sodomy itself, but somehow related, a member of a class so to speak. With this point we are already much closer to working out the puzzle since we do not any longer have to force Brunetto into a procrustean homosexual bed. The context is further amplified by what Biblical commentators of Dante's time said about the story of Sodom (found as part of Genesis, chapters 12 through 19) in the standard reference books. According to the commentaries, the evil citizens of Sodom were "exposed" to the nature of Abram's God by the victory of Abram's tiny force over the four kings who had plundered Sodom and by Abram's kindness and generosity in returning their goods to them (all this in Chapter 14). To the commentators, the significance of God's works in the presence of the Sodomites is that they amount to a revelation of the nature of God, that is, something the citizens of Sodom could not have learned by unaided reason alone. When the angels visit Lot in Chapter 19, however, the Sodomites behave as if this revelation had not been given them. Lot saw the strangers at the city gate and invited them home with him where he fed them.

> 4 But before they went to bed, the men of
> the city beset the house both young and old,
> all the people together. 5 and they called
> Lot, and said to him: Where are the men that
> came into thee at night? Bring them out
> hither that we may know them. 6 Lot went
> out to them, and shut the door after him, and
> said: 7 Do not so, I beseech you, my breth-
> ren, do not commit this evil. 8 I have two
> daughters who as yet have not known man:
> I will bring them out to you, and abuse you
> them as it shall please you, so that you do no
> evil to these men, because they are come in
> under the shadow of my roof. 9 But they
> said: Get thee back thither. And again:
> Thou camest in, said they, as a stranger, was
> it to be a judge? Therefore we will afflict thee
> more than them. And they pressed very
> violently upon Lot: and they were even at
> the point of breaking open the doors. 10 and
> behold the men put out their hand, and drew
> in Lot unto them and shut the door. 11
> And them that were without were struck with
> blindness from the least to the greatest, so
> that they could not find the door.

To the biblical commentators that Dante knew, the central issue was not that the townsmen wanted to rape the angels. Sodomy was a terrible sin, but only one aspect of the issue. Even intercourse itself seemed hardly to count, since, as we see, Lot offered the Sodomites his virgin daughters for whatever use the men wanted. The reason for this astonishing gesture, Lot explains, is that the men (angels) "came under the shadow of his roof." That is to say, that a guest-host relationship had been established, food had been shared and for Lot to give his guests up would violate a special and God sanctified trust. The men of Sodom should have understood generosity and courtesy because of the earlier revelation given to them through Abram's kindness. Their behavior contrary to revelation is specifically called sacrilege, which is to say, violence to the things of God or Nature. In the

extreme Medieval elaborations of this story the definitions of the sacrile-
gious acts clustered around the incident came to include such diverse things
as heresy, false prophesy, ingratitude and the refusal of responsibility
(among many others which Kay enumerates). In considering the sins of
Sodom, the Medieval exegetes apparently came to sodomy itself as the
least of it and then because the act was merely negative in that it prevented
something (procreation) ordered by God. In short, the sin with the seal of
Sodom is sacrilege, a violation of a law of nature, and is not restricted to
homosexual intercourse at all. It seems to me that here is another case
wherein Dante teaches us that we must know the context of particular
issues. He knew that his contemporary readers would be shocked by the
apparent accusation of sexual perversion against these famous people and
he apparently expected them to pursue the issue through the commentaries
to arrive at the truth. In that process they would not only learn of the true
errors of Brunetto and the others, but also about the true nature of sacrilege
even as the Pilgrim in his journey through Hell learns of the true nature of
sin. This case is analogous to the Francesca episode where he expected us
to know the "true" story of Lancelot and Guinevere or as in Canto XIII where
he clearly expects us to know Virgil's *Aeneid* well.

Kay's exhaustive research offers suggestions as to what exact
sacrilege Brunetto, Priscian and the rest committed. Other scholars have
naturally disagreed about the exact sin, but all researchers since Kay seem
to agree that we no longer can search only for evidence of homosexuality.
We will briefly summarize some of the various conclusions, but first let us
look at the text ourselves.

The Pilgrim has left Capaneus and travels along the edge of
Phlegethon, sheltered from the rain of fire by the vapor from the stream.
The long simile which compares the banks of the stream to dikes in Flanders
and Italy not only tells us how the river is contained (it must run above the
low lying plain, with the high banks keeping it from spreading out), but
keeps alive the image of the sea which makes up so much of the imagery of
Inferno. At the same time, the fact that the travelers are crossing a desert
place is part of the Exodus motif. Some commentators explain the falling
flakes of fire as inversions of the manna which fell for the Hebrews in their
exodus from Egypt. One can also recall Lansing's thesis (1981) of the Great
Chain of Being imagery throughout the circles of the violent and note that
here we have reached the level of the mineral soul, like sodomy, sterile.

Dante tells us (13) that he is so far from the wood that even if he had looked back, he could not have seen it. Not looking back on sin is symbolic of overcoming it, of course, but the passage also brings to mind the wife of Lot who looked back on the city of Sodom and was turned into the mineral salt. Lot's wife was told not to look back by an angel, so her error amounts to a violation of a revelation, that is, a sacrilege.

It's tempting to take Dante's reference to the distant wood as some sort of measure of the vastness of Hell, except that he tells us that the troops of souls which he now encounters have difficulty seeing him, by which we are informed that, falling flames notwithstanding, Hell is very dim and all things difficult to ascertain (17–21):

> each looked at us as men look
> at one another under a new moon at dusk;
> and they knit their brows at us as the old
> tailor does at the eye of his needle.

Here now, Dante and Brunetto recognize one another and both are astonished. As in other encounters, the Pilgrim obviously respects the sinner. In these others instances, we have seen that the respect is to some extent misplaced, as in the case of Farinata. A similar point is more difficult to make here, however, as Dante repeatedly affirms his respect for Brunetto and his indebtedness to him in ways which no evidence, internal or external, can contradict. His astonishment at finding Brunetto with the sodomites (and some of the running bands might be homosexuals) mirrors the astonishment the Poet expected to create in his readers who knew of Brunetto. (The real Brunetto Latini died in 1294, so it is possible for Dante's first readers to have known him personally.) I think that the most important clue to understanding the placement of this respect-worthy individual lies in the role of Virgil here. This variation of the canto format is nearly entirely taken up with the encounter with Brunetto. In the whole conversation Virgil utters only six words (99) and these are an aside to Dante, neither to or about Brunetto. Indeed, Virgil is not even named even though Brunetto specifically asks who he is in 48, "who is this who shows the way?" Brunetto knows that Virgil is the guide, not merely a companion or servant, but he does not know who he is. We can see the general sense of this. All sinners in Hell (except those in Limbo) are in some sense strangers to reason, but Brunetto is a unique case, seeing clearly the role of reason, without knowing its identity. As with all sinners, as he is in Hell, so must he have been in life. This is the necessary clue to the sin of Brunetto Latini.

The Pilgrim's evasive answer to Brunetto's question is also crucial in understanding the Pilgrim's stage of development. He summarizes his entire story in fewer than fifty succinct words (49–54):

> "There above in the bright life," I an-
> swered him, "I went astray in a valley, before
> my age was at the full. Only yesterday morn-
> ing I turned my back on it. He appeared to
> me, as I was returning into it, and by this
> path he leads me home."

In Canto XIII we saw the last of the Pilgrim's despair. Here we now see that he has comprehended his goal. Virgil is simply taking him home to his proper (in the Aristotelian sense) place with Beatrice and with God. Now we see why we can trust his assessment of Brunetto. The fearful, ignorant man who quarreled with reason, who misunderstood Francesca and Farinata, is no more and we who travel with him can be confident of his reactions as we face the fiercest wraiths of the very depths of Hell. This security is, of course, the point of Virgil's aside to Dante in 99, "He who notes it listens well" in reference to the Pilgrim's polite dismissal of Brunetto's prophesy of his future earthly ills. Fortune may do as she wills, one's true destiny is eternal and beyond her grasp. This is one of the *Inferno's* central lessons. In fact, it is a very simple idea to grasp, but see with what difficulty it is reached! At this middle point of the journey the veil of allegory is very thin and the moral Dante would teach shines through.

The central location of Brunetto is important (I think that there are twenty-nine sins which we see in Hell. Brunetto's is number fourteen). In significant ways he is very much like Dante himself, a scholar and writer, a master of rhetoric and a sometime official of the city of Florence. Like Dante, he was exiled when the flow of politics turned against him. Dante acknowledges the similarities by praising Brunetto as his teacher (in 86). We might guess then that whatever sacrilege Brunetto committed Dante might have been in a position to commit. It is true that Dante acknowledges Brunetto as teacher, but it is Virgil whom (In Canto I, 85) he calls "master" and "author." The difference between Brunetto and Dante lies in the difference between what Virgil and Brunetto teach. What does Brunetto teach? "How man makes himself eternal" (85). What does Virgil teach? The way "home." It sounds very similar, but Virgil's lesson leads to Paradise and Brunetto's eternity is in Hell. The Pilgrim regrets this distinction, but he does not actually question its justice (79-81):

> "If my prayer were all fulfilled," I an-
> swered him, "you would not yet be banished
> from human nature"

Someday, "not yet."

You can see where this leads. Most commentators have perceived that Brunetto is a very worldly man. He speaks of his own fame as a final goal (119-120): "Let my *Treasure*, in which I yet live, be commended to you, and I ask no more." He predicts Dante's fame as a result of his "star" (55) and because of "fortune" (70) and his escape from his enemies ("but the grass shall be far from the goat." (72)). These are purely earthly concerns. Brunetto does not mention the fortune of going "home," the truly good fortune. As we have already noted, the Pilgrim is courteous, but dismisses the issue.

> Then he turned back, and seemed like one
> of those who run for the green cloth in the
> field at Verona, and of them seemed he who
> wins, not he who loses.

These are the words of the poem which tells us of Brunetto's departure. Green is the color associated with the salvation in late parts of the *Comedy* and Brunetto "seems" like one who attains the green goal, but he is not. His race appears to be successful, but it is really the purposeless meanderings of Hell.

We can identify the cause of Brunetto's failure a little more exactly now. It is related to worldliness and it must involve sacrilege in the general sense that he must have in some way violated a revelation. This seems possible since to say that a person is worldly might mean a particular attitude towards a revelation as revelation is precisely how we know of otherworldly things. Of all the sins we might examine in *Inferno*, Brunetto's sin is the most abstract from our historical perspective. As an intellectual and a scholar he sins in an intellectual, scholarly way. Dante, also a scholar, judges Brunetto's work and finds the motivation for it lacking. Dante's judgement is idiosyncratic, peculiar to his time and to his own views, which sometimes are not typical of those of his contemporaries. It is not surprising that moderns should find the case of Brunetto difficult.

Kay's suggestion for Brunetto rests on the work which Brunetto himself mentions in the text. The *Treasure* was written while Brunetto was in exile in France. It is an encyclopedia of a type rather common in the Middle Ages, a compendium of knowledge with little pretense to originality. Given the principle of authority, originality was very little valued and no blame could be imputed to Brunetto for collecting the work of others. The book is really a handbook for politicians containing sections of both theoretical and practical knowledge. It stresses political science and rhetorical skills for the use of officials in a republican city like Florence. Brunetto as a Guelph despised imperial power. This itself is enough to cause Dante to reject the conclusion of Brunetto's work although he might admire its contents (the rhetorical teachings of Cicero) or the skill with which it was carried out. As we have seen, Dante was eager for well earned fame ("How man makes himself eternal.") The damnable aspect of Brunetto's work, according to Kay, was that Brunetto concentrated on earthly fame and ignored the more important issue of one's eternal fate, the facts of which are learned through a study of God's revelations to man. Ignoring revelation, "things" of God, is sacrilege. In addition, Brunetto misread the lesson of history as Dante saw it, in that he rejects the rule of the emperor whom Dante believed to be the agent of God ordained to establish peace and justice over the whole world. In that stable setting, the work of salvation could go forward. Since history was for Dante a revelation of God's intentions, opposition to imperial rule also amounted to sacrilege, the sin of Sodom.

Kay's work is complemented by that of Sally Mussetter (1984) who considers Brunetto's other important work, the *Tessoretto* or "Little Treasure." This is an autobiographical poem, like the *Comedy*, establishing yet another link between the two men. As for the *Comedy*, the purpose of the *Tessoretto* was to instruct Brunetto's fellow men. There are other important similarities. Brunetto lost the "high road" and found himself in a "strange wood" where he discovers a guide, the Goddess of Nature. Nature tells him that "Fortune" should be his goal. Eventually on his journey he comes to understand his spiritual needs and studies Christianity. Here

Nature and Grace have led him to the threshold of the fulfillment of the dual nature of man, both mortal and spiritual, but Brunetto turns back from religion and, poignantly, for those of us who read of the Pilgrim's success, reenters the wood to study astronomy with Ptolemy. Mussetter, correctly, I think, identifies this turning back into the wood as the motive of Brunetto's condemnation. Even as the turning back into the wood represents a turn from revelation and grace, Brunetto's support of Florentine Republicanism represents a turning back against God's historical plan which, in Dante's view, requires an empire.

Other scholars do reject Kay's theory altogether. Peter Armour (1983) rejects all the current hypotheses and suggests that Brunetto was a manichean heretic. A hypothesis which would imply a far looser structure to the *Inferno* than our experience would suggest.

The other sinners mentioned by name or allusion in Canto XV are all members of Brunetto's own band which is forbidden to mix with other bands (118). Since they are all members of the same group, their sin must be the same or very similar to Brunetto's. Most scholars think that the paucity of our knowledge makes it very difficult to say anything with certainty about them. The admirable Kay is not afraid to advance a theory about each. Kay believes Priscian to be condemned because, first, like Brunetto he was unnaturally concerned with fame and, second, because his work of Latin grammar, the *Instituitiones grammaticae*, sought to fix the rules of Latin once and for all. Dante believed the Latin language to be an important part of God's governance of the world since it allowed men at differing places and times to communicate. It is unclear how allowing Latin to change with the times could further its usefulness as a medium between times and places, but apparently Dante thought a frozen and rigid Latin grammar would become the property of specialists rather than the universal speech he had in mind. Priscian's interference with the natural development of Latin is again a kind of sacrilege.

Francesca d'Accorsa was a lawyer who committed the sin of sacrilege by advancing legal opinions which made the emperor subject to the pope. The error becomes a sin against revelation because Francesca based his opinions on the work of the decretalists, elaborators of the law, rather than on scripture or the church fathers. Andrea de'Mozzi, the "scurf" who left his "sinfully distended muscles" on the Bacchiglione, was archbishop of Florence. Himself a canon (that is, church) lawyer, his sin is similar to both that of Brunetto and Francesca. His concerns at Florence were almost entirely worldly and financial. He spent much of his energy on various lawsuits against members of his clergy. Dante thought the church should be above such earthly things and trust the providence of God. Indeed, the corruption of the papacy was caused by exactly such concentration on wealth. In addition, Mozzi was like Francesca d'Accorsa in that he ignored the teachings of the church fathers on important matters. Specifically, he heeded the injunction that bishops must preach (and Mozzi took this to mean for the good of his own soul, not necessarily the congregation), but he ignored the teaching of St. Gregory the Great about how the preaching should be done. Gregory warned bishops to preach simply and certainly not about things they themselves were ignorant. Mozzi preached sermons wherein he elucidated the power of God by comparing a turnip seed with a turnip and spoke of omniscience in terms of a mouse which lives on the beams of the ceiling of a house and knows all that goes on in it. Kay thinks that the "il mal poteste nervi" of 114 refers to this straining after comprehension which this overburdened intellect had to do.

To a modern mind, it might seem that Dante is here judging others in terms of his own intellectual, religious, and above all, political standards. To Dante, of course, they were all one, part of a single scheme of God's. Dante's view is essentially mystical in that mystical knowledge (revelation) always takes precedent over rational knowledge. Our eternal goal far transcends any mundane success or failures we might have. Revelation, like grace, is freely given, but once it is received we are required to behave according to its dictates. We might not be exactly sure how the individuals of Canto XV sinned, but we do know that for Dante sin is far more complex than we might suppose given Virgil's relatively clear cut catalog of Canto XI.

The three Florentines of the next canto present a similar case. Their concerns are earthly, the current state of Florence, and they demand information in the name of their fame. Furthermore, their movements are visualized with the same athletic metaphor used for Brunetto. Where he is seen as a participant in a race, these are seen as wrestlers (19–26, perhaps because they were soldiers) as well as runners. Their athletic performance, like Brunetto's, is impressive (86–89):

> Then they broke
> their wheel and in their flight their nimble
> legs seemed wings; an "Amen" could not

have been uttered so quickly as they van-
ished.

Brunetto has already told us that he cannot stop moving or he will
suffer the punishment of Capaneus and lie immobile on the burning sand for
a hundred years. These Florentines add more details to this aspect of the
contrapasso in their polite conversation with Dante (Kay). Three times they
refer to the fact that the Pilgrim has control of his body and mind. First in
32–33 they ask who he is who "thus securely move living feet through
Hell." Second in 64–65, "So may your soul long direct your limbs" And
third in 81, "happy you if you can speak thus at will." This underlines the
fact that their "sodomy" has caused them to cast off man's higher self-
willed characteristics and become objects of another will even as the
minerals of the plain on which they run. Their superb performance is not
their doing.

This band is separate from that of Brunetto which was all made up of
intellectuals. These are all soldiers and politicians. Dante's profound
admiration for them might come from the fact that they were all Guelphs
(supporters of the Florentine Republic). The young Dante had been a Guelph
and was a member of the republican administration of the city of Florence.
These individuals then represent the political affiliation of Dante's youth
which, however, he turned against after his exile when he became a
partisan of the hopeless Ghibelline (imperial) cause. Two of them are among
those the Pilgrim asked Ciacco about as those "who set their minds on doing
good" (VI, 81). Ciacco's answer, "They are among the blackest souls" tells
us how we are to take them now. Perhaps the paradox is partially solved
by the fact that these worldly soldiers and politicians honestly advocated a
position which, in Dante's view, became clearly wrong. Dante the politician
and soldier saw himself to be wrong and changed his allegiance from a
republican to an imperial position because of the spiritual mission of the
Emperor. Within their error, however, at least Tegghiaio and Guido tried to
do good when they opposed the Guelph expedition against Siena in 1260
(Singleton 1970).

The question the runners want answered is related to Brunetto's
ornate prophesy which the Pilgrim brushed off in Canto XV. Is the city still
characterized by courtesy and valor (67–68)? Dante's answer is not

directed to them, but to the city itself. He raises his face to where the sky would be and says (76–75):

> "The new people and the sudden gains
> have engendered pride and excess in you,
> O Florence, so that already you weep for it!"

The "sudden gains" surely include the new wealth of the city and refers to the destroyers of their own substance in XIII as well as to the usurers Dante will meet in XVII. The new people are those recent immigrants from the countryside (Singleton 1970) attracted to the city by economic growth. Brunetto's prophesy speaks also of corruption, but identifies its source as an old evil (XV, 61–66):

> But that thankless, malignant people, who of
> old came down from Fiesole, and still smack
> of the mountain and the rock, will make
> themselves an enemy to you because of your
> good deeds; and there is cause: for among
> the bitter sorb-trees it is not fitting that the
> sweet fig should come to fruit.

The legend of the founding of Florence had it that after the defeat of Catiline, the victorious Romans first destroyed the town of Fiesole which had sheltered him and then founded the new city of Florence. Generous, the Roman settlers allowed any Fiesolians who wished, to live with them. To Dante this mingling of the coarse stock with that of the aristocratic Romans accounted for the divisions in Florentine society. It is important in understanding the significance of this legend to Dante to know that Catiline's revolt was against Roman imperial power. The trouble making Fiesolians are symbols of the rejection of rightful government. Therefore, the agony of Florence is caused by greed on the one hand, a fairly recent evil, and rebelliousness on the other, with much longer roots.

Their question answered, the runners have no further interest in Dante and his guide (about whom they have not even inquired). They make the request for continued earthly fame we have come to expect from such as these and disappear.

CHAPTER 14

Cantos XVI and XVII

Geryon: Dante's Claim to Truthfulness

Since *Inferno* is a place memory system we should expect a major marker at this location. At Cantos XVI and XVII Dante and Virgil are half way along on their journey, at the dividing line between sins of violence and sins of fraud. The marker we are looking for is, of course, Geryon and the flight down the waterfall which sticks in the memory of every reader. Geryon's significance is emphasized by the fact that his advent is anticipated by the two references to the waterfall which frame the episode of the Florentine politicians. The first of these informs us of the existence of the waterfall and gives us a sense of its distance (XVI, 1—3):

> Already I was in a place where the re-
> sounding of the water which was falling into
> the next circle was heard, like the hum which
> beehives make.

The implication of the bee like hum is that we have a distance to go to the source. However, after the encounter with the politicians (during which Dante and Virgil stand still and the sinners circle) we travel only a short while and are suddenly at the falls and the sound is overwhelming (90—93):

> Wherefore it seemed well to my master
> to depart. I followed him; and we had gone
> but a little way when the sound of the water
> was so near we could scarcely have heard
> each other speak.

The cataract is so loud that had the travelers stayed too long, "it would have hurt our ears" (105). At this point, the figure of Geryon enters the scene of the waterfall and his episodes, XVI, 106—XVII, 34 and 79—136 frame the encounter with the usurers in the same way the waterfall references framed that of the politicians. This is formally very neat; description of area merges with the encounter with the demon and both aspects enclose interactions with sinners. For the structural development of the poem, it is important that whereas relations with demons at earlier stages had been marked by conflict, settled by Virgil's rebukes or (in the case of the fallen angels at the wall of Dis) divine intervention, the demons of violence, centaurs, harpies and the transitional figure of Geryon, pose no real threat to the more enlightened Pilgrim who has cast off despair and knows the goal and purpose of his journey. It is true that Dante is frightened of Geryon, but he masters his fear and mastered fear is a long way from despair.

Geryon has a central location and striking appearance and his behavior is as amazing as anything in Hell. Few modern commentators, however, have much to say about him other than he must, in some way, symbolize fraud. I have a little hope of adding some to this and, perhaps, we can elucidate some of the issues surrounding him.

Geryon is enticed to appear by Virgil at the end of XVI. Dante informs us of the nature of the waterfall by comparison with a location in Italy (93–105). This particular cataract is very steep and large at the flood, but not sheer (Singleton 1970). The cord which Dante hands to Virgil is explained by some commentators as an indication that Dante had something to do with the Franciscan order of friars whose members wore such a girdle (Ciardi 1954). As we will see, there is a cogent reason for bringing up the issue of the Franciscans at this point, although the exact meaning of the cord and the leopard which the Pilgrim once hoped to catch with it (107–8) are obscure. The leopard might be identified with the beast of Canto I, and it is true that of all the beasts encountered there the leopard is the least fearsome, as if the fugitive had at least a faint hope of overcoming it. However, his hope there was based on the symbolism of the stars and not the possession of the cord (I, 31–45):

> And behold, near the beginning of the
> steep, a leopard light-footed and very fleet
> covered with a spotted hide! And it did not
> depart from before my eyes but did so im-
> pede my way that more than once I turned
> round to go back.

> It was the beginning of the morning, and
> the sun was mounting with the stars that were
> with it when Divine Love first set those beau-

tiful things in motion, so that the hour of the
day and the sweet season gave me cause for
good hope of that beast with the gay skin;
yet not so much that I did not feel afraid
at the sight of a lion that appeared to me.

Most readers assume that Virgil throws one end of the cord down the waterfall, holding onto the other, although the text does little to support this. We are merely told that Dante hands Virgil the cord "knotted and coiled" (111) and that Virgil "Flung it some distance" down the waterfall. It's not unreasonable to think that he held onto it, but we are not told that he does so nor what he does with it after Geryon appears. The cord is never mentioned again. Clearly its literal function is that of a signal to Geryon, but what of its allegory?

I think the answer may relate to location. There are important similarities and significant differences between the episode here and the action before the walls of Dis. The waterfall is analogous to Dis in that it divides one major sector from another: Dis separates incontinence from violence and the waterfall violence from fraud. Other than being major markers in a spatial sense, the most obvious similarity between the two locations is that at both Virgil has a private conference with demonic forces. On the other hand, at the division marked by Dis, the Pilgrim and his guide are divided from one another by Virgil's presumptuous behavior. The Pilgrim is close to despair and Virgil tries to hide the nature of their difficulty; only divine intervention gets them past the walls. At this division, Virgil and Dante are well in tune with one another and Dante is content to go off a way and interview the usurers while Virgil arranges their passage. This solo journey by the Pilgrim is itself a mark of maturity and strength and reinforces my thesis that Dante, free of despair and sure of his goal, is coming to be the master of the journey. At Dis, remember, all the Pilgrim could do was hide in terror while Virgil approached the fallen angels. The cord, which Virgil uses to summon Geryon, is Dante's property. Therefore, it represents some strength which belongs to Dante himself. If we take it to be part of the uniform worn by those in Holy Orders, then that strength is related to divine power which Virgil, being pagan and representing only human reason, cannot himself possess. The cord, then, is analogous to the messenger at Dis in that it is that emblem of divinity which subdues evil. The Pilgrim had it with him at Dis, but intellectually he was not yet able to use it, as signified by his unsatisfactory relationships with human reason. Here, matured, he has no need of direct divine intervention, exercises his powers with the aid of reason and Geryon obeys without a demure.

Lines 115–136 are among the most packed in the poem. They narrate the action, reveal the Pilgrim's state of mind and the state of mind of the Poet who records the adventure. They testify to the truthfulness of the *Comedy* and marry the image of the monster to the motive of water (115–136):

> "Surely," I said to myself, "something
> strange will answer this strange signal which
> the master so follows with his eye."
>
> Ah, how careful one should be with those
> who not only see the deed, but have the wit
> to read one's thoughts! "Soon will come up
> what I look for and what your mind dreams
> of," he said to me; "soon must it be dis-
> covered to your sight."
>
> To that truth that has the face of a lie a
> man should always close his lips so far as he
> can, for through no fault of his it brings re-
> proach; but here I cannot be silent; and,
> reader, I swear to you by the notes of this
> Comedy - so may it not fail of lasting
> favor - that I saw, through that thick and
> murky air, come swimming upwards a figure
> amazing to every steadfast heart, even as he
> returns who sometimes goes down to loose
> the anchor that is caught on a reef or some-
> thing else hidden in the sea, who stretches
> upwards his arms and draws in his feet.

The Pilgrim expects something strange and the reader begins to anticipate whatever will arise with him. The language of the next few lines is replete with references to the power of sight which will reveal the thing: eye, see, read, look, sight, and this anticipation culminates in 130 when the Pilgrim *saw* the form rising through the air.

Now it is crucial here that the Poet tells us that he *saw* Geryon as Hollander tells us in his important *Dante Theologus-Poeta* (1980). By now serious readers of the poem will be convinced that it is something more than a mere fiction or adventure story; it is clear that Dante perceives himself to be telling us profoundly important truths about sin, salvation and the ultimate purpose of life in a deadly serious way. Surely by now we recognize that his disclaimer, "I am not Paul" in Canto II was a mistake of the Pilgrim and that the Poet clearly perceives himself to be Paul-like and his writings to be of a divine nature, possibly even divinely inspired like the works of Paul himself. Here the Poet tells us he understands the difficulty we must have in accepting the literal truth of his fantastic tale, "the truth that has the face of a lie." But, at the same time, he assures us by the *Comedy* itself, that he tells us the literal truth. The crux of this little knot is, of course, that we know that Dante the Poet is not telling the literal truth. Charles Singleton (1957) points the issue in his celebrated statement, "the fiction of the *Divine Comedy* is that it is not fiction." (See also Hollander 1980.) The introduction to this volume explains the essence of the "four fold method of exegesis" which most modern commentators believe that Dante used in constructing his great poem. That claim was made in the *Letter to Can Grande*. This particular moment is probably the strongest claim to this method in the poem itself. In making it Dante puts himself in opposition to some authorities who thought that poets could write moral tales, perhaps, but could never approach the level of revealed truth which was reserved for scripture alone. As we have just seen in the area of the violent, disregard or disrespect for revelation was sufficient grounds for damnation to Dante. It would seem that any attempt to create a false revelation would be particularly heinous.

All of this is what makes this particular issue, presented at this particular central location, so important. The student of the poem, it would seem, is being invited to consider exactly where the truthfulness of the poem is to be found. One aspect of the presentation is humorous. Surely Dante expects us to at least smile when he tells us that he has wandered into the afterlife, found a ghost for a guide, and among many other marvels, seen a huge creature part man, part reptile, part beast, part insect, with maybe a little mixture of rug thrown in! And it flies too. The poet specifically warns us about the dangers of presenting "truths that have the face of a lie" and immediately gives us a "foul image of fraud" (XVII, 7) with a benign, sweet face, the face of truth with the body of a lie. He swears to the truthfulness of all this by the very poem which contains the fiction (XVI, 27–130).

Beneath the humor, though, is the serious point which is not completely made here, but can be discerned by those who read the entire work through the *Paradiso*. That point is that Dante thought he knew truths every bit as vital as the truths found in the writings of St. Paul and he thought that those truths could be conveyed through the medium of poetry. Presumably Dante felt that the beguiling nature of poetry would help make his message perceptible to his audience (Geryon has a beguiling face, but underneath his aspect is evil). As Hollander (1980) claims, Dante is here clearly creating a new kind of poetic fiction: one in which the literal level of truth is only presumed, a kind of "suspension of disbelief" shared by the Poet and his reader, but which leads to allegorical significances fully as true as any in scripture itself. While Dante may have begun by disagreeing with St. Thomas about the truthfulness of poetry, I think he ends by agreeing with him about the nature of language: human language when it tries to designate the divine only creates pale images, never the real perception of the thing itself. Poetry, long divorced by church doctrine from the serious attempt to picture the transcendent, but with real power to make concepts palpable through metaphor and symbol could, in Dante's opinion and his masterful hands, play a real role. If it is to work, however, both poet and reader must be fully self-aware of the process by which truths are designated. Hence the importance of this central revelation. Right at the moment when we are to meet those who were deliberately deceptive, fraudulent, for evil purposes, the Poet reminds us of the shared process of image making in which we are engaged. *Poetic* truth, quite distinct from, but as valid as, *literal* truth is the beginning of our route to the vision of the divine.

If we now reflect that over the last few cantos the Poet has given us much evidence of the Pilgrim's growth in confidence and the perception of his goal, this testimony to his poetic power gains force; for poetic power is one of the remaining elements necessary to complete the Pilgrim's mission. He must, through his journey, achieve his own salvation is some measure, but if he is to fulfill the rest of the goal, stated in the *Letter to Can Grande*, "to remove those living in this life from the state of misery and lead them to the state of blessedness," he must be able to convey the lessons to us. Here Dante both claims and demonstrates to us his possession of that ability. His virtuosity in describing Geryon in the magnificent simile of the swimmer (anyone who has seen such a sight instantly responds to this description) is part of this and his acknowledgement of the poem's fictiveness while at the same time claiming truth for it is another part. How different from the Pilgrim who at the beginning of the poem had not words to describe what he experienced ("Ah, How hard it is to tell what wood that was" I, 4)!

One aspect of what is happening here is that the Pilgrim is beginning to surpass Virgil, both in his grasp of truth and in poetic power, even as the truths and poetry of paganism are surpassed by those of Christianity. Dante's eventual dominance is not reached, however, by a steady ascent. There are set-backs and hesitations in his growth which are still to come, but from this time forward his triumph over his teacher is inevitable.

When the beast appears, we are told exactly what to make of it. It is "the foul image of fraud" (7). This is one of the few places where Dante makes his allegory explicit; we are to be in no doubt at all and the mixed nature of the demon, as ambiguous as fraud itself, is described (XVI, 9–18):

> His face was the face of a
> just man, so benign was its outward as-
> pect, and all of his trunk was that of a ser-
> pent; he had two paws, hairy to the armpits;
> his back and breast and both his sides were
> painted with knots and circlets. Tartars or
> Turks never made cloth with more colors
> of groundwork and pattern, nor were such
> webs laid on the loom by Arachne.

As the Turks and Tartars are Moslem heretics and their prophet Mahomet is found in the Bolgia of the sowers of discord, the reference to their subtle weavings is significant. The mention of Arachne is intriguing. As always we must consider why the Poet chooses to mention a particular mythological figure. That Arachne was a weaver makes here an antique parallel to the contemporary Turks and Tartars and we know that Dante is pleased by such dualities, but there is this also: She was taught the art of weaving by Pallas, but, according to Ovid, denied that the goddess had taught her and was offended that her skill was divine in origin (*Metamorphoses* Book VI). For her presumption in denying her sacred sources and the sacred nature of her art, she was turned into a spider. The reference probably continues the attack on the Church's dogmatic denial of the role of poetry in revealing truth.

Geryon is announced at the beginning of XVII with a rhetorical figure of speech which contains clues to his significance (1–3):

> "Behold the beast with the pointed tail,
> that passes mountains and breaks walls and
> weapons! Behold him that infects all the
> world!"

Friedman (1972) has identified the beast "that passes mountains and breaks walls" with the figure of the Antichrist foretold in the Epistle of St. John. Friedman further points out that the iconography of Antichrist was an important concern of the mystics of the Franciscan Order in Dante's time. This tradition identified the figures of Gog and Magog from Ezekiel 38 with the Antichrist. Ezekiel 38, 18–20 contains the reference:

> 18 And it shall come to pass in that day, in the day of the
> coming of Gog upon the land of Israel, saith the Lord God,
> that my indignation shall come up in my wrath. 19 And I
> have spoken in my zeal and in the fire of my anger, that in
> that day there shall be a great commotion upon the land of
> Israel, 20 so that the fishes of the sea, and the birds of the
> air, and the beasts of the field, and every creeping thing that
> creepeth upon the ground, and all men that are upon the
> face of the earth, shall be moved at my presence: and the
> mountains shall be thrown down, and the hedges shall fall,
> and every wall shall fall to the ground.

The Antichrist, a false Christ, will make fraudulent revelations. This from St. Paul, II Thessalonians, 9–10:

> 9 and his coming is according to the working of Satan with
> all power and signs and lying wonders, 10 and with all
> wicked deception to those who are perishing. For they have
> not received the love of truth that they might be saved.

It is impossible to tell how closely Dante subscribed to the Francescan interpretation of such things, but if he did, it certainly adds weight to the identification of the cord of Canto XVI with an element of that order. To identify Geryon with the Antichrist is suggestive too since it allows this particular element, which straddles the central point of the poem, to look forward in the narration as well as reflect backwards. As we have already seen, much of the Geryon episode refers back to Canto IX and the wall of Dis. Identifying Geryon with Antichrist allows us to see him as a prefiguration of Satan who appears in the final Canto even as in the apocalyptic tradition the appearance of Antichrist precedes the appearance of Satan himself. Dante and Virgil's interaction with Geryon includes coming into physical contact with him even as they must come in contact with Satan. The Antichrist must be overcome before Satan can be defeated.

Geryon beaches himself like a German beaver (which was thought to dangle its tail as a lure for fishes, a fraudulent enticement) continuing the pervasion of the poem with nautical imagery. Dante and Virgil must deviate from their path to meet him and they turn to the right to do so. As the only other right turn was at Dis, this forms another link with that episode. Dante, for the first time, is told to go off on his own and encounters the "violent against Art," the usurers.

That Usury is an important sin to Dante is shown by his special treatment of it in Canto XI where we are informed that it violates God's direct command to mankind to prosper through labor. To Dante earning interest was a sterile replication of money by money and he blamed much of the corruption of Florence on the practice. Given his strong feeling, the encounter with the usurers is strangely flat. They are so burned as to be unrecognizable, although the coats of arms on their moneybags serve as a means of identification (Singleton's *Commentary* has the identifications). The most notable aspect of these sinners is their malicious desire to demean the reputation of others, by naming their fellow sufferers or by prophesying that one still alive will soon join them (72–73):

> "Let the sovereign
> Knight come who will bring the pouch with
> three goats!"

This animosity towards others contrasts sharply with the seeming courtesy and desire for continued fame of those above and is typical of the attitude of the more sinful below.

Dante returns to Virgil and finds him already mounted on Geryon. Many commentators have said that here Virgil performs a multifaceted act of education. Allegorically, the aim of the flight is to educate the Pilgrim in the means of overcoming sin; one aspect of that includes coming into actual contact with it as sin cannot be mastered from afar. Already mounted, Virgil provides the necessary example, his words encourage and reason with his student and his embrace protects his charge from any harm. Dante's continued references to his fear reveal what it is that education and reason enable men to overcome in the struggle with sin.

The description of the flight on the back of Geryon is one of Dante's most sublime creations. The test of its acuteness is that it reads so realistically to we twentieth century people who know so well the sensations of flight. Dante's genius imagination allows him to foretell what we actually experience. There is nothing comparable in any antique literature.

The description of the flight is illustrated with references to the flight of Phäthon, Icarus, and the disappointed flight of the failed falcon. Both Phäthon and Icarus attempted flight and failed; Phäthon when he tried to drive the chariot of the sun and was too weak for the task, Icarus when he disregarded the instruction of his father and flew too near the sun. Both of these are examples of flights which failed because they were in some sense illegitimate, unlike Dante's divinely sponsored journey. The falcon image, which concludes the canto, pictures a "sullen" bird which has disappointed both itself and its master, but it refers to Geryon whose master is Satan himself. Geryon is the defeated Antichrist. There now remains the confrontation with Satan.

CHAPTER 15

Canto XVIII and XIX

Fraud: Virgil's Limitations and the Corruption of the Church

"There is a place in Hell called Malebolge (XVIII, 1)." Thus the blunt opening to the first of the cantos of fraud. The opening to XIX is equally abrupt, "O Simon Magus! O you his wretched followers." The opening of Canto XX is especially singular, numbering the canto and spelling out the Poet's task, "Of new punishment I must make verses, and give matter to the twentieth canto of the first canzone, which is of the submerged." Some commentators find this last so strange that they prefer to attribute it to another hand than Dante's. However, the fact that it is clearly a statement of the Poet (rather than the Pilgrim) makes it consistent with the introits of the several surrounding cantos. Now the Poet voice is beginning to emerge in a crescendo of virtuosity and presence which will culminate in his apparent domination of Virgil and ancient poetry in general. We become more and more aware of the poet behind the narration who strongly contrasts with the lost and ignorant soul of Canto I who could not tell what the wood was (I, 4–5). The growth and strength of the Poet will continue to the end of the poem, but it will not be without setbacks.

Malebolge, where Geryon has dropped the Pilgrims in XVIII, is described as a series of ten concentric circles bridged by rock formations, "crags" (16), which seem to be "natural" rather than constructed like the banks enclosing the river of blood (XV, 10–12). There are several such bridges over each ditch, but all of them are broken at the sixth. At the center of the ten circles lies a pit "very wide and deep" (5). In the ditches (usually called bolgias in an Englished form of the Italian word) are punished those guilty of fraudulent acts committed against people in general, individuals to whom the sinner has no obligation other than those owed by anyone to his neighbors. To Dante, violations of our common bonds disrupted society in general, leading to mistrust and hatred and making the really important task of civilization, the fulfillment of man's earthly and spiritual potential, impossible. Worse, of course, than the violation of general obligations are the violations of special trusts such as those between subject and master. Such as these are punished in the central pit.

In Malebolge the sins of "simple" fraud begin with panderers and seducers and run through the falsifiers of Canto XXX. Malebolge begins with a sin which is a perversion of love as did the sins of incontinence which began with lust. The sins of violence do not have such an analogous structure.

Virgil moves to the left with the Poet following. As he looks to the right, he can see the sinners in the bottom of the ditch. Their progress is described in terms of the traffic across one of the bridges of Rome during the great Jubilee of 1300 which was proclaimed by Dante's nemesis, Boniface VIII. Boniface's festival is then going on during the fictional time of the Pilgrim's journey through Hell. The point of the Jubilee was that by visiting shrines and saying prayers, the faithful could win a plenary indulgence (full forgiveness) for their sins. People came by the thousands for the festival, the first of the jubilees. It appears that the Roman authorities made it possible for traffic to move by restricting those going in one direction to one side of the bridge and those moving in the other to the other side; an early example of "keeping to the right." Singleton (1970) says that if Dante was in Rome in 1300 he would have seen the Roman organization. Of course, Jubilee years also were a great opportunity for what might be called the Roman tourist industry and Dante might have known or suspected that a pope as interested in money as Boniface VIII might have had some involvement in such commerce. Certainly when large numbers of people gather together there is always a certain amount of "pandering and seducing." In any case, recalling the Jubilee at this reminder of licentious sexuality cannot be construed as flattering to the event at Rome. It is worth noting that Martin Luther attended such a Jubilee early in his clerical career and was horrified at the sexual excesses he saw there.

The sinners, panderers traveling in one direction, seducers in the other, are apparently punished by their nakedness, their ceaseless motion and the occasional lashing from the horned demons who patrol the bolgia. Here we have the first appearance of the demon who has become traditional for the twentieth century: horned and with an instrument of torture. Later we will meet some with pitchforks. The particular fitness of the *contrapasso* for sexual sins is a bit hard to see.

The sinner Dante addresses is one of those who walks towards him so that the sinner's face is visible. He is a panderer who sold his sister, Ghisolabella. Venedico Caccianemico is Bolognese and Singleton indicates that Bologna was considered to be a center of panderers. Already Florence and Padua have been singled out for criticism in the *Inferno* and Bologna adds to a list which will grow longer. Caccianemico is typical of sinners in lower Hell in that he makes it clear that he would prefer his identity to remain hidden.

Virgil and Dante easily ascend the bridge across the bolgia (an allegory of overcoming the sin) and turn to their right so that they can see the faces of those who previously had been going in the same direction they were (66–78). The sinner singled out for attention is Jason, a pagan figure to complement the contemporary Italian we have already seen. Jason was the leader of the Argonauts on the quest for the Golden Fleece. The story occurs in Ovid, Statius and Valerius Flaccus, sources available to Dante (Singleton 1970). In none of these is Jason a particularly complex character. He is driven by desire for adventure and gain and he is a successful seducer, subduing both Hypsipyle and Medea. In fact, however, both of the ladies involved are eager for Jason before he is for them. Perhaps the sin of the seduction lies in that Jason abandons them both. Given that Jason is rather colorless and certainly faithless, Virgil's exclamation, "What a regal aspect he yet retains!" (85) is meaningless unless it refers to Jason's merely physical beauty upon which all sources (and Hypsipyle and Medea) agree. If one thinks back over all the expressions of nobility ascribed to sinners in Hell, except in the case of those in Limbo, one finds that they all come from Virgil. Notably we remember Farinata and the sodomite runners whose shallowness is apparent. Virgil, misreading of character in the face of damnation, is an indication of the limits of purely human reason applied to questions of virtue. Virgil's confusion on this issue is again related to the fact of Dante's eventual superiority. That Jason was unworthy of praise is apparently rather a commonplace of medieval thought. The great Dutch historian Johan Huizinga (1921) relates that when Duke Philipp of Burgundy established the "Order of the Golden Fleece," his chaplain, Jean Germain, suggested to him that the name of the order be made to refer to the fleece of Gideon from the Old Testament, rather than that of Jason since Jason's treatment of women (one of the central issues of chivalric knighthood) was dishonorable. We should note in passing that

Jason was the commander of the first ship, the Argos, and that his quest after the treasure of the golden fleece is a type of Dante's own metaphorical voyage after the treasure of salvation. Jason, his ship and the voyage are alluded to in other places later in the *Divine Comedy*.

Whatever Virgil's admiration for Jason, he is quickly tired of seducers and panderers in general for he urges Dante along in a manner which is reminiscent of his disdain for the undecided of Canto III. There he said, "Let us not speak of them, but look, and pass on" (III, 31). Here, "let this suffice for knowledge of the first valley and those it holds in its fangs" (98–99).

Flatterers, the subjects of the next bolgia, are likewise briefly treated. In a pit filled with excrement, the sycophants squirm and scratch. Again we are presented a complementary pair, Alessio Interminei of Lucca and Thäis whom Dante knew from Cicero. The travelers are unable even to see the sinners until they are on the top of the bridge over the bolgia. If crossing the bridge signifies overcoming the sin beneath it, we should reflect that Dante was certainly never a flatterer of mankind!

If there is an implied criticism of Rome in the reference to the Jubilee of 1300 in Canto XVIII, Canto XIX is a full frontal attack on the papacy itself and since Dante blamed the corruption of the papacy for the ills of Italy, we should expect of the poet a full exercise of his powers. Indeed, the trumpet which sounds in line 5, is in addition to the trump of doom, the trumpet of Dante's poetry. Hertzman and Stephany (1978) point out that Dante's invocation in praise of the fitness of God's justice is in fact praise of the fitness of Dante's own invention (10–12):

> O Su-
> preme Wisdom, how great is the art which
> Thou showest in heaven, on earth, and in the
> evil world and how justly does Thy Power
> dispense!

The *contrapasso* for the sin of simony is, in fact, among the most highly developed in the *Inferno* and in that regard contrasts with the vague issues surrounding pandering, seduction and flattery. Simony is the selling of church office, a very difficult sin to commit today, perhaps, but a large issue in the corruption of the papacy in Dante's age. The story of Simon Magus (Simon the Magician) occurs in the Bible in the eighth chapter of Acts. The time is during the mass conversions after Pentecost after the

Holy Spirit had descended on the followers enabling them to speak in many tongues and to prophesy:

9 Now a man named Simon had previously been practising sorcery in that city and astounding the people of Samaria, claiming to be someone great; 10 and all from least to greatest listened to him saying, "This man is the power of God, which is called great." 11 And they gave heed to him because for a long time he had bewitched them with his sorceries. 12 But when they believed Philip as he preached the kingdom of God and the name of Jesus Christ, they were baptized, both men and women. 13 And Simon also himself believed, and after his baptism attached himself to Philip; and at the sight of the signs and exceedingly great miracles being wrought, he was amazed.

14 Now when the apostles in Jerusalem heard that Samaria had received the word of God, they sent to them Peter and John. 15 On their arrival they prayed for them, that they might receive the Holy Spirit; 16 for as yet He had not come upon any of them, but they had only been baptized in the name of the Lord Jesus. 17 Then they laid their hands on them and they received the Holy Spirit. 18 But when Simon saw that the Holy Spirit was given through the laying on of the apostles' hands, he offered them money, 19 saying, "Give me also this power, so that anyone on whom I lay my hands may receive the Holy Spirit."

But Peter said to him, 20 "Thy money go to destruction with thee, because thou hast thought that the gift of God could be purchased with money. 21 Thou hast no part or lot in this matter; for thy heart is not right before God. 22 Repent therefore of this wickedness of thine and pray to God, that perhaps this thought of thy heart may be forgiven thee; 23 for I see that thou art in the gall of bitterness and in the

bond of iniquity." 24 But Simon answered
"Do you pray for me to the Lord, that nothing of
what you have said may happen to me."

Of equal importance in understanding Canto XIX is the following
excerpt (in a translation by Robert Stoops) from the apocryphal *Acts of
Peter* which has Simon Magus competing with Simon Peter in the performance of marvels.

Simon was scorned and scoffed by the Roman crowd, and
he was not believed because the things he promised did not
come about. So he finally said to them: "Romans! Now
you think that Peter has overcome me as though he were
stronger, and you pay more attention to him. You are
deceived, for tomorrow I will leave behind you who are
thoroughly godless and impious. I will fly up to God, whose
power I am, though weakened. If now you have fallen,
behold I am the standing one, your son, they wished to
overthrow; but not heeding them, I returned to myself."

Already on the next day a great crowd gathered at the
Sacred Way in order to see Simon fly. But Peter had seen a
vision, and he came to the place to refute him again in this.
Simon stood in a high place, and when he saw Peter, he
began to speak: "Peter, now most of all, when I am about
to ascend in the presence of all these onlookers, I say to
you: If your God is able, the one whom the Jews killed- - -
and they stoned you who were chosen by him- - -let him
show that faith in him is from God! Let him show now
whether it is worthy of God! I, however, by ascending to
him will reveal to this whole crowd what sort of being I am."
Suddenly, when he was lifted into the heights, and everyone throughout the whole of Rome saw him lifted above the
city's temples and hills, the faithful looked to Peter.

When Peter saw the marvelous sight, he cried out to the
Lord Jesus Christ, saying, "If you allow him to do what he
has undertaken, all who have believed in you will now be
scandalized. All the signs and wonders which you gave
them through me will be discredited. Speed your grace,
Lord! Let him be deprived of power and fall down, but not
be killed! Rather, let him become powerless and break his

> leg [shank] in three places." So Simon fell down and broke
> his leg [shank] in three places. Then they stoned him, and
> each one went home, but from then on they trusted Peter.

The story of Simon Magus is a rich source for Dante's imagery. First of all, Simon misunderstands the significance of the apostles' powers and seeks to buy them thus providing a version of the sin of simony. (The actual prototype of the simoniac is Judas who sold Christ, himself.) For Simon's error he is quite literally invited to "go to Hell" (Acts 8:20) by Simon Peter, who was to become the first pope and was the rock (petram) upon whom Christ said he would build his church (Matthew 16:18). The contrast between the two Simons, one true, the other false, is the basic duality of the structure of the canto. The magician refuses to repent, asks Peter to do it for him, and thus compounds the sin. That Simon Magus, as a false prophet, is presented in the apocryphal story competing with the true Simon defines the issue. The simoniac popes, having gotten things wrong, pursuing wealth rather than spirituality, compete with the true forces of divinity and confuse the people. For this their punishment is forever to be imprisoned in a rock, a reference to the rock of the church which is Peter. First they are imprisoned in the holes in the rock that remind the Pilgrim of the baptistry of the Church of San Giovanni in Florence (13–18) and then, when their successor comes, pressed into the rock of Hell itself, mashed and flattened (73–75). The fact that they are upside down indicates their inversion of their proper activity, the pursuit of material wealth rather than spiritual gains for humanity. It also probably reflects the tradition that Peter convinced his persecutors to crucify him upside down, humbly avoiding appearing to be too much like Christ. Obviously this humility is not characteristic of Simon Magus or the simoniac popes.

Hertzman and Stephany, in the article referred to above, detail the many references to the sacraments, all inverted or perverted, to be found in this canto. In the sixteenth chapter of Matthew is not only Christ's designation of Peter as the first pope, the rock upon which the church is built, but also the delegation to him of the power to perform the sacraments (Matthew 16:15–19):

> 15 He said
> to them, "But who do you say that I am?"
> 16 Simon Peter answered and said, "Thou art

the Christ, the Son of the living God." 17 Then
Jesus answered and said, "Blessed art thou,
Simon Bar-Jona, for flesh and blood has not
revealed this to thee, but my Father in heaven.
And I say to thee, thou art Peter, and upon
this rock I will build my church, and the gates
of hell shall not prevail against it. 19 And I will
give thee the keys of the kingdom of heaven;
and whatever thou shalt bind on earth shall be
bound in heaven, and whatever thou shalt loose
on earth shall be loosed in heaven."

From this passage comes the tradition of symbolizing the papacy with two keys, a gold key of power and a silver key of discernment, which lock and unlock the treasury of merit. The locking and unlocking is accomplished by means of the administration of the sacraments which power Peter passed on to his successor popes by means of apostolic succession. (For an earlier discussion of the sacraments see Chapter 5.) These popes have perverted their power, use only the gold key of power, and are therefore subjected to perversions of the sacraments. References to other ecclesiastical perversions are made in the text.

The first of these images is the inverted baptism. In real baptism the "old" man, bound for damnation is "buried" and rises as a "new" man bound for salvation. (Note that in the baptistries of San Giovanni referred to here baptism could be by total immersion rather than only anointing, making this symbolism very graphic.) The Old Testament prefiguration is in the crossing of the Red Sea by which the Israelites are "reborn" and their Egyptian enemies symbolizing sin and idolatry are drowned. Dante refers to this traditional symbolism in his condemnation of the simoniac popes where he makes their lust for gold to be a form of idolatry (112–114):

> You have made
> you a god of gold and silver; and wherein do
> you differ from the idolators, save that they
> worship one, and you a hundred?

In this inversion there is no rebirth, no exit from the mouth of the vessel, but the victim is pushed down into the rock for a second stage of the punishment. The oily fire of the soles of the feet probably is a reference to the chrism or consecrated oil which is a feature of several sacraments (baptism, extreme unction) and is also used in the ceremony of appointing a bishop (the pope is the Bishop of Rome). Chrism, however, is applied to the head and brings with it grace, whereas this is on the feet and brings pain. Strandberg (1967) points out that these flickering flames are like the flickering flames of votive candles.

The second sacrament parodied here is the sacrament of confession wherein the pilgrim "confesses" Nicholas III. A proper confession, accompanied by contrition (true regret for having committed the sin), brings forgiveness. Here the confession brings more pain and no forgiveness since there can be no contrition in Hell. So that we should not overlook this confession image, the poet makes his allegory explicit (as he did before in the case of Geryon) with a graphic and truly horrible scene (49–51):

> "I was standing there like the friar who con-
> fesses the perfidious assassin who, after he is
> fixed, recalls him in order to delay his death"

The custom in Florence was for those convicted of murder to be executed by being buried alive upside down. They were bound to a post in a hole which was filled in. Their legs were left protruding as the legs of the simoniac popes protrude from their holes. Dante then is standing with his head lowered listening to Nicholas. It was Singleton (1965) who said that the protruding legs refer not only to this mode of execution, but also to the fate of Simon Magus whose "shank" was broken in three places in answer to Peter's prayer. Hence Dante's identification of this sinner as he "who was lamenting with his shanks" (44).

Other perversions of ecclesiastical things include the references to marriage in the text (3–4, 55–57, 111, 116). Of course a bishop was "married" to his post as Christ is "married" to the Church. The papal perversions reduce the relationship to rape, prostitution and fornication.

As apparently some sinners in Hell can, Nicholas can see the future, but even as Cavalcanti in Canto X, he is confused about the present moment. Hence his mistake of taking Dante for his successor Boniface VIII. His powers of prophesy are not impaired to the point that he cannot point to the coming reign of Clement V who will remove the Papacy from Rome to Avignon where it became an agency of French policy (82–87):

> "for
> after him [Boniface] shall come a lawless shepherd from
> the west, of uglier deeds, one fit to cover both
> him and me. A new Jason he will be, like
> him we read of in Maccabees, but even as to
> that one his king was pliant, so to this one
> shall be he who governs France."

This linking of Clement V to the Jason of Maccabees is a serious issue since this Jason not only bought the office of High Priest from the corrupt King Antiochus, but also defiled the temple by trying to import Greek religious practices and instituting the practice of male prostitution (II Maccabees 4). Like the Jason of the previous canto, this Jason is sexually corrupt and, by implication, so is Clement V. This implied challenge to this series of simoniac popes is made explicit in the long condemnation of Nicholas which the Poet puts into the mouth of his Pilgrim (88–117). Here the Poet, the intelligence behind the poem is at his most present. The issue of papal corruption is at the core of Dante's political theory and he lays his condemnation out clearly and precisely. Throughout it all, his respect for the office is apparent, indeed, only his "reverence for the Great Keys" (101) moderates his speech.

Virgil is pleased as he always is when his pupil strikes out at sin and carries him out of the pit even as he carried him down into it (31–45). The carrying motive must signify Dante's accord with reason in respect to the issues raised in this canto. Virgil not only carries the Pilgrim out of the bolgia, but entirely to the top of the arch of the next bridge: a concentrated image of surmounting a sin (130–133):

> Here he gently set down
> his burden, gently because of the rugged and
> steep crag, which would be a hard passage
> for goats; and from there another valley was
> disclosed to me.

A hard passage for an avaricious goat (a standard medieval symbol), but possible for the Pilgrim assisted by reason.

One other issue needs to be addressed, the mystery of the meaning of the Poet's address to the reader where he refers to an autobiographical detail, the breaking of one of the baptistries at San Giovanni (13–21):

> Upon the sides and upon the bottom I saw
> the livid stone full of holes, all of one size
> and each was round. They seemed to me
> not less wide or larger than those that are
> made for the baptizings in my beautiful
> San Giovanni;
> one of which, not many years ago, I broke to
> save one who was drowning in it - and let
> this be the seal to undeceive all men.

None of Dante's early commentators have an adequate explanation for this story. Nokes (1968) points out the unlikelihoood of a literal truth to the notion that Dante saw someone drowning in such a container and then, in order to rescue him, broke the stone. Since the baptistries were made for people to stand in, surely all that would be necessary would be to reach in and pull the victim out. Breaking heavy stone is unnecessary and would require tools which would have to be fetched, impossible if someone were drowning. Fortunately, we have already seen that the "literal" level of the *Comedy* is fiction. The profundities lie in the allegory. Nokes' suggestion is that the episode is an allegory referring to a vow the leading citizens of Florence took to preserve the city's independence in the face of the threat of invasion by Charles in 1300. The vow, which required the citizens to put aside factionalism, was made on the baptistries at San Giovanni as symbols of civic unity. Dante broke the vow when he became a partisan of imperial rule, thus he "broke the baptistry," but only for a higher good, to save the city from drowning. The higher good would be the divine social order which places secular power in the hands of an emperor chosen by God. Breaking sacred vows is a serious issue, but it is possible under certain circumstances as the Pilgrim will learn in *Paradiso*. This reference both justifies Dante's action and prepares for the further discussion of vows in Heaven.

CHAPTER 16

Canto XX

Fortunetelling: The Pilgrim's Triumph

The issue of foretelling the future is an important and complex one for Dante since, because his poem contains predictions, he is open to the charge of divination (fortunetelling) or of false prophecy (claiming to be a spokesman for God). While divination was not necessarily illegal, (many of the great courts had resident prognosticators, some of whom Dante places among the sinners of this bolgia) it certainly was a sin; a sin in which the diviner attempts to preempt the power of God to know the future, a power largely denied to mankind. Dante believed divinely inspired prophesy possible, but I do not think he claims that power for himself. In Canto XIX he is concerned with illegitimate prophesy, either fraudulent or misguided and with separating himself from either sort. The canto also has important lessons concerning the relationship of Christian and pagan poetry.

There are many statements about the future in the *Inferno*. Most of them are "poetic predictions" such as those about the rule of Clement V and the Avignon captivity of the papacy in the last canto, which had, by the time the Poet put the prediction in a character's mouth, already happened. Certainly any attempt to pass predictions such as these off as real would be unsuccessful since the date of the poem's composition was well known. Clearly we are to be as aware of their symbolic and poetic nature as we are to be aware of the fictitiousness of the literal level of the poem.

There are two types of predictions in the *Inferno* which seem to be "real" as opposed to "poetic." There is a single example of a real political prediction. This is the statement about the "Veltro" (Hound) in Canto I (100–111):

> "Until the Hound
> shall come who will deal her a painful death.
> He will not feed on earth or pelf, but on wis-
> dom, love, and virtue, and his birth shall be
> between felt and felt. He shall be the salvation
> of that low-lying Italy for which the virgin

> Camilla and Euryalus, Turnus, and Nisus
> died of their wounds.
> He shall hunt her through every town till he
> has thrust her back into Hell, whence envy
> first sent her forth."

Like most such predictions, this one is obscure and oracular. Scholars understandably disagree about exactly what it means, but some think it is a reference to Can Grande della Scala who gave the real Dante a refuge at Verona during his exile from Florence and to whom the *Paradiso* is dedicated. In any case, since it refers to the defeat of the wolf of avarice and the unification of parts of Italy, it clearly had not happened by the time the *Comedy* was finished. Perhaps it is merely a hyperbolic compliment to Can Grande, who while he may have been a moral ruler, certainly could not have been imagined capable of accomplishing what this prediction implies. Such flattering statements about patrons were a common feature of literature in Dante's age and afterwards, but Dante has just shown us what happens to those who flatter immodestly, and this would seem to imply that the Veltro prediction is not simply hyperbole. (This discussion admittedly leaves out the question of whether the famous *Letter to Can Grande* itself is an example of immodest flattery, but Dante himself raises and refutes this charge in the letter, at least to his own satisfaction. This shows us that Dante had indeed considered his relationship to Can Grande in these terms.) One clue to the nature of the Veltro prophesy and to the issue of prophesy and fortunetelling in general, is the fact that the Veltro prediction is made by Virgil and not by the Pilgrim. Its placement in the mouth of the Roman rather than the Christian poet determines our reaction to it.

The high regard for Virgil in the Middle Ages partly rested on his reputation as a prophet. His famous *Fourth Eclogue* written in 37 B.C. was taken by Augustine and others to be a prediction of the birth of Christ (*Eclogue* IV), 5–10):

> Now is come the last age of the song of Cumae;
> the great line of the centuries begins anew. Now
> the Virgin returns, the reign of Saturn returns; now
> a new generation descends from heaven on high.
> Only do thou, pure Lucina, smile on the birth of the
> child, under whom the iron brood shall first cease,

and a golden race spring up throughout the world!
Thine own Apollo now is king!

In Dante's reading of this passage it was not necessary that Virgil understand the import of his own prediction. Indeed, as the pagan world was to be fulfilled by Christianity, the fact that it took Augustine to see the real significance of the passage is fitting. It is in the nature of paganism to have only dim glimpses of the truths revealed through Christ. It might be likewise in the case of the Veltro prediction. Placing the words in the mouth of Virgil, relieves the Poet of the necessity for ever making the prophecy true in a literal sense, or of even making it understandable, since it can be taken as a pagan groping towards truth. The extent to which the Christian poet, Dante, surpasses the pagan Virgil by the end of *Inferno* makes it possible to accept Virgil's prediction at the beginning of the poem as "partial" or incomplete. Whatever is uncertain about the prediction, however, it is clear that it is an optimistic statement about the future of Italy. And this, in general terms, is what Dante meant to signify by it. As the Pilgrim has learned to deal with predictions about his own coming earthly misfortune by comparing it with his coming future bliss as one of the elect (getting his priorities straight, so to speak), so can the Poet deal with the present and future misery of Italy, by reflecting that, as all history is providential, a part of God's perfect plan, there must ultimately be peace and unity for Italy. In the canto of the suicides, Dante warns against despairing in the face of a false and gloomy vision of the future (characterized by the false prophesy of the harpies). In fact, this same point about the optimistic character of God's creation is inherent in Dante's characterization of his poem as a *Comedy*, a story beginning badly in the dark wood, but ending well in Heaven. Similarly all human history has a tragic beginning, the fall of man, but will have a triumphant ending with the coming again of Christ. Dante's sacred purpose is to teach individuals to participate in the comic aspects of history and to avoid being trapped by the tragic. Therefore Dante's Veltro prediction can be seen as in no way out of accord with the commonly held vision of history. Its lack of specificity and its "pagan" source keeps Dante from having to account for its details. Dante fortunately lived before the time when it became very dangerous to make prophetic statements which might confuse the authorities. Giordano Bruno was burned in 1600 for similar oracular pronouncements which the orthodoxy took wrong. Still we should note that while the Veltro prediction is orthodox doctrinally, it is not necessarily so politically, as it seems to portend the rise of a great secular ruler as advocated in *De monarchia*, certainly an unfavorable conclusion to papal politicians. Disagreeing with church politics, however, is very different from a disagreement with church doctrine and, at any rate, Dante was already in exile, condemned for his politics.

The other sort of prediction in the *Comedy* which appears to be real (but isn't) is the frequent prediction of the eternal state of an individual soul. With great certainty, the Poet distributes the souls of those he knew, or knew of, throughout the three stages of the afterlife. Some, still living, he predicts will find their eternal future in Hell. This is very serious business, as Italy in the Fourteenth Century was a very violent place and, in addition to any possible charges of divination the Poet might be open to, people had a very highly developed sense of personal honor and blood feuds were common (Burckhardt 1954. See also Canto XXIX for a feud in which Dante was involved). One of the most frequent questions students ask is, "How did he get away with it?" a question to which there is no easy answer given the state of our knowledge. Probably he picked his targets carefully and made sure that he was protected at all times by someone who valued him, someone such as Can Grande or Guido Novella who sheltered him at Ravenna. Indeed, Guido's aunt was the Francesca of Canto V, so it is possible that some people might even have been flattered by the inclusion of their relatives in the great work—even in Hell. More important than whatever personal animosity Dante's book might have aroused, is the fact that his placement of souls in various places in the after life, a placement about which no one can possibly have any information, looks very much like divination. This is one of the central issues of Canto XX. First let us review its details in light of modern commentary.

Thinking now about Dante's apparent involvement with divination, we can perhaps understand a bit better the self-conscious air of the beginning of this canto. The previous sins of simple fraud, pandering, seduction and simony had no temptations for the Poet, so his Pilgrim surmounts them (symbolized by crossing the bridges over the bolgias) easily. His triumph over simony is so sure that he can even lecture a pope about it. Divination is a different thing altogether.

The reference to the sinners of this bolgia as the "submerged" (3) apparently merely means "placed in the mid'st of Hell" although it does continue the water motive of such importance to *Inferno*. Water indeed suffuses this entire canto: the souls are "bathed with tears of anguish" (6), their tears "bath[ing] their buttocks at the clef" (23-24). Dante himself weeps (25). Later (61-81), the founding of Mantua is described in terms of water flowing from the Alps to end in a swamp. All these images echo the hydraulic structure of Hell itself where the tears of sin and pain flow towards the central pit. The image of the sinners bathed in their own tears recalls the Old Man of Crete, the image of unredeemed humanity.

Neither the Pilgrim nor the reader is ever told the sin of the inhabitants of this circle; both must deduce it from the context, the listing of the souls found here. Once that connection is made, however, the *contrapasso* of the twisted necks, the reversed vision, the necessity of backing ahead is appropriate enough. The first action of the canto is when Dante weeps and invites us to share in his weeping (19-30):

> Reader, so God grant you to take profit of
> your reading, think now for yourself how I
> could keep my cheeks dry when near at hand.
> I saw our image so contorted that the tears
> from the eyes bathed the buttocks at the
> clef. truly I wept, leaning on one of the
> rocks of the hard crag, so that my guide said
> to me, "Are you even yet among the other
> fools? Here pity lives when it is altogether
> dead. Who is more impious than he who
> sorrows, at God's judgement?"

Now, this passage is very active on several fronts. First of all, if the Pilgrim is weeping because of the fate of the fortunetellers, then such sorrow represents a retrogression on his part as he has previously begun to see the justice of Hell and even in certain instances (the last canto comes again to mind) thoroughly approves of the punishment. Still, no one's education is without setbacks and Virgil's momentary reemergence as the dominant figure can symbolize a false step on the Pilgrim's part. However, if the Pilgrim weeps at the punishment, the Poet weeps at the distortion of "our image." In Dante's theology, our image is God, as man is made in His image and to distort the image of man is to distort the vision of God, even as the fortuneteller's false claim to omniscience is a distortion of God's omniscience. If Dante is then weeping at mankind's willing distortion of the

things of God, then Virgil's criticism is misplaced and based on a misunderstanding of the object of sorrow. Both senses are implied by the passage.
Virgil's question, "Who is more impious than he who sorrows at God's
judgment?" could refer to the Pilgrim who weeps or to the diviners who
weep at God's judgement for all eternity. The poet's implied question, would
the reader have wept, requires both a no and a yes, no at the fate of evil
doers, yes at the distortion of humanity it represents.

Virgil directs our attention to the first of five classical diviners. The end
of the canto deals briefly with a number of contemporaries, but the
emphasis is on the ancient world. Hollander (1980) is the best authority on
these sinners and perhaps something can be added to his discussion.
Amphiaraus is a figure from the *Thebaid* of Statius, one of the seven kings
who set out on the quest to overthrow the city of Thebes. Amphiaraus was
also a soothsayer and in Statius he joins forces with Melampus, prays for
revelation and sees the future in the flight of birds. This future includes his
death and the death of all the other kings. Dante has by now taught us that
we need to know his sources to grasp his meaning. If we read Statius, we
find that Amphiaraus, having seen his own death, repents of divination and
the voice of Statius condemns the practice (*Thebaid* III, 547–565):

> Affrighted thus by the future's dire import, and having
> suffered all under a sure image of things to come, the seers
> are held by terror; it repents them that they have broken in
> upon the councils of the flying birds, and forced their will
> upon a forbidding heaven; though heard, they hate the gods
> that heard them. Whence first arose amongst unhappy
> mortals throughout the world that sickly craving for the
> future? Sent by heaven, wouldst thou call it? Or is it we
> ourselves, a race insatiable, never content to abide on
> knowledge gained, that search out the day of our birth and
> the scene of our life's ending, what the kindly father of the
> gods is thinking, or iron-hearted Clotho? Hence comes it
> that entrails occupy us, and the airy speech of birds, and
> Thessalia's horrid rites. But that earlier golden age of our
> forefathers, and the races born of rock or oak, were not thus
> minded; their only passion was to gain the mastery of the
> woods and the soil by might of hand; it was forbidden for
> man to know what to-morrow's day would bring. We, a
> depraved and pitiable crowd, probe deep into the councils

of the gods; hence comes wrath and anxious fear, hence
crime and treachery, and importunity in prayer.

Augury is impious and it distracts us from our proper work in the fields
and woods. Although knowledge of the future is forbidden, the gods may
hear our requests. The result is sorrow, "though heard, they hate the gods
that heard them." This statement of pagan skepticism is so convenient for
Dante's point about divination, that it would be preferable to see it as
Christian. So Dante chooses in a remarkable rewriting of history. When we
meet Statius in *Purgatorio* XX and XXI, Statius relates a strange tale, how
he had been lead to poetry by Virgil's *Aeneid* (*Purgatorio* XXI 94–102) and
converted to Christianity by the *Fourth Eclogue* (*Purgatorio* XXII 64–89):

> "You [Virgil] it was who first sent
> me towards Parnassas to drink in its caves,
> and you who first did light me on to God.
> You were like one who goes by night and
> carries the light behind him and profits not
> himself, but makes those wise who follow
> him, when you said, ' The ages are renewed;
> Justice returns and the first age of man, and
> a new progeny descends from heaven.'
> Through you was I a poet, through you a
> Christian; but that you may see better what
> I outline, I will set my hand to color it. Al-
> ready the whole world was big with the true
> faith, sown by the messengers of the eternal
> realm, and those words of yours I have just spoken
> were so in accord with the new preachers
> that I began to frequent them. They came
> then to seem to me so holy that when Domi-
> tian persecuted them, their wailing was not
> without my tears and, while I remained
> yonder I succored them and their righteous
> lives made me scorn all other sects. And be-
> fore I had lead the Greeks to the rivers of
> Thebes in my verse, I received baptism."

The import of this is that Statius was converted to Christianity with the
aid of the *Fourth Eclogue*. This conversion, while no one knew of it save
Dante, was not inconsistent with the way the *Eclogue* was considered by

some in the church. Further, Statius says he was baptized, "before I had lead the Greeks to the rivers of Thebes in my verse" In other words, before he wrote of Amphiaraus and his divination. This allows Dante to treat Statius' condemnation of divination as the word of a Christian and therefore to mirror his own properly Christian attitude to this sin.

To this point I have followed Professor Hollander closely whose work on the issue of truth in the *Comedy* and on the diviners of Canto XIX is so helpful. I would now like to make an observation. The reader has seen that the demon Geryon has brought to a head the issue of what is true in the poem and what is symbol. Dante's claim is that he can begin with a poetic fiction and arrive at allegorical, moral and anagogic truths. Here, with Statius's Amphiaraus, we arrive at the moral that true divination may work, but its results will not be pleasing to us. It is far better for us that we work in the sphere allotted to us, symbolically the "woods and the fields." Dante's poetic divination is appropriate, however, because it doesn't pretend to be real. Instead it is a series of images, metaphors, which lead us to higher truths. Geryon isn't real and yet the Poet, in his fictional person of the Pilgrim, says he "saw" it. If Geryon wasn't seen then neither are any of the individual and named souls seen. The literal fiction, then, extends to all particulars.

If we acknowledge that Dante modeled much of his *Comedy* on Virgil's *Aeneid* (see the references to Hollander's work on this aspect in Chapter 1), then a look at Aeneas' trip to Hades in that work might reveal some helpful details. Before the mouth of the cave which is the mouth of Hades there is an elm tree (*Aeneid* VI, 282–294):

> In the midst an elm, shadowy and vast, spreads
> her boughs and aged arms, the home which, men
> say, false Dreams hold in throngs, clinging under
> every leaf. And many monstrous forms besides of
> various beasts are stalled at the doors, Centaurs and
> double shaped Scyllas, and the hundredfold Briareus,
> and the beast of Lerna, hissing horribly, and the
> Chimaera armed with flame, Gorgons and Harpies,
> and the shape of the three-bodied shade. Here on a
> sudden, in trembling terror, Aeneas grasps his sword,
> and turns the naked edge against their coming; and
> did not his wise companion warn him that these
> were but faint, bodiless lives, flitting under a hollow

semblance of form, he would have rushed upon them and
vainly cleft shadows with the steel.

The first thing the reader of the *Comedy* is likely to notice, is that
Dante has borrowed several of Virgil's demons for his own Hell. From the
list we know centaurs, gorgons, harpies and, most important here, the
"three-bodied shade" which is Geryon. It is interesting that Dante leaves to
Virgil a bit of proprietary interest in these beings in the *Inferno* as the
centaurs, gorgons and Geryon are all the subjects of negotiations between
themselves and the Pilgrims, all these negotiations carried out by Virgil
himself. More germane here, in Virgil's poem these monsters, objects of
dread, are depicted as unreal. They are false dreams, forms, faint, "hollow
semblance of form." If Aeneas had acted against them, the act would have
been one of fruitless futility. Surely Dante, who expects us to know the
Aeneid, wishes us to see that any view of the afterlife we might conjure up
is populated with empty images, reflections of our own ignorance and fear.

Virgil also addresses the issue of prophetic knowledge in a way which
Dante would have found sympathetic. When Aeneas finally finds the shade
of his father Anchises, he is given a long list of prophecies concerning the
future history of Rome. Like his pupil Dante, Virgil is careful not to have
prophesied anything which had not already taken place by the time of the
composition of the poem. These statements are the models, in fact, for
Dante's own poetic prophecies. There is an example which Virgil gives,
however, of the futility of real foreknowledge. Aeneas sees the shade of
Palinurus, his helmsman, who had fallen overboard only a few days before
and apparently drowned. The problem is that the prophecy had been made
that this Palinurus would complete the voyage and arrive safely in Italy
(*Aeneid* VI, 341–361):

> "What god, Palinurus, tore thee from us and
> plunged beneath the open ocean? O tell me! for
> Apollo, never before found false, with this one
> answer tricked my soul, for he foretold that thou
> wouldst escape the sea and reach Ausonian shores.
> Lo! is it thus his promise holds?" But he: "Neither
> did tripod of Phoebus fail thee, my captain Anchises'
> son, nor did a god plunge me in the deep. For by
> chance the helm to which, as was my charge, I clung,
> steering our course, was violently torn from me, and

I dropping headlong, dragged it with me. By the
rough seas I swear that not for myself felt I such
fear as for thy ship, lest, stripped of its gear and reft
of its helmsman, it might fail amid such surging
waves. Three stormy nights over the measureless
seas the South drove me wildly on the water; scarce
on the fourth dawn, aloft on the crest of a wave, I
sighted Italy. Little by little I swam shoreward,
and even now was grasping at safety, but as, weighted
by dripping garb, I caught with bent fingers at the
rigged cliff-peaks, the barbarous folk assailed me
with the sword, in ignorance deeming me a prize.
Now the wave holds me and the winds toss me on
the beach."

Here in Virgil is a lesson similar to that in Statius: even if augury is successful, it will do you no good. Amphiaraus saw his own death and was destroyed by the vision. Palinurus thought himself safe only to see the prophecy fulfilled in an ironic and fatal manner. In either case, it is possible to see the foolishness of trying to gain anything by divination. I think that the necessity of making these points here, that divination is fruitless and that the apparent predictions of future events and the future state of individual souls are poetic rather than real, explains the use of Geryon as the guardian of the bolgias of fraud. Commentators have frequently wondered about his suitability for his post. Geryon, a king of Erytheia in traditional mythology, was a monster with three bodies who was killed by Hercules when the latter stole his cattle. Nothing in his story is involved with any form of fraud. Why then should Dante use him to symbolize that sin? The answer is that fraud is the sin of false appearances, of the unreal which appears as truth. It is Geryon's appearance in Virgil's Hades as a demon without substance which makes him appropriate for Dante's use of him in this context. Dante, the Poet, is very careful to let us know that about things we cannot know, we can only speak in symbols, metaphors. The imagination can give rise to dark images, the art of poetry turns them into a vision of truth.

Further evidence of the hypothetical nature of the Poet's judgement of individual souls is found in the *Paradiso*, Canto XX, where the Pilgrim finds the souls of some who were thought to be pagans, but who were, in reality, Christians. These include Ripheus, a very minor figure from the

Aeneid. Mentioned only in passing before, in *Aeneid* II, 426–27, he receives an epitaph:

> Ripheus fell,
> A man uniquely just among the Trojans
> The soul of equity

Dante places him in Heaven to indicate the unknowableness of God's judgement (*Paradiso* XX, 67–69):

> Who would believe, down in the erring
> world, that Ripheus the Trojan was the fifth
> of the holy lights in this circle?

And later the final comment of the canto in the mouth of the eagle (129–138):

> "O predestination, how remote is thy root
> from the vision of those who do not see the First
> Cause entire! And you mortals, keep your-
> selves restrained in judging; for we, who see
> God, know not yet all the elect. And to us
> such defect is sweet, because our good in this
> good is refined, that what God wills we also
> will."

If the elect in Heaven do not know the disposition of all souls, what can Dante the Poet know?

So far in this discussion we have seen how Dante uses the canto to condemn divination while at the same time exculpating himself from any charges of that sin. His complex argument has a good deal to do with his vindication of poetry as a means of speaking truthfully without speaking a literal truth. These issues are not the only ones on Dante's agenda here, however. The other major point concerns Dante's relationship to Virgil and to ancient poetry in general. Many commentators have noticed that Dante's versions of the stories of the pagan diviners, retold in this canto, differ in one aspect or another from the versions told in his sources, Statius, Lucan, Ovid and Virgil. Some earlier commentators try to explain the deviations away by suggesting that Dante's copies of the works of these famous classical authors must have differed from those we have today. More modern scholars, Robert Hollander among them, believe Dante's revisions of the stories to be deliberate and, further, that he intended us to notice them.

Some of the classical diviners mentioned, Amphiaraus, Tiresias, Aruns and Manto were, in the original telling, virtuous prophets whose work was not only successful, but honored. Even Amphiaraus' unfortunate vision of his death was successful and Dante does not tell us in what sense it was fraudulent. Tiresias's entire career, Dante reduces to his change of sex. An event which in Ovid came before his career as a successful soothsayer. The most telling alterations, however, are those which touch on the work of Virgil: the story of the founding of Mantua and the inclusion of Eurypylus as a soothsayer.

In the case of Manto, Virgil has it in *Aeneid* X, that Mantua was founded by Manto's son who named it after his "prophetic mother." Virgil's explanation in *Inferno* directly contradicts this, having the place settled by the neighboring people after the death of the hermit Manto. They named the place after her, but only because she was the first inhabitant. There was (93) no other reason. Now this does have the virtue of separating the city of Mantua from any connection with divination, but its real purpose is to discredit Virgil and the *Aeneid*. Indeed, in testimony to the truthfulness of this account Virgil says (97–99), "Therefore I charge you, if you ever hear other origin given to my city, let no falsehood defraud the truth." This gives the Pilgrim license to correct Virgil's poem.

Eurypylus, like Ripheus, is an extremely minor character in the *Aeneid*. He is mentioned in passing by the lying Greek Sinon as he persuades the Trojans to accept the wooden horse. He claims the Greeks were discouraged and sent to the oracle for instructions (*Aeneid* II, 113–114):

> Perplexed, we send
> Eurypylus to ask the oracle of Phoebus.

First, Sinon is lying (we will meet him further down in Hell where he suffers for it) and second, Eurypylus is only the messenger. In the earlier event, where the prophet Calchas indicated the moment for the Greek fleet to sail, Eurypylus is not even mentioned. Again Dante has amended and corrected Virgil and in Virgil's own tongue. Through Virgil, Dante assures us that he knows what he is about in his corrections. Virgil says of Eurypylus (112-114):

> "and thus my high Tragedy sings of
> him in a certain passage - as you know well,
> who know the whole of it."

These alterations of Virgil and the other classical poets are not done by a careless reader, but with intent and indicate the superiority of Christian poetry over pagan and of Dante over the classical poets including his "master and author," Virgil.

CHAPTER 17

Cantos XXI–XXIII

The Grafters: Humor in Hell

Two themes strongly addressed in the last several cantos are also important elements of Canto XXI–XXIII. These are the issues of the vindication of the Pilgrim from his purported sins (divination in the last canto, barratry here) and the by now thematic issue of the Pilgrim's relationship to his mentor, Virgil. Dante was exiled from Florence accused of corruption in office and takes the opportunity, in the place where that sin is punished, to proclaim his innocence. On the older theme, Dante continues to delicately indicate the fallibility of his model while at the same time preserving the sense of respectful admiration and indebtedness with which the relationship began. Cantos XXI–XXIII contain the longest sustained episode in the entire *Inferno*. The narration of the adventurers' doings with the military demons lasts for 347 lines or two and one-half cantos. Even then the subject is not really put to rest until the very end of Canto XXIII.

For many commentators the first striking characteristic of the episode is the barbarity of the language, the cruelty and coarseness foreshadowing the thoroughly debased speech of the still more bestial damned to come. One has only to remember the courtly speech of Francesca or Pier della Vigne to understand much of Dante's point about the hierarchical nature of sin. Yet even so, maybe because of the self- conscious crudeness, the reader cannot help but recognize this episode for the burlesque it is. As the great Viennese symphonists were accustomed to relieve the intensity of their masterpieces with a popular third movement (Haydn and Beethoven even called such movements *Scherzi*-jokes), Dante here recalls the broad and popular humor of the theatricals held outside the churches from time to time. During these productions costumed "demons" ran about the crowd insulting matrons, frightening children and young girls and violating the dignity of the self-important in exactly the sort of festival beloved of the popular mind at all times. Yet, even as beneath Haydn's gaieties lurk musical profundities, the reader must not here assume the burlesque surface is all there is or that we are here invited to a vacation from intellectual concerns.

Indeed, Canto XXI begins with two mysteries:

> Thus from bridge to bridge we came
> along, talking of things of which my Comedy
> is not concerned to sing, and we had reached
> the summit, when we stopped to see the next
> cleft of Malebolge and the next vain lamenta-
> tions; and I saw it strangely dark.

We must wonder what Virgil and Dante talked about! The last time we were so pointedly excluded was in Limbo when the Pilgrim was taken into the company of distinguished poets (IV, 103–105):

> Thus we went
> onward to the light, talking of things it is
> well to pass in silence, even as it was well to
> speak of them there.

The reader might suspect poetry and its mysteries to be the subject there, but here the possibilities are wider and more intriguing. It seems unlikely that Dante the Poet would specifically mention that his characters carry on conversations not reported unless we are being invited to speculate about them. Working on the supposition that the most likely subject would be the most recent events, dare we guess that the conversation was about Virgil's embarrassing confession of the error in the *Aeneid* about Mantua? Dante's genius can create three dimensional figures with a very few deft strokes. Think of Francesca and how well we know her! We know Farinata, too. And Virgil? The Poet has had more space to develop the character of Virgil than any other character save the Pilgrim himself. We are beginning to know him well. He is not only the best guide to be had, he is a wonderful companion. He is not hardened to Hell; we have seen him moved at Limbo. He respects the remnants of dignity that some few sinners still possess as he revealed in the circle of the sodomites. At the same time he is very proud, even vain, and concerned not to have his competence or knowledge challenged, hence the incipient quarrel between the pair at the walls of Dis. Might it be that a blow to Virgil's pride such as that dealt by the revelation about Mantua might cause him to react to the demons of these cantos as he does, claiming more competence in dealing with them than he should? Particularly if he thought his handling of the centaurs and Geryon had made the Pilgrim forget his failure at the gate of Dis, he might want to continue to appear in control. The intricate quirks of his intellectual and psychological makeup and the necessity to recover his pride after the embarrassment of Mantua might cause Virgil to make the mistake of trusting the Malebranche.

The second mystery is the darkness of the pit. Much of Hell has been dark, but here it is dark and seemingly empty, "I saw nothing save the bubbles raised by the boiling" (19-20). Emptiness is futility. Hell *is* futile, of course, but the futility always has beings subject to it: futile motion, pain, futile humiliation. The futile pitch calls forth the opposite image in the simile of the Venetian Arsenal, scene of purposeful, manifold (and nautical) activity. The Pilgrim gazes, his memory teased by the associations of the pitch, and the quiet explodes in the warning of Virgil (23), "Guarda, guarda!" The calm, the intimacy (whatever private matters it contained), is broken and we are caught up in the ceaseless activity and threat of the demonic burlesque from which there is not a moment of respite until the forced calm of the hypocrites of Canto XXIII. The mystery itself remains, but not for long, as the fitness of the sticky pitch as *contrapasso* to the barrators' sticky fingers is crystal clear. Bologna ("Saint Zita's elders") is singled out as the specific center of corruption as Dante continues his catalog of Italian cities.

As the simoniacs parodied the sacraments in XIX, so the newly arrived soul parodies worship as he involuntarily genuflects in the pitch. "Here's no place for the Holy Face" (48), a reference to a favorite icon of Bologna and a terrible pun on the "face," his posterior, which the sinner presents to the demons. As low humor rejoices in scatology so this canto is filled with rump references. It is the "haunches" of the sinner we see first (35), then the rump of the genuflection. Dante is made to "squat." (59, *t'acquatta* in Italian, as ugly a word in that language as "squat" is in English.) Called forth, he is designated "you that sit asquat" (89, *quatto, quatto,* even uglier). We have the rump of 101 and the culmination of the famous signal of the last line.

Virgil knows such rough company is dangerous, but given his recent successes and, I think, embarrassment about Mantua, is willing to play the "what is willed in Heaven" (82) gambit again. It worked with the centaurs

(XII, 91–93), he may have used it with Geryon, but we were not present during that interview. His assurances to Dante are ambiguous (61–63):

> "and whatever outrage be
> done to me, be not afraid, for I know about
> things here and was in a like fray once
> before."

On his previous journey (IX, 22), Virgil must have passed this way, but of the "like fray" we know nothing at all. Virgil's challenge to Malacoda seems to work, at least Malacoda orders the others not to strike Dante (87):

> "Omai non sia feruto."   "Now let no one strike him."

"Omai" might mean "Now" or it might be ironic, "O well" or even "Gosh!" With hindsight we know the ironic interpretation is correct, but Dante suspects it all along as he tells us the action triggers his memory (93–96):

> I feared
> they might not keep the pact. Thus I once
> saw the soldiers afraid who were coming out
> of Caprona under pledge, seeing themselves
> among so many enemies.

Dante had served with the Guelph forces at both the battles of Campaldino and Caprona in 1289. At Caprona, the Ghibellines surrendered under a pledge of safe conduct. Exactly what happened is uncertain. some authorities record only the defeat (Singleton 1970), others suggest a bloody conclusion in which the prisoners were slaughtered despite the promises which were given. If this second and darker version is the true one, it adds significance to Dante's recollection in this particular instance.

We can see that Dante's experience and instinct are at odds with Virgil's confidence; to Dante's warning we hear Virgil's breezy reply (130–135):

> "If you are as wary as you are wont,
> do you not see how they grind their teeth
> and with their brows threaten to harm us?"
> And he to me, "I would not have you be

> afraid; let them grind on as they please, for
> they do it at the boiled wretches."

We know who is correct.

At the heart of this episode is Malacoda's speech. Part lie and part truth, it fixes the exact time of events and completes the trap into which Virgil is to fall (104–117):

> Then he said to us, "To go farther by this
> crag will not be possible, for the sixth arch
> lies all shattered at the bottom; but if it is
> still your pleasure to go forward, then proceed
> along this ridge: nearby is another crag that
> affords a way.
>
> Yesterday, five hours later than now, com-
> pleted one thousand two hundred and sixty-
> six years since the road was broken here. I
> am sending some of my company that way,
> to see if any is out taking the air. Go with
> them for they will not harm you."

First let us deal with the truthful part of Malacoda's speech, that is what time it was. Way back in Canto I we were able, by calculating Dante's age, to determine that the year of the journey was 1300. Further, by means of the astrological signs explained to us, we could tell it was Easter season (I, 37–41):

> It was the beginnning of the morning, and
> the sun was mounting with the stars that were
> with it when Divine Love set those beau-
> tiful things in motion, so that the hour of the
> day and the sweet season gave me cause for
> good hope.

Since then, we have been able to keep track of time by indications in the text (For details of the astronomy see Singleton 1970.):

> II, 1–3 (The evening of first day)
> VII, 94–99 (It is now midnight)

XI, 112–115 (4 A.M.)
XX, 124–128 (6 A.M.)

Malacoda's statement now allows us to calculate the day of the year. According to Luke 23:44, Christ died at the "sixth hour" reckoning from the traditional beginning of the day at 6 A.M., thus Christ died at noon of Good Friday. Christ's death is accompanied by the tearing of the veil of the temple. Matthew 27:51 says that there was also an earthquake at that moment which tradition linked to the story of the Harrowing of Hell. We were told in XII, 37–45 of the moment when "the universe felt love," the gate of Hell was broken open, the bridges over the bolgias broken down and the souls released from Limbo. Yesterday noon, noon of Good Friday, was 1,266 years after the death of Christ. Christ was believed to have been thirty-four years of age at the time of his death (Christ's age was calculated from the incarnation). Thus for the year we again get 1300, a year in which Good Friday was April 8. It is now 7:00 A.M. on the morning of Holy Saturday, April 9, 1300. We might have suspected that Dante's journey took place over Easter weekend before, but now we can be certain. Dante will emerge from Hell, as Christ did from the tomb, at dawn of Easter Sunday. Dante's use of the Pilgrim as a type of Christ is one of the ways he emphasizes the sacred character of his message.

The lie is simpler. Malacoda simply says there is one remaining bridge over the sixth bolgia and makes up an excuse, which Virgil accepts, to have ten of his demons accompany the travelers, saying that they will be safe as far as the nonexistent bridge (124–26), that is, not safe at all. Barbaricca is given command of the troop, a *Decade*, ten men like a platoon. No one is certain about the meanings of the demons' names, but Barbaricca means Curlybeard and Malebranche, the collective name for the Demons (see 37), was the name of a family of Lucca.

The obscene military ceremony and the Poet's comment on it form the transition between XXI and XXII, where the spoof reaches its climax. Wolff (1969) comments that the Pilgrim gets rather familiar with the demons in Canto XXII, and this is only one of the incongruities. The Poet, seeming to indicate a suppression or forgetting by the Pilgrim of his great fear of the demons, enters into the ribald spirit of things with his long comment on military signals (1–12) and, in what seems like a shrug of assent to it all, comments (13–14), "in church with saints and with guzzlers in the tavern!"

The Pilgrim, careful to have learned all the demons' names (37–39), seems to ignore them and concentrate on the passing scene (16–18):

> My
> attention was all on the pitch, in order to see
> every condition of the pouch, and of the peo-
> ple who were burning in it.

The demons and sinners are almost frivolous; they play hide and seek and tricks on one another while the hellishness of the situation is barely acknowledged in only a few instances. The memory of it appalls the Poet (31), the trapped sinner mentions the heat (54), and later his desire to cause sorrow (111), a demonic attitude in itself.

Again, Wolff suggests that the numerous animals mentioned in this canto serve to emphasize the bestial nature of the demons and also to indicate the level to which the humor has sunk. In addition we might say that if Virgil is in error about his competence to judge the trustworthiness of the Malebranche, the Pilgrim is in danger of an error of decorum which he will commit in Canto XXX, the fault of too much interest in and identification with the mere things of Hell.

Dante makes fun of the ridiculous soldiers by referring to their corporal as "marshal" (94, 123), but they need little help to appear foolish given the job they do on themselves in their double dealing negotiations with the nameless sinner of Navarre (48). The climax, when Alichino and Calabrina fall into the pitch themselves can be seen coming a long way off. Dante and Virgil, having each in his own way come to his senses, steal away.

The fable referred to in the first few lines of Canto XXIII is a bit of a puzzle since no one is sure what fable is being referred to. The point seems to be that the tricksters are tricked and, like the demons, become the victims of their own treachery. Nastiness has its own appropriate rewards, thank goodness. That the demons might seek revenge for their humiliation (after all, one reason the Navarrese was let go was to fetch more Italians for the Pilgrim) occurs therefore to Dante and he suspects they might come (18), "fiercer than the dog to the leveret [hare] he snaps up." The dog and his victim are the end of the long series of animal references which began in XXII. It begins with men (XXII, 1,4) and includes (in order): dolphin (a fish, not a mammal), frog (amphibian), otter (aquatic mammal), mouse, cat (terrestrial animals), bird, duck, falcon and hawk. The conclusion is with the frog and mouse of the fable and the present dog and hare. The suggestions of a meaningful sequence are tantalizing, but the meaning is obscure.

More certain is the suggestion of unity in Virgil's ready agreement to Dante's suggestion that they flee (25–30):

> And he, "if I were of leaded glass, I should
> not draw to me your outward semblance more
> quickly than I receive your inward. Even
> now came your thoughts among mine, with
> like action and like look, so that of both I
> have made one counsel."

This is significant since the pair are at a potentially quarrelsome moment. The business about Mantua, Virgil's error in trusting the Malebranche, Dante's wandering attention, potentially could cause another division, but the circumstances demand unity. The passage is also important in that it contains the first reference to mirrors in the poem. The symbol of the mirror joins the nautical metaphor and will appear in *Paradiso* as the culminating metaphor of the poem. That it is here connected with a success (the unity of man with reason, the successful escape from the demons) foreshadows its use to image divinity. Dante is united with reason as child to mother (38, 51) and Virgil slides into the pit of the next bolgia. The demons, trapped in their location by their nature cannot follow.

CHAPTER 18

Cantos XXIII-XXV

Hypocrisy and Theft: St. Thomas and the Interrelations of Sins

Virgil's slide brings us abruptly to the hypocrites and the tone of the poem abruptly becomes serious once again. With the grafters we have reached a point where we can begin to understand one of the great questions which the poem raises. We are now among the fraudulent, specifically those who, according to Virgil, committed fraud against those who had no special reason to hold the sinner in confidence and therefore broke "only the bond of love which nature makes" (XI, 56). Virgil's catalog in Canto XI mentions specifically hypocrisy, flattery, sorcery, lying, theft, simony, pandering, graft and in general terms "like filth" (XI, 60). The question raised here is simply what principle dictates this particular arrangement, why these sins and not others? What is meant by the category of "like filth?" Further, what is the nature of the sin of Ulysses and Guido da Montefeltro in Cantos XXVI and XXVII, fraudulent counsel, which is not mentioned at all by Virgil? On a deeper level all this refers to the real and constant question of the poem which is what is it that Dante is teaching us, on what are we to reflect? One thing that we do know now is that Virgil's catalog in Canto XI is only a summary and general ordering and we cannot expect it to guide us to the moral meaning of the poem. Many critics (notably Markulin 1982) have recognized that no one is in this particular section of Hell for any one specific sin. In the stories of these wretches there is a pattern of habitual sinfulness and failure of repentance. The issue is clearest in the cases of Ulysses, who is not in Hell simply for his last voyage, and Guido da Montefeltro who is damned by many things in addition to his advice to Boniface VIII. Moreover, it is likely that the sins of these bolgias are related by something other than the bald fact that they are all "frauds."

It is characteristic of the medieval mind to seek out the relationships among all things. Indeed the belief that there is a single relationship that ties the entire universe together is the climax of the *Divine Comedy*. Medieval theology sought out the relationships amongst sins. I would like to claim that the organization of Cantos XXI through XXVII can be understood in the light of two passages from the *Summa Theologia* of St. Thomas Aquinas. The suggestion I am to make cannot, of course, exhaust the possibilities of Dante's relationships, but since it is a set of medieval relationships directly concerned with the subject matter of this section, it does reveal much of the unstated principle behind the poem and the medieval "frame of mind" that produced it. Part of what I want to indicate by referring to the *Summa* is that Virgil's catalog of Canto XI does not fully explain the organization of the sins in Hell. That this should be the case we now know to be appropriate, since Virgil's catalog represents a pagan, not a Christian, understanding.

The first passage from St. Thomas that I have in mind is this one concerning hypocrisy. Thomas cites Augustine (*Sum.* 2a 2æ. III, 2):

> So also Augustine notes, "just as stage players (hypocritae) take off other people," i.e. play the part of someone they are not, "the one who plays the part of Agamemnon not really being he, but pretending to be - so in the Church and in all of human life one wishing to appear to be what he is not is a hypocrite. He plays the good man without being one."
>
> From this we conclude that hypocrisy is deception; not, however, just any form of deception, but only that whereby one poses as someone else, as in the case of a sinful person pretending to be virtuous.

The second defines a larger category of sins, vainglory, of which hypocrisy is only one of the "daughters" (*Sum.* 2a 2æ. 132, 5):

> As we said earlier, the vices naturally ordered to attain the end of any capital sin are termed its daughters. Now the end of vainglory is to display one's own excellence, as is clear from earlier discussion...When it is by words, it is boasting; when it is by actual deeds that cause some wonder, it is passion for innovation, which men usually admire more than familiar things; if deceit is used, it is hypocrisy.

I think these definitions and classifications can be used to find our way through some of the issues in Dante's web of meaning. One of the essential points of this movement within the poem concerns the growing competence and self assurance of the Pilgrim and the question of the appropriateness of his utilization of his virtuosity. That the poem from Canto XXI of the grafters through Canto XXVII of Guido da Montefeltro is a virtuoso performance none will deny. Particularly the imagery and the dialogue show the Pilgrim's continued growth, but as we saw in Canto VIII, an increase in poetic powers does not always coincide with an increase in moral stature (Kleinhenz 1986). Such, I believe, is the case here. The Pilgrim does make progress throughout this section, but he also misapplies his poetic virtuosity. In short, he is guilty of "displaying his own excellence" and of a "passion for innovation," mainstream vainglory. To completely see this we must try to keep many things in mind. Some of these are: the continuing motive of the victory of Christianity over both Hebrew and Latin antiquity, the relationship of the Poet to the Pilgrim, the motive of the education of the Pilgrim and the nature of particular sins, hypocrisy, theft and "fraudulent counsel," and the relationships among them. We readers who must struggle to understand the masterpiece, might begin by seeing all of these things as separate issues, but of course in the mind of Dante, and finally in ours, they are not separate at all. To his genius the relationships among things is clear and the threads of his fabric never slip from his fingers. If we follow him humbly, as his Pilgrim humbly follows the footsteps of Virgil, the marvelous ability of the poem to educate its faithful students will continue to prove itself.

For a long moment, caught up in the foolishness of the demons pretending to be an army and participating in the "games" of the sinners, there was the danger of forgetting that this is truly Hell. Certainly the Pilgrim seemed to disregard his earlier fears and enter into the spirit of things until his musings brought him to his senses. Here is a place to remind ourselves of whose eyes through which we see. Only rarely do we see Hell as the refined Poet remembers and reflects upon it. Rather, he allows us to see it as his fictional earlier self, the Pilgrim, saw it. That way, we, too, learn the lessons by recreating in ourselves the experience. Did we not have fun with the demons? And now we have learned how perilous it is to think that evil, however humorously presented, is trivial. Even as the Pilgrim (and Virgil!) has learned to be cautious, so too have we learned to evaluate the inhabitants of Hell with great care. This underlines the importance of always distinguishing between the Poet and the Pilgrim. When I said earlier that this section contains examples of misapplied poetic virtuosity, I certainly did not mean that the Poet was deficient in any sense. I meant that the Poet writes the poem in such a way that we are allowed through the poetry to see the deficiencies of the Pilgrim. I don't think we should spend a great deal of time on this issue, for it is a maze of paradox, but briefly, if the poetry doesn't "work," it's because the Poet doesn't want it to "work" and he wants us to perceive that fact. We are to interpret that fact not as a deficiency of the Poet who has journeyed all the way to Heaven and seen God, Himself, but as a deficiency of the Pilgrim still struggling in the depths of Hell. To use "poetic insufficiency" to show us the deficient development of his Pilgrim of course means that, in one sense, the poetry is anything but insufficient. In fact, it is clearly a work of great genius. Paradox, but not one that will confuse a thoughtful reader.

When we find ourselves with the hypocrites, there is not much danger of any misinterpretation. The fatigue of the hypocrites reminds us of the eternal misery of damnation; their tears make an irony of the membership of some of them in the order of "Jovial Friars." What can be the meaning of this change in the poem's character? The answer, I think, is one of the keys as to how this movement ties together.

Loderingo and Catalano were appointed by Pope Clement IV to mediate between the Guelphs and Ghibellines of Florence. In actual practice they worked in the Pope's interest and therefore favored the Guelphs, indeed making it possible for that party to exile many of the Ghibelline aristocracy and destroy their property (mainly in the Gardingo district of Florence, hence the remains of the "peace" that "still appears around the Gardingo" of 108). As the two friars were from Bologna their condemnation here continues the criticism of Bologna which began with the first sinner in the pitch, but now ties that condemnation to Florence itself. For us, the important issue is the nature of their hypocrisy, to paraphrase St. Thomas as quoted above, they pretended to be good men without being so.

As we will see, this is the basic definition of hypocrisy, but it is itself a ramification of a larger issue. It is related to all forms of fraud in that all who would commit fraud must hide their guile from their victims by pretending to be virtuous toward them.

The simple hypocrisy of the two friars, however, pales into insignificance compared to the hypocrisy of Caiaphas who advised the Jews to crucify Christ and the *contrapasso* of whose punishment is therefore particularly appropriate as he must bear the weight of all hypocrisy, as the others in their leaden cloaks pass over him who is crucified on the ground, even as Christ, crucified, bore the weight of all sins. Caiaphas was the first of the chief priests and pharisees to see the necessity (from their point of view) of the death of Christ. In explaining his case, the Divine Will made him speak the truth about the necessity of the death of Christ (as seen from the divine point of view) which he himself could not know in the same manner that Virgil speaks truths beyond his comprehension in the *Fourth Eclogue*. Thus the famous passage in John 11:

> 45 Many therefore of the Jews who had come to Mary, and had seen what he did, believed in him. 46 But some of them went away to the Pharisees, and told them the things that Jesus had done. 47 The chief priests and the Pharisees therefore gathered together for a council and said, "What are we doing? for this man is working many signs. 48 If we let him alone as he is, all will believe in him, and the Romans will come and take away both our place and our nation." 49 But one of them, Caiaphas, being high Priest that year, said to them, "You know nothing at all; 50 nor do you reflect that it is expedient for us that one man die for the people, instead of the whole nation perishing." 51 This, however, he said not of himself, but being high priest that year, he prophesied that Jesus was to die for the nation; 52 and not only for the nation, but that he might gather into one the children of God who were scattered abroad. 53 So from that day forth their plan was to put him to death.

The irony of Caiaphas's speech is apparent to anyone with any knowledge of Christianity. Dante expects us to know the passage, of course, and the circular nature of Caiaphas's speech perfectly reflects his circular and ironic fate as he who counsels crucifixion ends up as the eternally crucified one. Still, this passage does not explain Caiaphas's condemnation as a hypocrite. In fact, his speech is very straightforward and not at all deceptive; he wants to protect the priest's position and the political independence of Israel. To do this, calm must prevail and Jesus is a trouble maker. This aspect of Caiaphas is not hypocritical (Caiaphas might even have thought it to be virtuous), but is part of the more general category which we have encountered before (as in the case of Semiramis in Canto V) of individuals who oppose God's plan of history which, in Dante's under-standing, required the peace of Rome over the whole world in order for the doctrine of Christianity to spread. In the context of this passage, Dante sees Caiaphas merely as another who works against the necessary domination of the world by Rome in the same way as Loderingo and Catalano, in the context of Dante's time, work against the necessary stability of imperial rule by doing the Pope's disruptive work. This passage does, however, reinforce my point that Caiaphas (like the other sinners around here) is "generally sinful" in directions other than hypocrisy. The specific hypocrisy of Caiaphas is revealed when it is time for the trial of Christ. Christ is brought before Caiaphas, the High Priest and the Sanhedrin (Matthew 26:59):

> 59 Now the chief priests and all the Sanhedrin were seeking false witnesses against Jesus, that they might put him to death, 60 but they found none, though many false witnesses came forward but last of all two false witnesses came forward, 61 and said, "This man said, 'I am able to destroy the temple of God, and to rebuild it after three days.'"

So this is why the soul of Caiaphas eternally parodies the crucifixion; he sinned not by mere hypocrisy himself, but by urging others, to be hypocrites. The startling image of the crucifixion, retribution for a compound version of hypocrisy, which brings us up so sharply after the lightheartedness of the demons, is the keynote here. Understanding Caiaphas enables us not only to begin to understand the sinners of simple fraud, whose sins turn out not to be so simple at all, but also to comprehend the next step in the development of the Pilgrim himself. Back in Canto XI, Virgil catalogued the sins of fraud in this way (XI, 52–60):

> "Fraud, which gnaws every conscience, a
> man may practice upon one who trusts in
> him, or upon one who reposes no confidence.
> This latter seems to sever only the bond of
> love which nature makes; wherefore in the
> second circle hypocrisy, flatteries, sorcerers,
> falsity, theft, simony, panders, barratry, and
> like filth have their nest."

Typically, Virgil does not name the sins in the order they appear and this particular section is complicated by the use of the general term "like filth" which implies that sins other than those specifically mentioned might be found in the second circle. Now this is no problem as we do not always see all of a circle. By the same understanding, that Virgil's listing is general, we are not surprised when Guido da Montefeltro is condemned because "he gave the fraudulent counsel" (XXVII, 115) even though that sin is not specifically mentioned by Virgil. Hatcher (1970), Musa (1983), Thompson (1974) and Truscott (1973) have engaged in a lively controversy over exactly what fraudulent counsel might be. Is it to give fraudulent advice, or to suggest that someone behave fraudulently? Guido certainly does this second, but Ulysses in XXVI, usually tarred with the same brush (since he is in the same circle as Guido), does not, nor can his "counsel" to his crew be said to be fraudulent. Wrong, sinful, mistaken perhaps, but not fraudulent. Like finding "mad bestiality" (Chapter 9) attempts to pin the sin down seem futile, yet the similar case of "mad bestiality" might give us some guidance with it. Remember that bestiality turned out to be a general category of sin which Dante refers to in order to make a point about general categories. I would suggest that fraudulent counsel is similar and points out that the whole category of simple fraud is made up of interrelated and interlocking sins. I don't know that anyone has noted in print that Caiaphas's sin involves counseling someone to do something fraudulent and that it is in the act of counsel that his hypocrisy lies; he and the Sanhedrin counsel others to give false witness and make hypocrites of themselves. Now in XXVII, Guido will counsel Boniface VIII to hypocritically promise his enemies safety and then kill them. In short, he will counsel Boniface to be hypocritical even as Caiaphas counseled the pharisees to be hypocritical. Of course, one cannot advise hypocrisy without being hypocritical, so Guido is as much a hypocrite as Caiaphas or Boniface who "advised" Loderingo and Catalano. Now leaving out for a moment how Ulysses fits into this, let me make my point: The key phrase in Virgil's description of the second circle is "like filth" which indicates a unity of nature among these sins. We should seek enlightenment by noting similarities as well as differences. I think all the fraudulent souls of this area ("like filth") are tainted with hypocrisy and connected through that sin to all the other daughters of vainglory. Further, I think that the Pilgrim himself, recently cleared of charges of divination and barratry, now confronts vainglory (displaying one's own excellence) himself. Vainglory is, of course, a form of pride which is a very deadly Deadly Sin and, in the Medieval view, the root of human error.

If hypocrisy can be seen to permeate this area so too can the other daughters be perceived. Certainly Caiaphas meant to protect his own position, ("display his own excellence") and to do so by deceit, lying to the people through false witnesses, so he properly is punished for hypocrisy. Ulysses's quest is certainly "passion for innovation" whereas Guido's advice is surely again deceitful. This leaves displaying one's own excellence by words, boasting, and this is the sin of which the Pilgrim is here in danger. Since the Pilgrim is presented in *Inferno* as novice poet, the boasting will be poetic boasting and will result in the poetry being insufficient or inappropriate.

In the cantos of the grafters, we saw the Pilgrim on a slippery slope from which he has extracted himself with credit, barely. While he saw the danger of the Malacoda (and Virgil did not), he did allow his attention to wander and he did present a view of that section of Hell which was perhaps a bit too lighthearted for the reality of the situation. The canto of the hypocrites brings everyone up short. Its very leadenness and its reminder of the crucifixion return us to a serious state of mind.

The meaning of the contrast in tone between the description of the grafters and the hypocrites is indicative of the great gap between the Pilgrim of the "now" of the poem and the greater understanding of the Poet who has completed the journey. And since the issue of Geryon and his unreality has made us acutely conscious that the poem is metaphorical, a poetic construction intended to reveal ultimate truth, I think we can understand the Poet here allows us to see the mind of the Pilgrim at an earlier level of understanding, the thought of the poet as he was, not yet the master of his art, not yet having completed his purification.

This assumption, that the movement of the poem shows the incomplete understanding of the Pilgrim at this stage of the journey, is supported by the fact that the other poet involved, Virgil, is also shown here to be deficient in understanding. Of course Virgil has been obviously underrating evil for some time; here we see him begin to understand. Ryan (1982) has already pointed out that Virgil's amazement over Caiaphas is caused by his ignorance of much of Christianity. Virgil knows of the Harrowing of Hell, and thus of the existence of Heaven. He does not seem until this moment to come to face the fact of the crucifixion (124–126):

> I saw Virgil wonder over him who was thus
> outstretched as on a cross, so vilely in the
> eternal exile.

On his earlier journey before the crucifixion, Caiaphas would not have been there. The crucifixion is not the only thing Virgil learns about here; he also learns of his misunderstanding which caused his failure with the demons. Informed that no bridge stands over the sixth bolgia, he grasps that he has been lied to by Malacoda (139–42):

> My leader stood for a moment with bowed
> head, then said, "He that hooks the sinners
> back yonder gave a poor account of the matter."

Ryan notes that Friar Catalano's comment is the most common of Christian truisms (142–144):

> "At Bologna once I heard
> it said that the devil has many vices, among
> which I heard that he is a liar and the father
> of lies."

So common, in fact, that it is well known even in sinful Bologna, but news to Virgil, who, being pagan, has no understanding of the real nature of evil. This explains why Virgil was so easily mislead by the demons while Dante, the Christian, was suspicious, at least until his own lapse into inattention.

So Dante the Christian poet is again one up on Virgil and yet, we see that he too has insufficiencies and a long way to go before he learns all the lessons of Hell. That he must learn some of these lessons from Virgil seems obvious, but by now we understand that Virgil's perfection is the limited perfection of fallen man, man without the crucifixion. Dante will surpass his master wherever Christian insight is required as it was with the Malebranche.

Canto XXIII ends with Dante following in the footsteps of his beloved master, beloved, as all humans must be, in spite of their faults. XXIV begins with a long simile about that angry look which Virgil wears as a result of having been fooled by Malacoda. We must return to this simile, but for now note simply that the look of anger disappears, replaced by that "sweet look

which I saw first at the foot of the mountain." (21–22) We were not told
of that look in Canto I, but now we are told that it was there and here it
serves as a sign of yet another reconciliation between the pair. What this
reconciliation introduces is the scramble up the ruins of the bridge, out of
the bolgia of the hypocrites, and then along the ridge to the brink of the
bolgia of the thieves. It is clear that this exhausting effort should be seen as
a continuation of the motive of education. It has many similarities with the
episode of the mounting on the back of Geryon, for instance, in that the
student is exhorted and protected by Virgil in the climb up the cliff.

This represents a return to the "proper" relationship between the two,
but it is not the final form of that relationship which is not only the relationship of Dante and Virgil as individuals, but is also the allegory of the
relationship between pagan and Christian poetry themselves. It is clearly an
important stage in both as the importance of the moment is shown by
success in the climb. Indeed, "It was no road for anyone wearing the
mantle" (34), notes the poet, a climb impossible for a hypocrite. Dante and
Virgil are not hypocrites nor is the poem hypocritical in its defenses against
divination and barratry. (But if Dante is free of hypocrisy, he is not
necessarily free of other forms of vainglory.)

There is a clear distinction between hypocrisy and putting the best
face on a difficult situation as the exchange between Dante and Virgil shows
(41–60):

> We, however, came at length to the
> point where the last stone is broken off. The
> breath was so spent from my lungs, when I
> was up, that I could go no farther, but sat
> down as soon as I got there.
>
> "Now it behooves you thus to cast off
> sloth," said my master, "for sitting on down
> or under coverlet, no one comes to fame,
> without which whoso consumes his life leaves
> such vestige of himself on earth as smoke in
> air or foam on water. Rise, therefore; conquer
> your panting with the soul that wins every
> battle, if with its heavy body it sinks not
> down. A longer ladder must be climbed; it
> is not enough to have left these spirits. If
> you understand me, now act that it may

> profit you." I then rose, showing myself
> better furnished with breath than I felt, and
> said, "Go on, for I am strong and resolute."

If the Pilgrim's efforts to become "strong and resolute" can best be aided by putting on the face of that he wishes to be, there can be no hypocrisy in the acting. This would seem to be a self-evident truth, yet coming where it does, immediately following the testimony that Dante is not a hypocrite, it bears investigating. St. Thomas speaks of hypocrisy versus non-hypocritical pretending by again citing St. Augustine (*Sum.* 2a 2æ. III, I):

> As Augustine remarks, "To pretend is not always to lie, but
> only when there is nothing behind the meaning of the pre-
> tence. When, however, our pretence has reference to some
> further meaning, there is no lie, but truth in a figure."

Inasmuch as Dante's pretence to be strong depicted what he wished to be and was bending his efforts to become, it was not hypocritical. In the same way, the poem itself depicts through figures a truth beyond the pretense of the poem, but is not thereby deceitful. The importance of this passage includes not only the distinction between hypocrisy and non-hypocritical pretending, but extends, then, to the validity of figurative speech, poetry, itself and is then a part of
Dante's defense of the poetic conception itself (The making of "truth in a figure.") as a divine act conveying truth which we last saw in the Geryon episode with its mention of Ariadne (XVII, 18).

Virgil's view of the conversation, however, is more limited and our sense of the limitation is reinforced by our new knowledge of how ignorant Virgil is of the facts of Christianity and of the goals of the proper life. Virgil knows that his charge can attain the bliss which is denied to himself because of the lack of baptism. He spoke to Dante of this in Limbo. However, of the nature of that bliss he must be ignorant. Most of Virgil's comments in this exchange can be interpreted in Christian terms, that is, the soul burdened with its heavy body, the long ladder to be climbed, the root of the soul's delay in sloth are all Christian images. Virgil's suggestion that the goal of it all is fame, however, is not. In fact, it sounds very much like that vainglory, "displaying one's own excellence," of which St. Thomas spoke. When Virgil speaks of victory in his exhortation to the Pilgrim, he naturally does so in terms of that fame which in the ancient world was a proper goal of much of life since there was no conception of the higher goal of salvation. Virgil, of course, did realize that there were more important things than individual fame as his own claim to it rested on a poem whose greater purpose was the reunification of a divided Roman Republic. Still, in terms of the individual, since the attainment of salvation was not possible, fame was a primary goal. Like Virgil, many of the souls we have met in Hell accede to this "incomplete" view hence their desire to be remembered even in the face of the futility of mere fame considering the fact of their damnation. The Poet certainly thought that earthly fame was desirable and he eagerly sought it, but it was fame won in pursuit of a higher goal: his own salvation and the salvation of others. His mistaken (and temporary) search for fame on merely earthly terms (in *Convivio*) was the cause of his being lost in the dark wood in the first place. Fame can be good, but it cannot be all. Here again Virgil, the mouth of paganism, speaks in terms which can bear a Christian interpretation, but he, himself, does not know of those meanings.

But it is the Poet who understands these issues. The Pilgrim has not yet understood the relation of fame to salvation and this is the root of the empty error he is about to make. At this moment in the poem, when progress is spoken of as a difficult climb after fame, the reader is allowed to see the soul's struggle for purification in the struggle to properly make the poem itself. The soul's struggle is reflected in the struggle to write the poem. We can understand it in this way: Dante the Pilgrim, having struggled with the things of Hell and reached a firm understanding of his own destiny as one of the saved, has begun to triumph over his mentor Virgil. The triumph is not, of course, of the Pilgrim's own making; it began with the sense of fear in the dark wood (the "first gift of the Holy Spirit"), it continued with Beatrice's intervention and it has been honed by the revelations the Pilgrim has been permitted to experience in his journey. Indeed, Virgil himself has been the medium through which Dante has learned many of the lessons which lead to his victory. Virgil, we understand, represents the ancient world in general and ancient poetry in particular. In Dante's historiography, the ancient world and its poetry existed in order to be fulfilled by Christianity, therefore, Dante's eventual triumph over Virgil and, in a sense, on his shoulders, is not only inevitable, it is just. It is a part of the necessary movement of God's plan itself. We have just seen the Pilgrim's superiority where Christian knowledge is required; we are now to witness the next step.

The complex relationship we now confront involves the sins of simple fraud as forms of vainglory (hypocrisy, deceit, passion for innovation) and the Pilgrim's own struggle with vainglory which takes place under the surface of the narration and which must be uncovered by careful reading. Much of what we must note concerns Dante's eventual triumph over ancient poetry which he so boldly challenges among the thieves. The issue here is not that Dante as Christian poet will or will not best the ancient poets. He must do so given the divine scheme of history. What is at issue is the precise nature of that triumph and the Pilgrim's vaingloriousness.

We have already seen the beginnings of the struggle. The canto of the grafters is a masterpiece of comic invention and hugely entertaining. The fact that such a tone is subtlety out of place is shown by the fact that the poets find themselves in serious danger and must perform a slapstick scramble to escape and find themselves face to face with, of all things, hypocrisy. Hypocrisy, as we learned from St. Thomas is a form of vainglory as is proclaiming one's own excellence. Now to be a comic poet is a fine thing, if that is your role, but is it Dante's appointed task? Rather he must show us the fate of those who have lost "the good of intellect." The Pilgrim has for a moment lost sight of his high purpose, but the Poet has arranged things so that we see through the error. Of course, we are allowed to enjoy the spoof for the thing it is, perhaps a necessary relief from the gravity of the rest of the poem, while understanding the error of those who would reduce Hell to ribaldry. It is much like watching a comedy about war. Our attention must be somewhat divided: with one part of our mind we experience with the Pilgrim, with the other, we learn from the Poet.

The next marker in this struggle to find the proper poetic voice for the high subject is the famous and lengthy simile which begins Canto XXIV. We have already noted that this simile forms part of the reconciliation and cooperation motive which pervades this section. It sets the stage for the cooperative scramble up the broken ledge and for the perfect agreement to the descent into the ditch of the thieves. Many critics have written about this simile (notably Economou 1976) noting that it is a villanelle, that is, a poem with a rustic subject, that it is concerned with a set of metamorphoses (as the episode of the thieves will be) wherein the supposed snow becomes hoarfrost which disappears and the peasant's despair turns to joy, and that for all its length, it accomplishes very little. It tells us that Dante was troubled when Virgil frowned and encouraged when he smiled again. Certainly, it is a fine little bit of high flown poetry, but oddly empty and unconvincing. What shepherd could be so ignorant and unskilled in his calling to mistake frost for snow in the first place? To say nothing of making the error for so long as to be actually discouraged? The whole thing is as out of place as the spoof of the demons, but in a totally different direction. Here the error is too much refinement of language at the cost of a lack of content.

Remember that I am arguing that the Poet was perfectly aware of the inappropriateness of both the spoof and the villanelle and that they are presented while the Pilgrim is in the middle of a number of errors. The inappropriate poetry is to be taken as indicative of the limitations of the fallen Pilgrim, not of the perfected Poet.

The Pilgrim's request to descend into the next pit is met with perfect agreement by Virgil (XXIV, 76). That it is the Pilgrim who makes the suggestion to which Virgil simply agrees is another sign of the complicity between the pair and of Dante's growing competence. On the one hand, he makes errors; on the other, he gains. The Poet is very realistic in his depiction of the development of his character. There are gains. there are missteps, sometimes both at the same time.

What the Pilgrim finds are the thieves who are subjected to constant metamorphoses reflecting the way they changed the goods of others to their own hands in their lifetimes. The fact that the metamorphoses involve snakes might be a reflection of the hidden nature of theft, but at least one of the thieves we are to meet, Puccio Sciancato (XXV, 148) is remembered for the very openness of his thefts (Singleton, 1970). More probably, the snakes are to remind us of the serpent in the Garden of Eden who counseled the first theft, that of the fruit of the tree, falsely promising Adam and Eve that it would make them "as gods, knowing good and evil (Genesis 3:5)." That this is the intended reference is supported by the fact that the serpents "thrust through their loins the head and tail which were knotted in front (95–6)" in a manner reminiscent of Adam and Eve's futile attempts to hide their nakedness. It is significant that this reference again raises the issue of fraudulent or hypocritical counseling (on the part of the snake) in its primary appearance in the Garden of Eden.

From the images of Eden the poem quickly evokes the image of the Resurrection in the figure of the Phoenix. The reader is expected to see the irony of the continuous and futile "resurrections" of the sinner Vanni Fucci. This *contrapasso* is a Christological image of which the crucifixion of Caiaphas is another example.

Vanni Fucci is, like all the other thieves we are to see in this and the next canto, not an ordinary thief. Dante wastes no ink on mere petty thieves, but presents to us only men famous for their thefts, virtuoso thieves. All are mentioned in the chronicles of the time and their identifications are fairly certain (Singleton 1970). These are men of uncommon talent who misused their great gifts even as Caiaphas, a persuasive and talented leader, misused his gift of leadership and persuasion. Such misused virtuosity is, I believe, another thread which ties this movement of the poem together even including the role of the Pilgrim as novice poet. For what is Dante if not a man especially gifted by God who might, through ignorance or willfulness, misuse his talents?

Vanni Fucci is condemned for his theft from the sacristy or treasury of the church of San Zeno at Pistoia (which city is now added to the catalogue of cities, (see also XXV, 10–12) even though the Pilgrim says he thought of him as a man of violence, "I have seen him as a man of blood and rage." (129). He is at least verbally violent, however, as he, in a manner typical of the more fierce wraiths utters his dark prophesy specifically to grieve the Pilgrim. This sinner speaks reluctantly; we will not see any more individuals eager to speak in hope of the futility of fame, but in the case of Vanni Fucci, his reticence is not motivated by shame. Like Farinata of Canto X and Capaneus of Canto XIV, he is trapped in his obstinacy, one of St. Thomas's daughters of vainglory. Both Capaneus and Vanni Fucci are spoken of as "unripe" (XIV, 48 and XXV, 18) and in both cases it is flames, falling from the sky or from the mouth of the dragon (XXV, 23), which will ripen them. Farinata, who like the other two is punished by flames, utters prophesy designed to grieve the Pilgrim (Dante says, "the words...seemed hostile to me (X, 123))" and, in a sense, speaks of his eventual ripening when his intellect will be void.

Just before Virgil requests Vanni Fucci's story, there is a brief Address to the Reader (XXIV, 119):

> Oh power of God! how severe it is, that
> showers down such blows for vengeance!

This comment is reminiscent of the invocation in XIX, 10–12:

> O Su-
> preme wisdom, how great is the art which
> thou showest in heaven, on earth, and in the
> evil world! and how justly does Thy Power
> dispense!

There, thinking about the metaphorical nature of the poem we noted Hertzman and Stephany's point that in fact the praise of God's judgement is in fact praise of the appropriateness of Dante's own invention. Here the same point can be made, but in both cases on the literal level of the poem the appropriateness of crediting justice to God is also a valid interpretation. Here, in light of what is to come, the literal interpretation is the predominant one. The pious acknowledgement of the primacy of God's judgement is repeated in XXV, 4–9 in the Pilgrim's further approval of Vanni's punishment for his supreme act of defiance:

> From
> this time forth the serpents were my friends
> for one of them coiled itself about his neck, as
> if it said, "You shall say no more," and an-
> other about his arms and bound him again,
> so riveting itself in front that he could not
> give a jog with them.

For a moment, the Pilgrim's responses are appropriate, but he then begins to make his next great error. As the three spirits appear (33–34), Dante dismisses Virgil by giving him a sign to remain silent because of his concern that his attention might wander (44–45):

> Wherefore, in order that my
> leader might remain attentive, I placed my
> finger upwards from my chin to my nose.

Virgil's attention wander? Surely Virgil has made errors of overconfidence and out of ignorance, but he has never failed to pay attention. The Pilgrim is about to assume the ascendancy, perhaps rashly. Another Address to the Reader, similar to XVI, 124–136 which brings us face to face with Geryon and all that he implied, alerts us to something exceptional (46–48):

> If, reader, you are now slow to credit that
> which I shall tell, it will be no wonder, for I
> who saw it do scarcely admit it to myself.

The description of the punishment of the thieves which follows is graphic and lengthy as descriptions of punishments in Hell go. However, given that we have accepted the poetic premises of the poem already, premises which include the acceptance of a supernatural world wherein the ordinary laws of nature are suspended, it is difficult to see why we should be slow to credit this experience. After all, we accepted Geryon as well as many other marvels. Why should we be suspicious here? What follow are two metamorphoses: descriptions of changes in the form or substance of a person. In this case in the form of the souls of the thieves. These two metamorphoses are, of course, linked to the metamorphosis of Vanni Fucci which we saw in Canto XXIV which involved Vanni's reduction to ashes at the bite of a serpent and his subsequent reformation (XXIV, 97–105). In the description of Vanni's changes, no mention is made of what happens to the serpent that bit him. It is this detail that distinguishes the two metamorphoses that follow here in XXV as the first describes how two creatures, serpent and sinner, combine into the same form (XXV, 49–78) and the second (79–138) describes how serpent and sinner exchange forms. Obviously, an important part of the issue is this crescendo of poetic virtuosity, but, as we noted, in this area of Hell the question of the proper use of virtuosity is central.

The *contrapasso* of this action is well designed as it is appropriate that those who stole from others should have their single remaining possession, their form, stolen from them and that the nobility of the human shape be reduced to that of a reptile, a veritable sign for evil nature. Dante devotes nearly 100 lines of exact description to these changes. Clearly, the sheer literary quality of the metamorphoses are a clue to what it is that we should find incredible here, as the literary character of the villanelle of Canto XXIV was a clue to its nature. This supposition is confirmed by the interjection in the middle of the third transformation. (XXV 94–102):

> Let Lucan now be silent, where he tells of
> the wretched Sabellus and of Nasidius, and
> let him wait to hear what now comes forth.
> Concerning Cadmus and Arethusa let Ovid
> be silent, for if he, poetizing, converts the one
> into a serpent and the other into a fountain,
> I envy him not; for two natures front to front
> he never so transmuted that both forms were
> prompt to exchange their substance.

Now Ovid is the poet most associated with describing metamorphoses because of his work *Metamorphosis* and Lucan in the *Pharsalia* relates episodes of such changes, perhaps in imitation of Ovid. Both of these were among those who welcomed Dante into the company of high poets in Limbo. We have seen how Dante's Pilgrim has shown himself to be superior in some regards to his guide Virgil, one of whose allegorical burdens is to represent ancient poetry. Dante's ascendancy over Virgil, however, has been markedly courteous, only just verging on the rude, before the encounter with Farinata in Canto X. Further, Dante's superiority has always consisted of more accurate knowledge or insight and has never been couched in terms of poetic virtuosity or technique. Here the challenge to antique poetry is open, self-conscious and technical (Dante says he will describe a metamorphosis more complex than any attempted by Ovid). It is presumptuous since the Pilgrim/Poet presumes to challenge the ancient poets on their own ground, the device of a metamorphosis, which he could only have learned by study of the very poets he now abruptly challenges. If it were that the challenge was successful, that would be self evident to anyone who knew the poetry of Ovid and Lucan. Without the open challenge Dante's triumph would be gentle and courteous, as was his triumph over Virgil in the issue of Mantua, but no less real. It would seem that the parallel here is again the Poet's rash behavior towards Filippo Argenti in Canto VIII (Kleinhenz 1986), wherein the Pilgrim's participation in the punishment of the sinner is understandable, but perhaps impious. The challenge and the display of increasingly complex metamorphoses is vainglorious in accord with St. Thomas's definition: it is designed to display

Dante's own excellence and at the expense of the reputation of Ovid and Lucan. Even given that Dante does triumph over Lucan and Ovid, the effect is boasting.

Singleton (1970) has cited the various passages from Lucan and Ovid which are related in form and content to Dante's versions. Here is one example from Lucan's *Pharsalia* in a slightly longer citation than Singleton's (*Pharsalia* IX, 763–787).

> When a tiny seps stuck
> the leg of the hapless Sabellus and clung there with
> barbed fang, he tore it off and pinned it to the sand
> with his javelin. Though this reptile is small in
> size, no other possesses such deadly powers. For
> the skin nearest the wound broke and shrank all
> round, revealing the white bone until, as the
> opening widened, there was one gaping wound and
> no body. The limbs are soaked with corrupted
> blood; the calves of the legs melted away, the knees
> were stripped of covering, all the muscles of the
> thighs rotted, and a black discharge issued from
> the groin. The membrane that confines the belly
> snapped asunder, and the bowels gushed out. The
> man trickles into the ground, but there is less of
> him than an entire body should supply; for the fell
> poison boils down the limbs, and the manner of
> death reduces the whole man to a little pool of cor-
> ruption. The whole human frame is revealed by
> the horrible nature of the mischief: the ligaments
> of the sinews, the structure of the lungs, the cavity
> of the chest, and all that the vital organs conceal,-
> every part is laid bare by death. The shoulders
> and strong arms turn to water; the neck and head
> are liquefied; snow does not melt and vanish more
> quickly before the warm South wind, nor will wax
> be affected faster by the sun. It is little to say that
> the flesh was consumed and dripped away in the
> form of matter: fire also can do this, but no pyre
> ever made the bones disappear. They also vanish:
> following the corrupted marrow, they suffer no
> traces of the quick death to survive. Among the
> plagues of Africa the seps bears off the palm for

> destruction: all the rest take life, but it alone
> carries off the dead body.

Well might one argue that Dante has chosen worthy opponents and that his compound transformations are "better." However, the description is too self-conscious to be "poetic." The Poet uses the effect of the self-conscious poetry to reveal the incomplete development of the Pilgrim at this moment in the poem. In his vainglorious assault on ancient poetry the poet in the person of the Pilgrim is close to the daughters of vainglory: hypocrisy, passion for innovation and boasting. That the Poet intends this is shown by the address to the reader at the end of the canto (142–144):

> Thus I saw the seventh ballast change and
> transmute - and here let the novelty be my
> excuse, if my pen goes aught astray.

Readers who have not yet read *Purgatorio* and *Paradiso* should realize that not all issues raised in *Inferno* are resolved in *Inferno*. This issue of the proper humble use of poetic power is not completely concluded until the very end of *Paradiso* itself. Another example is the question of the guilt of Caiaphas and the necessity of Christ's crucifixion which is finally explained in *Purgatorio*.

CHAPTER 19

Canto XXVI

Ulysses: Overreaching Presumption

Here is Ulysses, another of the great sinners of Hell in the class of Francesca, Farinata, Brunetto Latini and Pier della Vigne. Soon we will see Guido da Montefeltro and later Ugolino who also belong to this league. All of these figures are a severe challenge to the Pilgrim and as such they represent obstacles that must be overcome in order to conquer sin. A constant element of the challenge in these cases is that we have to learn to perceive truth as it lies beneath the surface of language; for instance, we had to see past Francesca's poetic speech to the lust under it; we had to detect Farinata's rage, Brunetto's indirection and Pier's servile self-pity. There is a comparable issue here and we are alerted to expect it by the fact that Ulysses is bound in Hell to another figure, Diomedes, who does not speak. Most of the figures who thus confront our understanding are found in Hell bound to other souls who are silent or secondary in some way: Francesca to Paolo, Farinata to Cavalcante, Brunetto to his group of the unnatural. Pier della Vigne is alone, but he speaks of a time when he will be "with" his body, though separate from it.

The history of the criticism of Canto XXVI is similar to the history of the other cantos in the group. Earlier critics tended to see these sinners as sympathetic and, in the most romantic cases, to see them as "misplaced" inhabitants of torment. Many modern critics see this issue differently and begin with the assumption that characters are damned because they are of an evil nature. The trick is to see how this is so.

Ulysses, like Francesca, has generated a large library of criticism. Readers who want some idea of how large should consult Anthony Cassell's lengthy bibliography (1981b). In this analysis, which cannot be exhaustive, I would like to address two major issues: One is that Ulysses is demonstrably a sinner and the other is that Ulysses' voyage has an intimate relationship to the Pilgrim's own journey. In addressing these, I will try not to lose track of the question of language and of the continued development of the Pilgrim and of the fact, discussed in the last chapter, that rigid categories of sin do not provide an adequate explanation for the organization of Lower Hell.

A sympathetic impression of Ulysses is still generally received by students in their early readings of the poem and any modern Westerner can understand why this is so. In spite of the fact that the Poet has made Ulysses explicitly condemn himself from his own mouth (as in the case of Francesca), the figure of the intrepid explorer who defies fate to gain knowledge and glory corresponds so much to our present definition of the heroic that, at first, readers must force themselves to see the condemnations on the page before them.

Dante's different vision of Ulysses is that he is an impious and devious personality; that his steadfastness and intelligence are misused in the service of his vainglory. One way to get to Dante's vision of Ulysses is to consider his sources of the story. First, remember, Dante didn't have Homer who is the source of most modern impressions of Ulysses. We can't be sure of all of Dante's sources, but it seems that he knew Ulysses through Virgil, Statius, Ovid and Cicero and these Roman versions of the story generally conform to the Roman civic mythology which sees the Greeks as the enemies of the Trojan ancestors of Rome and, therefore, evil. In addition, it seems likely that Dante refines and Christianizes his interpretation through the strictures of St. Thomas in the *Summa* (Truscott 1973).

Virgil has Aeneas tell the story of the wooden horse in Book II of *Aeneid* and in that telling the emphasis is on the treachery of the Greeks in general and Ulysses in particular (*Aeneid* II, 41–53):

> "Then foremost of all and with a great throng
> following, Laocoon in hot haste runs down from the
> citadel's height, and cries from afar: 'Oh, wretched
> citizens, what wild frenzy is this? Do ye believe the
> foe has sailed away? O think ye any gifts of the Greeks
> are free from treachery? Is it thus ye know Ulysses?
> Either enclosed in this frame there lurk Achaeans, or
> this has been built as an engine of war against our
> walls, to spy into our homes and come down upon
> the city from above; or some trickery lurks therein.
> Trust not the horse, ye Trojans. Whatever it be, I
> fear the Greeks even when bringing gifts.' So saying,
> with mighty force he hurled his great spear at the
> beast's side and the arched frame of the belly. The

> spear stood quivering and with the womb's rever-
> beration the vaults rang hollow, sending forth a moan."

The Trojans are persuaded to take the horse into the city by the lies of Sinon whom, Virgil makes clear, is the agent of Ulysses.

Statius's tale of how Ulysses seduced Achilles from the arms of Deidamia to the forces of Agammemnon explicitly associates Ulysses with fraud in the passage about how the Greek hid the arms and armour in the gifts for the women (*Achilleid*, I, 841–848):

> The troop [of women among whom Achilles is hidden]
>   disperses amid applause, and they seek
> again their father's threshold, where in the central
> chamber of the palace the son of Tydeus [Ulysses] had long
> since set out gifts that should attract maidens'
> eyes, the mark of kindly welcome and the guerdon
> of their toil; he bids them choose, nor does the
> peaceful monarch say them nay. Alas! how simple
> and untaught, who knew not the cunning of the gifts
> nor Grecian fraud nor Ulysses' many wiles!

In Ovid, the picture of a scheming Ulysses is even stronger than in Statius. Roman patriotism always disparages the Greeks to exalt the Trojans (a motive Dante pursues as we have seen) and frequently attacks Ulysses's character to make this point. In his relation of the debate between Ajax and Ulysses for the possession of the armour of Achilles, Ovid allows Ulysses to win because of his superior intelligence and rhetorical skill, but still implies that he lacks sincerity (*Metamorphoses* XIII, 128–134):

> "If my prayers and yours had availed, O Greeks,
> there would be no question as to the next heir in this
> great strife, and you, Achilles, would still have your
> own armour, and we should still have you. But since
> the unjust fates have denied him to me and you"
> (and with his hand he made as if to wipe tears from
> his eyes) "who would better receive the great
> Achilles arms than he through whom the Greeks
> received the great Achilles?"

Ulysses' story in *Inferno* is of a voyage in search of knowledge. He dies on that voyage and yet Dante's point is not that the search after knowledge is evil in itself or doomed to failure. After all, his Pilgrim is on a voyage much like Ulysses' in search of the knowledge "of human vice and worth" (XXVI, 99). Like Ulysses the Pilgrim will arrive at the foot of the Mountain of Purgatory. The Pilgrim will proceed beyond that place because his voyage is authorized by Divinity itself whereas Ulysses' ends there because it is in defiance of all sanctity. Ulysses tells us that he and his crew passed through the Straits of Gibraltar "where Hercules set up his markers, that men should not pass beyond" (108-109). This line contains the central point of the canto, but like many points made in *Inferno* (including the Pilgrim's vainglorious attack on ancient poetry in the last canto) one must wait for a later canticle for it to become clear. In *Paradiso* XXVI Adam explains to Dante the very essence of the original act of sin (115-117):

> Now know, my
> son, that the tasting of the tree was not in
> itself the cause of so long an exile, but solely
> the overpassing of the bound.

Further clarification comes from St. Thomas in the *Summa*. Ulysses overpasses the bounds and finds himself in seas which he cannot navigate. If we consider this in the context of St. Thomas' daughters of vainglory, we can see that Ulysses' "passion" for innovation has led him beyond his personal competence. Indeed, this is the point St. Thomas makes in his discussion of presumption (*Sum.* 2 2æ. 21, 4):

> ON THE OTHER HAND are the words of St. Gregory that, *presumption where extraordinary things are concerned*, is a daughter of vainglory.

> REPLY: As already pointed out, there are two kinds of presumption. One of these involves relying confidently on one's own abilities, attempting what in actual fact lies outside personal competency as though this were not so. Presumption of this sort obviously comes from vainglory, for the fact of seeking a great deal of personal glory leads a person to attempt things beyond his powers, especially things that tend to stir up greater admiration. This is the significance of St. Gregory singling out, *presumption where*

> *extraordinary things are concerned,* as a daughter of
> vainglory.

We will return to St. Thomas for the second type of presumption later. For now, recall in the earlier citation of St. Thomas from 2a 2æ. 132, 5 we saw the list of "daughters of vainglory" to include "passion for innovation." There the issue was "displaying one's own excellence." Here the context expands to presumption if the thing attempted is outside one's competence. This is a good place to remind ourselves that Thomas's list of vainglory's daughters also included boasting by words (as in the case of the Pilgrim in XXV) and hypocrisy as in the case of Caiaphas.

Ulysses crosses the limits set by the divine Hercules and becomes a pagan type of Adam who crossed the limits set by God. (Franco Fido 1986 has written beautifully about correspondences between *Inferno* XXVI and XXVII and those cantos in other canticles.) It is not in seeking knowledge that sin lies, but in going beyond that which is possible to man unaided by divinity. The sin also consists in the resulting neglect of those things that do lie within man's competence and his duty. Ulysses's speech shows us exactly what he neglects in his search for "experience of the world and of human vice and worth" (98–99). A search which he paradoxically makes in "the world that has no people" wherein he can only learn of the vices and worth of himself and his own small crew (Cassell 1981a). He neglects specifically the claims upon him of his family (93–97):

> "neither fondness for my son, nor
> reverence for my aged father, nor the due love
> which would have made Penelope glad, could
> conquer in me the longing."

By implication he neglects all other claims of proper duty also including statecraft, the proper government of Ithaca, substituting the illegitimate leadership of "that small company" (101–102), the body of men who are the objects of his "fraudulent counsel" in his "little speech" (122). So is Ulysses condemned for presumption as in Thomas's definition? Is he guilty of "fraudulent counsel" (in the sense that his advice to his crew is bad advice, craftily intended to further his own mad pursuit of vainglory)? Surely, both of these conclusions are correct, but Virgil's catalog of the sins of Ulysses and Diomedes adds to the list (58–63):

> and in their flame they
> groan for the ambush of the horse which
> made the gate by which the noble seed of
> the Romans went forth; within it they la-
> ment the craft, because of which the dead
> Deidamia still mourns Achilles, and there
> for the Palladium they bear the penalty.

Ulysses' exhortation to his men to force the gates of Hercules is fraudulent counsel since with it he exhorts them to sin. In the ambush of the horse, called by Dante's source, Statius, "fraud" (*Achilleid* I, 846), a critical element is that Ulysses persuades Sinon to sin and bear false witness to the Trojans. The stratagem by which Ulysses made Achilles throw off his female disguise and impiously leave his family, as Ulysses himself did, again involves persuading someone to sin. The theft of the sacred Palladium, as pointed out by David Thompson (1974) is accomplished by Ulysses by persuading the Trojan Antenor to steal the image for him. In all cases Ulysses' powers of elocution and persuasion are used to make others commit sin, in exactly the same way Caiaphas hypocritically persuaded others to sin. The point here is that Ulysses' sins are as mixed as are all the sins of simple fraud. Fraud, hypocrisy, theft, intertwined in what Virgil calls "like filth," all related to St. Thomas's "daughters of vainglory." Certainly Ulysses' passion for the unknown with which he infects his crew in his "little speech" is related to Thomas's "passion for innovation" and the whole range of Ulysses' devious activities are examples of misused virtuosity.

With this preliminary discussion as background, let us look at the text of the canto.

The apostrophe to Florence which beings the canto is one of the series of condemnations of Italian cities which we have noted. It is artistically important because of the image of useless flight (1–3), "Rejoice, O Florence, since you are so great that over sea and land you beat your wings, and your name is spread through Hell!", which foreshadows Ulysses's "mad flight" of 125. The Pilgrim's development is such that he can here wish for God's judgement as he accepts Virgil's help in climbing the steep slope (15). Since Virgil had been presumptuously silenced by the Pilgrim in XXV, this coopera- tion represents a return to a more correct relationship which is underscored by the address to the reader (19–24):

> I sorrowed then, and sorrow now again,
> when I turn my mind to what I saw; and
> I curb my genius more than I am wont, lest
> it run where virtue does not guide it; so that,
> if a kindly star or something better has
> granted me the good, I may not grudge my-
> self that gift.

If, as most readers agree, the canto of Ulysses is more beautiful than the cantos of the thieves, in spite of the latter's technical virtuosity, this is the reason. The Poet, having absorbed the lesson of Ulysses' vainglory, has advanced beyond the vainglorious Pilgrim of XXV. There, remember, an excuse, novelty (passion for innovation), was offered for the extremes of poetic virtuosity and the Pilgrim admitted his confusion (XXV, 142–146):

> Thus I saw the seventh ballast change and
> transmute - and here let the novelty be my
> excuse if my pen goes aught astray. And
> though my eyes were somewhat confused
> and my mind bewildered.

Now language is restrained within proper limits and we are presented with a simile which echoes the intemperate villanelle of XXIV, but which presents a very different picture (25–33):

> As many as the fireflies which the peasant,
> resting on the hill - in the season when he
> that lights the world least hides his face from
> us, and at the hour when the fly yields to
> the mosquito - sees down along the valley,
> there perhaps where he gathers the grapes
> and tills; with so many flames the eighth
> ditch was all agleam, as I perceived as soon
> as I came where the bottom could be seen.

The "intemperate" villanelle was also concerned with a peasant and carefully designated the time of year. That peasant, however, was agitated and his perceptions were confused. This one is quite the opposite; he is at rest and not in error, even as the Pilgrim, his sense of propriety restored, correctly understands the nature of the flames even before Virgil's explanation of them.

The following simile, that of Elisha's vision of the ascent of Elijah, explains how each flame steals away a sinner, but it also juxtaposes the issue of proper advice (Elijah's counsel was not fraudulent) with an authorized ascent to the eternal regions (Elijah comes to Heaven "as pleased another"). The method of identifying Elisha by the line "And as he who was avenged by the bears" (34) is puzzling. As always we must question why Dante wishes to recall particular images to our minds, in this case, one of the strangest images of the Old Testament. The story is found in 2 Kings, 2, 23–24:

> 23 And he [Elisha] went up from thence to Bethel: and as he was gong up by the way, little boys came out of the city and mocked him, saying: Go up, thou bald head; go up, thou bald head. And looking back, he saw them, and cursed them in the name of the Lord; and there came forth two bears out of the forest, and tore of them two and forty boys.

Little children torn by bears! And this given us as a throwaway line merely to identify Elisha? Perhaps the purpose is a warning to the impious, presumptuous and ignorant of the danger of mocking God and, more specifically, mocking his spokesman. In which case the line might stand as a vindication of Dante himself, an "authorized" traveler to Purgatory, like Elijah and unlike the "unauthorized" Ulysses. If, as may commentators think, Dante claims a true role as a spokesman for God for himself, then the warning against mocking one who would "go up" is particularly pointed.

In this canto, allusion follows upon allusion. The next one is the comparison of the flame that contains the sinner whose identity the Pilgrim questions to "the pyre where Eteocles was laid with his brother" (53–54). Many commentators have noted that the connotation of the comparison is negative. Polynices and Eteocles are themselves guilty of violence; they brought war upon the people of Thebes and, if they were in Hell, presumably would be in the river of burning blood. To some extent, also, Ulysses and Diomedes are warmongers. But beyond that, Polynices and Eteocles hated one another to the extent that, when on their common funeral pyre, the flame above them divided. It seems reasonable that their enmity must reflect on the relationship of Ulysses and Diomedes who are together in the present divided flame. As we have seen in previous instances of souls united in torment, the unification always adds to the penalty and we need to consider that issue here. How does Diomedes contribute to the punishment of Ulysses and the contrary? Mark Musa (1978) has considered this question and concludes that as Diomede was one of Ulysses' band convinced by the "little speech" to undertake the sinful voyage, his attitude must be one of hatred of Ulysses and this is the explanation of the "punishment" in the pairing. Undoubtedly this is so and I think the hypothesis is given further credence if we look again at the speeches of Ajax and Ulysses over the arms of Achilles in Ovid. Both orators stress how much Diomedes gave himself to Ulysses. First Ajax attacks Ulysses on the point (*Metamorphoses* XIII, 95–103):

> "But if I may speak truth, the arms claim greater
> honour than do I; they share my glory, and the
> arms seek Ajax, not Ajax the arms. Let the Ithacan
> compare with these deeds his Rhesus and unwarlike
> Dolon, his Helenus, Priam's son, taken captive, and
> the stolen Palladium: nothing done in the light of
> day, nothing apart from Diomede. If you are really
> giving that armour for so cheap deserts, divide it
> and let the larger share in them be Diomede's."

Ulysses' reply emphasizes Diomede's loyalty (238–242):

> "Finally who of the Greeks praises you or seeks
> your company? But Diomede shares his deeds with
> me, approves me, and is ever confident with Ulysses
> at his side. Surely, 'tis something, alone out of the
> many thousand Greeks, to be picked out by Diomede!"

Ulysses' second reference to Diomede in the speech includes the image of a fighter as a man of the "right hand," a thinker as a man of the "left," and explains Diomede's subjugation of himself to the man of thought (354–356):

> "And if Diomede
> did not know that a fighter is of less value than

a thinker, and that the prize was not due merely to a
right hand, however dauntless, he himself also would
be seeking it"

So, yes, Diomede must hate Ulysses, must feel he invested his life in a man whose leadership brought him to Hell. How does the reciprocation work on Ulysses? I think the answer to this question points out the singular nature of the character whose portrait Dante creates, for Ulysses is in a sense more self-aware than most of the great sinners of Hell. Most of these, Francesca, Farinata and the rest seem to be victims of their own self deception. This is particularly apparent in the case of Francesca and Pier, but Ulysses seems to understand his sin. His speech makes it clear that he realizes how his neglect of duty was wrong and he calls his final voyage a "fool's flight." In fact, Ulysses' punishment consists as much in burning regret as it does in the burning flame. Is part of his punishment regret for the fate of Diomede? Regret for his hatred? I suspect this is so, because of Ulysses' acute intelligence about which all the sources agree. It is precisely Ulysses' gifts of intelligence and understanding which permit him to commit the sins cataloged here. His virtuosity is exactly that which is misused. The *contrapasso* is that his punishment consists in understanding his sin. This does not mean that he repents since one of the "laws" of Hell is that condemned souls are not permitted repentance. Indeed, the persistence of Ulysses in his sin is in his beautiful speech by which he attempts to persuade Dante and Virgil, and the reader, to pity. That he is frequently successful, with readers at least, is shown by the record of criticism.

There remains the issue of Virgil's address to the flames. Virgil speaks to the souls for Dante, but no one is sure why. One suggestion is that the shade of Virgil is recreating the actual line by which Dante learned of the exploits of Ulysses, the Roman report of Greek literature. Others suggest that there is a kind of division of historical responsibility here since in this canto Virgil speaks to an ancient sinner, but in the next urges Dante to speak with a modern representative of the same sin of fraudulent counsel. Mark Musa (1978) reminds us that Virgil's address to the Greeks is a bit deceptive (79–84):

> "O you who are two within one fire, if I
> deserved of you while I lived, if I deserved of
> you much or little when in the world I

> wrote the lofty lines, move not; but let the
> one of you tell where he went, lost, to die."

Ulysses and Diomede, dead before Virgil wrote *Aeneid*, probably do not know what he says about them in it. We know that it is not flattering. Virgil says, "if I deserved of you much or little," thus leaving the question open, but Ulysses does respond, hoist on his own petard, so to speak by a brilliantly deceptive speech. But Musa's point goes beyond this. His understanding is that when Virgil inserts himself into the conversation between Dante and Ulysses with the words, "leave speech to me, for I have understood what you wish" (73–74), what he means is that he understands the *sort* of thing the Pilgrim wishes to hear, not a specific issue. The sort of thing would be simply something memorable and thus the tale of the last voyage, "where he went, lost, to die." It is again Virgil, jealous of his prerogatives, eager to be in control taking an initiative to which the Pilgrim graciously assents.

CHAPTER 20

Canto XXVII

Guido da Montefeltro: Prideful Presumption

St. Thomas explains in the *Summa Theologiae*, 2 2æ. 21, 4, that there are two kinds of presumption, the first, we have seen, helps bring Ulysses to Hell.

> there are two kinds of presumption. One of these involves relying confidently on one's own abilities, attempting what in actual fact lies outside personal competency as though this were not so. Presumption of this sort obviously comes from vainglory, for the fact of seeking a great deal of personal glory leads a person to attempt things beyond his powers, especially things that tend to stir up greater admiration. This is the significance of St. Gregory singling out, *presumption where extraordinary things are concerned*, as a daughter of vainglory.

The other variety of presumption damns Guido da Montefeltro.

> Quite different from this is the other kind of presumption which, relying on the divine mercy or power, but in a distorted way, expects to obtain eternal life therefrom without having merited it, and pardon apart from repentance. This sort of presumption appears to spring directly from pride; implying, in effect, that one thinks so much of himself that he imagines God will not punish him nor exclude him from eternal life in spite of his continuing in sin.

Guido is presumptuous because he manufactures the form of repentance without its substance. He tells us of his conversion in what seem sincere words (XXVII, 84):

> When I saw myself come to that part of my
> life when every man should lower the sails
> and coil up the ropes, that which before had

> pleased me grieved me then, and with re-
> pentance and confession I turned friar, and -
> woe is me! - it would have availed.

Anna Hatcher (1970) points out that this is rather unconvincing. That Guido, self-described as guilty of the sins of the fox (75), seems here merely to have made a rational, as opposed to heartfelt, arrangement for the afterlife. His conversion lacks true contrition, as Hatcher has it, "he would make a deal with God." My claim is that this fits neatly into St. Thomas's definitions. Guido expects to obtain eternal life without deserving it, an act of presumption. Further, Guido blames his failure on Pope Boniface VIII who asks for his advice in his war with the Colonna (67–71):

> "I was a man of arms, and then a corded
> friar, trusting, so girt, to make amends; and
> certainly my hope would have come full, but
> for the High Priest - may ill befall him! -
> who set me back in my first sins."

Readers, their antennae tuned by the education we have received in the poem, will have little difficulty with this one. It is a familiar chord, one played by both Francesca and Pier della Vigne: someone else made me do it. We know, given the premise of God's perfect justice, that this cannot be so. If Boniface has any role in Guido's damnation at all it is that he returned Guido to sins he customarily committed in the past, he, "set me back in my first sins," which as Hatcher says, Guido had never repented in the first place. The evidence for this is pretty clear since if he had repented the "sins of the fox" he wouldn't commit them again as he clearly does. Guido's whole explanation is hypocritical and he is guilty of encouraging the Pope to be hypocritical, to make "long promise with short keeping" (110). This complex of hypocrisy is subtly emphasized by the reference to Boniface as "High Priest," the title, of course, of Caiaphas the arch hypocrite.

Joseph Markulin (1982) has detailed the many ways in which Guido's elaborate language is deceptive from its fawning (if noisy) prologue to the outright lie at the end. In addition, we can see that the simile of the Sicilian bull, which tells us exactly how noisy Guido's approach was, also serves another purpose (7–18):

> As the Sicilian bull
> (which bellowed first with the cry of him --
> and that was right -- who shaped it with
> his file) was wont to bellow with the voice
> of the victim, so that, though it was of brass,
> yet it seemed transfixed with pain

Since we have left the bolgia of the grafters we have met no common sinners. We have seen breathtaking hypocrites, masterful thieves, stunning Ulysses and now Guido. In addition, the poetry which has presented these figures to us has been of a consummate order, revealing as it does the moral state of the Pilgrim's soul. Reflecting, we can see that another theme of this section has been virtuosity, its proper use and its misuse. Most, if not all, of this group of sinners are men who were especially gifted and who put those gifts to evil use. The theme of gifts and talents is an important one throughout the *Comedy* and is strongly involved in the development of the Pilgrim himself. Readers who pursue the work through the end will come to see how vital a theme it is. Here in this instance, the virtuosic builder of the brass bull, Perillus, was the first to die in it, a just recompense for an evil use of talent. Singleton (1970) quotes Valerius Maximus as a possible source of the story.

> There was a savage fellow who invented a brazen bull in
> which victims were enclosed and a fire kindled beneath;
> they suffered a long and hidden torture for he so arranged it
> that the moans that were torn from them sounded like the
> lowing of a bull, since if they sounded at all like human
> voices, they might plead for mercy from the tyrant, Phalaris.
> Now, since he was so anxious to torment the unfortunate,
> the artisan himself was the first to experience the efficiency
> of his hideous invention.

Since we have learned that investigating Dante's sources frequently yields dividends, we can look at Ovid's version of the story which strikes the same note (*The Art of Love*, I, 655–656):

> there is no juster law than that contrivers of death should
> perish by their own contrivances.

The Christian writer Orosius picks up the same moral stating that the unjust Perillus was justly punished (*The Seven Books of History Against the Pagans* I, 20).

This is neat for Dante since it is a pagan example of perfect *contrapasso* perfectly suited to the present issue. Perillus, the evil virtuoso, is "hoist by his own petard" even as Guido, who offers the advice to Boniface that, "long promise with short keeping will make you triumph on the High Seat," prompted by Boniface's promise of long bliss in Heaven. This promise is shortly broken when the black Cherubim comes for Guido. Thus the opening simile and the closing scene create a frame for the canto.

Following the simile Guido addresses Virgil, a Latin poet, who apparently has been speaking the Lombard dialect to the Greek Ulysses. The meaning of these linguistic relationships is not clear. It is complicated by the fact that Virgil deems it fitting that Dante should converse with Guido for, "he is Italian" (33). Guido makes the familiar request for news of his homeland, here Romagna, and receives from the Pilgrim a lengthy list of who rules where in that country. Singleton (1970) sorts the list out. Some of the rulers have been Dante's protectors or employers during his exile and the list includes both the family from which Francesca comes and the family into which she marries. It may be that this is Dante's device to bring the case of Francesca and her misuse of language to mind since Guido is deceptively smooth and polite and his intent is clearly to shift the blame for his fate from himself to Boniface (Markulin 1982). Markulin thinks that Guido knows perfectly well that the Pilgrim is no ordinary denizen of Hell in spite of his claim that he is sure that Dante will never return to the world above.

> "If
> I thought that my answer were to one who
> might ever return to the world, this flame
> would shake no more; but since from this
> depth none has ever returned alive, if what I
> hear is true, I answer you without fear of
> infamy."

If Markulin's hypothesis is true, then Guido's speech is another example of the hypocrisy which pervades this entire section. Guido hopes to persuade the visitors that his comments are entirely disinterested, a claim belied by his intense eagerness to speak.

Guido's characterization of Boniface VIII is, in fact, Dante's characterization (85–93):

> "The Prince of the new Pharisees, having
> war near the Lateran - - and not with Saracens
> or with Jews, for his every enemy was Chris-
> tian, and none had been to conquer Acre, nor
> been a merchant in the Soldan's land - - re-
> garded neither the supreme office and holy
> orders in himself, nor in me, that cord which
> used to make its wearers leaner"

Dante's position was not that the Pope should be unwarlike, but that holy wars should be directed against proper targets, the Saracens and the enemies of the faith in the holy land. Boniface sins by making war on Christians.

Guido sins again (he has never truly repented of his previous sins) when he agrees to accept Boniface's absolution before he reveals his solution to the Pope's problem. Markulin says, and we must agree, that Guido's account of his trip to Hell is at least somewhat fallacious. It is inconceivable that St. Francis would have been deceived by Guido's phony repentance, but the account of the black Cherubim's reasoning must be accurate. Guido never truly repented and the effort to reduce the power of the Papacy (of the keys) to a mere legalism is absurd.

CHAPTER 21

Canto XXVIII

The Sowers of Discord: Scandal and Schism

We have learned over the course of the last several cantos that the arena of "simple fraud" is more complicated than Virgil's catalog would have lead us to think. Far from punishment merely for fraudulent acts against people in general, "upon one who reposes no confidence" (XI, 54), the movement from the grafters to the "fraudulent counsel" of Guide da Montefeltro expands to include the misuse of talent and the forms of vainglory. It can be seen to include as well an essay on the interrelatedness of all sin and a psychological study of the consistently sinful nature of the damned. Virgil's listing in Canto XI is only a generalized and schematic map of Hell; its threefold divisions (incontinence, violence and fraud) do not comprehensively define the essence of sin. Too, we have come to understand that the shortcomings of Virgil's catalog are in part the result of the shortcoming of the spirit himself. Virgil is pagan man, he is reason unassisted by revelation; unbaptized, he is inherently inferior to the Christian poet whom he guides. His understandings proceed no further than the pagan knowledge of Aristotle and Cicero who are his sources. We and the Pilgrim have the advantage of Christian insight.

Canto XXVIII in important ways is a continuation in the sense that the sins here are not simply fraud. This bolgia, the ninth bolgia of the eighth circle, is given over to those guilty of the twin sins of scandal and schism. Schism, we were led to expect by Virgil; scandal is added to the list by Mohammed (XVIII, 30–36):

> "Now see how I
> rend myself, see how mangled is Mohammed!
> In front of me goes Ali weeping, cleft in the
> face from chin to forelock; and all the others
> whom you see here were in their lifetime
> sowers of scandal and of schism, and there-
> fore are thus cleft."

In modern English scandal simply means an act that shocks the sense of propriety. To Thomas Aquinas, it had nothing to do with shock. It was a specific sin with two separate aspects. In the one, a person performs an act which is an obstacle to another's salvation, as, say, by setting up a heretical religion. In the other aspect, a person takes the act of another as an occasion for one's own sin, as when the sight of another's wealth leads one to the sin of envy (*Sum.* 2a 2æ. 43).

Now schism, again according to Thomas, is a sin against the unity of the church. It does not necessarily have to do with heresy, although Thomas quotes Jerome to the effect that schism certainly leads to heresy, "there is no schism which does not make up a heresy for itself in order to make leaving the church seem right." (*Sum.* 2a 2æ. 39). It is possible that Dante was thinking of Mohammed in exactly these terms since there was a medieval tradition that Mohammed was a renegade Christian bishop (Singleton 1970). Mohammed's heresy, Islam, then is only a kind of excuse for his prideful rebellion against the authority of Rome.

It is something of a shock to realize, if we are thinking in terms of Virgil's organization, that neither of these sins has anything directly to do with fraud. In fact, a schismatic who, to justify his rebellion, creates a heresy (and thereby a scandal, an obstacle to another's salvation), is almost certainly sincere in his error and in no sense hypocritical. J. S. T. Tatlock (1932) surely has Dante's intention correctly when he says that the essential unity of these sins with fraud is that they operate against the ties binding men together, even as do the kinds of frauds which work against the general sort of confidence we should expect of one another. This seems a clear example of how Dante develops an understanding of sin in terms of underlying relationship rather than as a simple catalog. In this regard, Dante works like Thomas, who is also careful not to create a rigid system. In his discussion of schism and scandal, Thomas specifically points out the ambiguity of the issues, "Circumstances," he says (*Sum.* 2a 2æ. 39, 2, speaking of schism), "are particular and can vary in an infinite number of ways." Here is Thomas on the relative severity of schism and heresy, which he here calls "the denial of faith," (*Sum.* 2a 2æ. 39, 2):

> 3. Charity has two objects; the principal one which is the divine goodness, and the secondary object, the good of our neighbour. Schism and sins like it attack charity through its secondary object, which is less than the object of faith, God

himself. Such sins then are less than denial of faith. Hating God, which attacks charity through its principal object is not less. However, among sins against our neighbour schism seems worse because it attacks the spiritual good of the multitude.

In other words, if we think of schism and heresy in terms of their effect on our fellows, schism is worse because it is always a social sin whereas heresy can very well be private. In absolute terms though, heresy is worse because it is a form of direct attack on God himself. It seems then, again as noted by Tatlock, that the Poet is aware of these ambiguities and presents us a poetic interpretation which transcends Virgil's legalistic formula.

Canto XXVIII is a sort of intermezzo, concerned as it is with sins that are not strictly speaking fraud, between the large movement of Cantos XXI–XXVII and another movement which will conclude with the first simile of Canto XXXI. It contains two of the most striking physical images of sinners in the poem, the rent Mohammed and the haunting figure of Bertran de Born. The stage for these images is set by two means, first, by the expression of the difficulties of language, speech and memory of the first six lines and, second, by the comparison of the nature of the pit to the list of those maimed and torn in the list of wars and battles of the next fourteen lines. This passage is linked to the development of the Pilgrim by the compliment to Livy of line 12 which assists in his reconciliation with Pagan authorities which began after his attack on them in the bolgia of the thieves.

Mohammed names the sins of schism and scandal. Like his successor Ali he is split, a *contrapasso* intended to make clear that the essence of these sins is that they divide one from the other or, that even they divide people from their correct (Christian) selves. Typically, the punishment is circular as the sinners circle round the pit uselessly healing only to be split anew when they reach the demon. Dante's intent in this canto seems to be very general. There is no obvious thread which ties all the figures who are mentioned closely together. Some are sinners in this pit, others are merely named in the course of the various predictions which are made. Mohammed and Ali certainly are guilty of schism and scandal and heresy as well. They are sunderers on a grand scale. Mohammed splits Islam from Christianity and Ali further divides Islam (Singleton 1970). The individual mentioned by Mohammed, Fra Dolcino was a Christian heretic. The next figure who speaks, Pier da Medicina, is unknown by any direct information, but the traditions about him claim that he separated people by whispering false tales to increase his own reputation and enrich himself (Singleton 1970). If these stories are so, then this Pier is guilty of falsehood, but not necessarily schism (which is specifically dividing the church) or scandal. Dante's theme seems to be divisiveness in general. The pair named by Pier, Guido and Angiolello, are merely helpless victims and their killer, Malaspino, only a murderer.

The next two figures fall more easily into a familiar pattern in the poem. The first of these is pagan, Curio, who encouraged Julius Caesar to cross the river Rubicon, thereby causing the Roman civil war and making the fall of the Republic inevitable. We have already seen how in Dante's moral view of history the sundering of Roman unity is such an evil. Dante's parallel from the Christian era is the disruption of the Florentine Republic. Mosca is the man who, when the feud between the Guelphs and the Ghibellines was still fermenting, made the split inevitable with his comment, "A thing done has an end." This comment (a scandal) lead the Florentines to murder Buondelmonte de'Buondelmonti dividing the Florentines among themselves and to the true schism of the strife between the Pope and the Emperor (Singleton 1970).

The last figure in the bolgia who confronts the Pilgrim and speaks to him is Bertran de Born. There are many things here which indicate to the reader that Bertran is one of the important sinners of Hell. The first of these is the appearance of his shade. He carries his head in his hand by its hair. We are made to understand that the head is separate from the body and independently aware (118–126):

> Truly I saw, and seem to see it still, a
> trunk without the head going along as were
> the others of that dismal herd, and it was
> holding the severed head by the hair, swing-
> ing it in hand like a lantern, and it was
> gazing at us and saying: "O me!" Of itself
> it was making a lamp for itself and they
> were two in one and one in two - how this
> can be, He knows who so ordains.

It is a spellbinding image, especially when the thing raises its head above its neck up to the level of Dante who is standing on the bridge above it (127–135):

> When he
> was right at the foot of the bridge he raised
> high his arm with the head, in order to
> bring near to us his words, which were, "See
> now my grievous penalty, you who, breathing,
> go to view the dead: see if any other is so
> great as this! And that you may carry news
> of me, know that I am Bertran de Born, he
> who to the young king gave the evil counsels."

In addition to the image, the importance of this figure to the poem is indicated by the fact that it is the shade of a poet. Part of Dante's claim to authority in the writing of his *Comedy* is that he is the superior poet, not only of his time, but of all time. Throughout the *Inferno* he has gradually gained ascendancy over Virgil and all of ancient poetry. Once before, in Canto X, he claimed superiority over a contemporary poet, Guido Cavalcante whose poetry was apparently deficient in its relation with the antique. In *Purgatorio* Dante will meet other poets, one of whom will attest to Dante's ascendancy. Bertran de Born was a troubadour poet who was a courtier of Prince Henry, son of Henry II, King of England. King Henry had his son crowned while he himself was still on the throne in order to secure the succession. This assurance of his own eventual kingship lead Prince Henry to rebel against his father. Some sources known to Dante said that Bertran was the "evil counselor" who lead Prince Henry to rebel and caused the division in the English kingdom (Singleton 1970).

Marianne Shapiro (1974a) says that if Bertran is the cause of this, his evil counsel must be contained in his poetry, which, indeed, consistently praises violent warfare. Therefore, he is another example of misused virtuosity, one who, unlike the Pilgrim, has not repented of his sin. The spots where the poem touches on the Pilgrim's own life are often climaxes. Both Shapiro and Teodolinda Barolini (1979) detail how much of the preceding material of the canto is reminiscent of the poetry of Bertran de Born. Such references are lost to modern readers who know nothing of Bertran's poetry and read in translation, but it is to Bertran's bloody poetry that Dante owes the inspiration for the list of horrible battles which begins the canto and even the image of the split Mohammed which also comes from his work. Because of these hints, argues Shapiro, the moment when Bertran de Born finally appears after such preparation is the climax of the canto.

Even if we do not detect the traces of Bertran's poetry before we reach his divided image, we are alerted to its importance by the Poet's disclaimer quoted above, "Truly I saw, and seem to see it still" so reminiscent of the similar disclaimer at the sight of Geryon in Canto XVI. This reminds us that, of course, Dante didn't see Bertran any more than he saw Geryon, but that which is to follow is an example of high poetic creativity designed to carry significant meaning.

Bertran de Born is divided in two and he carries his head like a lamp. Dante is bemused by how a single consciousness can be divided into two entities, "How this can be, He knows who so ordains." This is a faint prefiguring of the greater question, answered later in the poem, of the Trinity, one being in three persons. The futile lamp of Bertran's head, his cognitive part, therefore his poetry, should be remembered when Statius compares Virgil's poetry to a lamp that lights the way for others in *Purgatorio* 67–68:

> "You it was who first sent
> me towards Parnassus to drink in its caves,
> and you who first did light me on to God.
> You were like one who goes by night and
> carries the light behind him and profits not
> himself, but makes those wise who follow
> him, when you said, ' The ages are renewed;
> Justice returns and the first age of man, and
> a new progeny descends from heaven.'"

If we take Thomas Aquinas as the ultimate authority on sin, what Bertran does, dividing a kingdom against itself, is not schism, which is dividing the Church. In Dante's mind, however, the stability of governments is a part of divine ordering since the work of the church cannot go on in the midst of political turmoil. He therefore equates Bertran's sundering with schism. To do this he links Bertran with Ahitophel who encourages Absalom's rebellion against his father, King David, raising the whole issue to the level of scripture. For this sin is Bertran de Born's head separated from his body; as he says, "Thus is the retribution observed in me" (142). In Italian, retribution is *contrapasso*. Bertran's importance is emphasized by the fact that it is exactly here, and in no other place, that the nature of eternal punishment as retribution, *contrapasso*, is exactly explained.

CHAPTER 22

Cantos XXIX-XXX

Alchemy: The Pilgrim's Shameful Pleasure

The next section of the poem, one of the internal "movements," begins at line 36 of Canto XXIX. Lines 1–35 are the ending of the previous movement, but some issues are raised in them which continue throughout so that they function as a transition.

The images which the poet has presented since the bolgia of the grafters have become stranger and stranger. The torn figure of Mohammed and the bifurcated Bertran de Born are a momentary climax of the grotesque; no wonder then, that the Pilgrim reels under their impact (XXIX, 1–12):

> The many people and the strange wounds
> had made my eyes so drunken that they
> longed to stay and weep; but Virgil said to
> me, "What are you still gazing at? Why
> does your sight still rest down there among
> the dismal mutilated shades? You have not
> done so at the other pits. Consider, if you
> think to count them, that the valley circles
> two and twenty miles; and already the moon
> is beneath our feet. The time is now short
> that is allowed us, and there is more to see
> than you see here."

Not only are the Pilgrim's eyes "drunken," but his guide is testy. He is sarcastic about the Pilgrim's supposed wish to count the damned. His assertion that Dante has not previously become engrossed in the sights of Hell is not strictly true. It is belied by Dante's own statement in Canto XXII, 16–18:

> My attention was all on the pitch, in order to see
> every condition of the pouch, and of the peo-
> ple who were burning in it.

There the concentration on the sinners led to the neglect of the demons, a serious error, so perhaps Virgil's rebuke (for that's what it is) has validity. However, Virgil seems primarily to feel pressed for time, although there is just a hint that the concentration on "dismal, mutilated shades" is distasteful. The point returns at the end of this movement (XXX, 130–148) when the Pilgrim again becomes fascinated by the sinners and is again rebuked by Virgil. The motive in this way forms a frame and sets this section of the poem off. Readers who pursue the journey through Purgatory and Paradise will encounter the issue of Dante's attention several more times. There seems to be here a resumption of the tension between Dante and Virgil which we have not seen for some time. Dante's response to the rebuke is petulant (13–15):

> "If you had given heed to my reason for
> looking," I answered then, "perhaps you
> would have granted me a longer stay."

This speech is delivered while the Pilgrim patters along after Virgil who has simply turned and walked away. The ensuing discussion explains the identity of Geri del Bello. Singleton (1970) suggests that the pity which Dante expresses for his unavenged relative in line 36 is the sense of *pietas* which has to do with respect for family ties. In any case, during his explanation the Pilgrim does address Virgil respectfully as "my leader" so that the temporary irritation is healed.

Commentators note that this passage contains the first specific reference to the size of Hell. There is a similar measurement given in the next canto (82–87) which allows us to see for certain that Hell is a funnel shaped pit. The passage is also another time marker, it now being 1:00 in the afternoon.

Now the new movement proper begins. We are at the lip overlooking the last bolgia of simple fraud, that of the falsifiers, who are not only those who lie, but also counterfeiters and imposters: falsifiers of words, things and persons. The crescendo of weird images continues, characterized by an atmosphere of sickness. Dante says the scene is like the hospitals of Valdichina and Maremma combined. In Canto XXX, the increased intensity of the scene is indicated by comparing it all to insanity, sickness of the mind rather than that of the body (XXX, 1–21).

The travelers descend into the pit and into one of the high themes of the poem. The indefatigable Robert Hollander, to whom modern students of Dante owe so much, shows us that here the Poet makes one of his strongest claims to reliability (58–66):

> I do not believe it was a greater sorrow to
> see the whole people in Aegina sick, when the
> air was so full of corruption that every ani-
> mal, even to the little worm, fell dead, and
> afterwards as the poets hold for certain, the
> ancient peoples were restored from the seed of
> ants, than it was to see, through that dark
> valley, the spirits languishing in divers heaps.

Hollander (1982) sees that Dante is continuing his disparagement of the ancient poets. Dante reminds the reader of the fabulous story of the destruction of the whole population of Aegina (by a plague, reinforcing the atmosphere of sickness) and its repopulation by the transformation of ants into men. The story is from Ovid and, as Dante solemnly assures us, "the poets hold it for certain." The poets, however, frequently lie, even as do those souls punished in this pit, even as Virgil lied about the founding of Mantua in the *Aeneid*. Hollander says that this is the Poet's way of reminding us of the peculiar claim to truth that he is making: a poetic falsehood upon which is raised a structure of divine truth. Dante has just reminded us that poetry is literally false; the claim to truth for Dante's poem is found in the lines just previous (52–56):

> We descended onto the last bank of the long
> crag, keeping ever to the left, and then my
> sight was clearer down into the depth, where
> the ministress of the High Lord, infallible
> Justice, punishes the falsifiers whom she reg-
> isters here.

Over the years, there has been confusion about where "infallible justice" registers the falsifiers. The poem says "here" and most commentators understand this to mean "in the world of the living" or conversely "in this bolgia of Hell." Hollander's insight is that it means that it is here in the text of the poem that the falsifiers are "registered." Thus, Dante speaks with the voice of Justice. I would assert that Dante's claim to accuracy does not extend to the names of individual sinners, a point already made in the discussion of the significance of Geryon, but to truth in some more abstract sense. Again, this is an issue which does not culminate until late in the entire *Comedy*.

The first of the "sick" (69) whom the travelers encounter are alchemists. One of them, he "of Arezzo" (109) is condemned for his alchemy although he was executed for falsifying, claiming he could teach Albero of Siena to fly. The other, Capocchio, is a counterfeiter who used his alchemical processes to disguise his fraud. Mayer (1969) details some of the many alchemical references in this text, but readers should understand that not all alchemy was sinful. In its highest form, the search for the "philosopher's stone" (or the elixir of life) and the attempt to change a base metal into gold was not to be taken literally. The alchemist was performing a metaphor. Searching for the stone which grants eternal life is a symbol of the search for salvation. To move lead, a base metal, to the status of gold is to symbolize the necessary movement of the perfection of the soul. The philosopher's stone was taken to be that which grants health, hence the image of sickness among these illicit alchemists. Illicit alchemy was simply the use of the manipulations of alchemy to disguise fraud and counterfeiting, as here.

It is interesting that just at the moment when he has reminded us of the metaphorical truthfulness of poetry correctly written, Dante raises the issue of alchemy which is a similar art in that it is a fictional operation which, through images, leads to the contemplation of high truths.

These alchemists, however, are not "correct" alchemists even as poets whose works are only lies are not correct poets. Dante uses the imagery of alchemy to show the shortcomings of such individuals. Many of the involved processes of alchemy included the use of distasteful substances such as excrement so Dante gives us the sense of foulness throughout the movement. The vocabulary of the practice was biological. Substances were said to "die" to "putrefy" (said even of metals) and to be "reborn" or "regenerated." These false alchemists are trapped in the stage of putrefaction (hence the itch and the scales) and are never reborn. The nested pans of line 74 are the crucibles of the alchemical practice and the shape of Master Adam of Canto XXX is that of an alembic, a type of retort used in transmutation (Mussetter 1978).

Canto XXX opens with two accounts of classical madness, both taken from Ovid as was the story of the pestilence of Aegina in the last canto. Thus sickness becomes the insanity of the shades of Gianni Schicchi and Myrrha. Perhaps it is because they were imposters who counterfeited the forms of others that they are transformed into pig-like beasts here.

Dante's attention is now caught by "one shaped like a lute" (49). Sally Mussetter (1978) calls him "Dante's Counterfeit Adam." He is surely the major sinner of this bolgia and like other important figures in Hell, his image carries a great deal of meaning. Mussetter's claim is that Master Adam is not accidentally named, that he is a type of the "Old Adam," sinful man incapable of perceiving the goods of God and thus of attaining salvation. Christ, of course, is the "New Adam" who regenerates mankind. (Remember, too, that Virgil is the highest type of "Pagan Man" who can foresee the coming of Christ, but does not understand his own prediction, and that Dante is the type of "Christian Man.")

Mussetter shows how limited Master Adam's understanding is. He tells us how he longs for the cool waters of his native Casetino in phrases that remind us of the waters of Eden. The memory does not comfort him, however, but adds to his torment even as the memory of Francesca's "love" torments her. The inutility of water, though, is most strongly shown by the fact that Master Adam, to undermine the Florentine coinage, counterfeited the florin, a coin "stamped with the Baptist" (74). This image should have been a constant reminder of the forgiveness possible in the water of baptism and a constant reproach to his continuing sin. All his attention is on the coin, but he fails to understand the significance of its symbol. Mussetter goes on to show that Master Adam's retort like shape, bloated with polluted waters, is emblematic of an incomplete or failed alchemical process, even as the original Adam's spiritual quest was an incomplete failure.

Questioned about his companions, Master Adam names them as Sinon who, impersonating a Greek turncoat, convinces the Trojans to admit the wooden horse into the city and as Potiphar's wife who, unable to seduce Joseph in the Old Testament tale, falsely accuses him of making improper advances to her.

What is wonderful here is the marvelously ugly quarrel which follows this identification. Sinon and Adam, both thoroughly evil and corrupt, quarrel about who is the worse sinner, as if, in this stage of their existence, the question any longer had any meaning. The accusations one levies against the other can just as easily be turned back against the one who made them. Sinon's intent, at the instigation of Ulysses, was to bring down Troy, the great city of antiquity, by introducing into it the false horse. Adam's intent, at the instigation of the dukes of Romagna, was to bring down the city of the present, Florence, by introducing into it the false coinage.

The quarrel of Sinon and Adam is ended, for us, by the resumption of the quarrel of Dante and Virgil (130–132):

> I was standing all intent to listen to them,
> when the master said to me, "Now just you
> keep on looking a little more and I will.
> quarrel with you!"

Which interjection brings us back to where we started at the beginning of Canto XXIX where Dante too was accused of absorption in the sinners. This time, it suddenly becomes clear to the Pilgrim exactly what is wrong (133–135):

> When I heard him speak to me in anger,
> I turned to him with such shame that it
> circles through my memory even yet.

The shame is the shame of prurient *interest* in sin, like an interest in pornography or violence, in the thing for its own sake, rather than for its moral lesson. The Poet tells us that this shame "circles through my memory even yet," another of the poem's constant emphasis on the role of memory in moral affairs. We might, perhaps should, forget the sin itself, but the memory of the shame will keep us from committing it again. In Canto II, 1–9, the Poet extolls the role of memory in moral affairs:

> Day was departing, and the dark air was
> taking the creatures on earth from their la-
> bors; and I alone was making ready to sus-
> tain the strife, both of the journey and of the
> pity, which unerring memory shall retrace.
> O Muses, O high genius, help me now! O
> Memory that wrote down what I saw, here
> shall your worthiness appear!

Here memory is called "unerring." Later, when the Poet speaks of the highest things, memory will fail, but it is completely competent to deal with sin if we use it. The problem of Guido da Montefeltro, for instance, is that if he did truly repent, as he said he did, he did not remember his repentance when Boniface VIII tempted him again. The Pilgrim's regret for his unwholesome delight in the vile is caught in the following simile (136–139):

> And as is he who dreams of something hurt-
> ful to him and, dreaming, wishes that it were
> a dream, so that he longs for that which is,
> as if it were not, such I became that, unable
> to speak.

This vacillation between the real and the unreal not only pictures the Pilgrim's confusion, it also images the vacillation between the unreality of the poetry and the real moral significance of the poem. Dante's embarrassment leads to a great boon (140–148):

> I wanted to excuse myself, and did
> excuse myself all the while, not thinking I
> was doing it.

> "Less shame washes away a greater fault
> than yours has been," said the master, "there-
> fore disburden yourself of all sadness; and do
> not forget that I am always at your side,
> should it again fall out that fortune find you
> where people are in a similar dispute, for the
> wish to hear that is a base wish."

The boon is forgiveness, earned by shame or repentance. Because the Pilgrim is truly repentant, his fault is truly forgiven. This action is a parody of the sacrament of confession. In that sacrament, the confessant, truly contrite, confesses his sin to the priest who can assign a penalty and does forgive the sin. Here, Dante's show of shame takes the part of the confession by word and the embarrassment of the recognition of fault is penalty enough for the sin. Virgil's forgiveness is Christ-like. His adjuration, "do not forget that I am always at your side" reminds the Christian of Christ's words at the end of the book of Matthew, "Lo, I am with you always even to the end of the world." The line, "if fortune find you where people are in a similar dispute." predicts Dante's return to the present world and to Italy where such conditions manifestly hold.

Surely this perfect act of contrition, achieved at the end of the bolgias of simple fraud, should be contrasted with Guido da Montefeltro's imperfect performance of the same act, but that is not all. Canto XXXI begins with a final comment about the episode which includes a reference to Achilles (XXXI, 1–6):

> One and the same tongue first stung me
> so that it tinged both my cheeks, and then it
> supplied the medicine to me; thus I have
> heard that the lance of Achilles and of his
> father was wont to be the cause, first of a
> sad and then of a good gift.

We know by now that Dante's allusions require us to consider the entire context. In this case, we need to remember that Achilles not only had a miraculous lance, but that he was also made invulnerable by virtue of having been dipped in the river Styx. His lance, according to the poet, could heal the wounds it caused by a further touch. The formulation "thus I have heard" indicates that the tale exists in the realm of poetic lies (Singleton 1970). We take Achilles' lance to be a metaphor of rebuke and subsequent forgiveness by the Church, we do well to remember that it is only an apparent similarity. Achilles lance could actually no more heal than his apparent baptism in the river Styx conferred true immortality on him. In both cases, the fiction of the old stories points to something that is true, baptism makes one immortal, the Church rebukes and forgives, but the pagan stories are not true themselves. In this way, we should think of Virgil's parody of confession and penance. Though Virgil imitates Christ, Virgil is not Christ or even Christian. He cannot forgive in any but the human sense. Though this episode may point to Dante's eventual salvation, it cannot be the salvation itself. Salvation cannot be earned in Hell, it is a gift of the higher realms.

CHAPTER 23

Cantos XXXI–XXXII

The Giants

Dante will now end *Inferno*, but he will not bring the momentum of the *Comedy* to a halt. There surely is a feeling of conclusion at the end of the first canticle, but the many unresolved issues which the poem has raised tell us that we are only at a station along the way. Indeed, one of the poem's great morals, Dante's optimistic (or comic) view of the universe, is contained in the fact that only one-third of the work is concerned with the world's human failures and the rest with great successes who will achieve or have achieved salvation.

Some of this sense of finality within process is the result of the fact that the Pilgrim's journey through the nether world has all along imitated the final events in the earthly life of Christ (Cassell 1979, Cook and Hertzman 1979, Freccero, 1965 a,b): the crucifixion, the harrowing of Hell, and the resurrection. These events, as everyone educated in a Christian context understands, imply both an ending, that of the old dispensation and of the hopeless era of mankind, and the beginning of the new time of hope. Our discussion of the last four cantos will be sometimes concerned with the Christological images to be found in them.

There are important formal issues to be mentioned first. Canto XXXI is structurally related to Canto IX, the transition from incontinence to violence, and to Canto XVII with its description of Geryon and the transition to the bolgias of fraud. At all three locations the motion from one division of Hell to another is assisted by a spiritual being and is connected in some way with water. In Canto IX, the Pilgrim was assisted by the heavenly messenger in a passage that was associated with the water of the swamp. In XVII, the descent was made possible by the monster Geryon and was associated with the waterfall. In XXXI the movement is from simple, indiscriminate fraud, to treason involving the betrayal of those who have a special reason to trust the traitor. Dante and Virgil are assisted by the giant Antaeus and the water motive appears in the ice of Cocytus. The physical relationship between Dante and Virgil during the descent is another structural element. In the episode with Geryon, the Pilgrim clung to Virgil on the back of the beast. Here Virgil holds Dante: "of himself and me he made one bundle" (135). The allegory is probably again of the relationship of the pilgrim soul with reason and with the fact of evil. It returns again in the encounter with Satan.

Of the figures which dominate the canto, the pagan giants, Ephialtes and Briareus have been alluded to earlier in the poem. Capaneus, the blasphemer of Canto XIV, on the ground in the rain of fire, compares his own defeat at Thebes to the defeat of the giants at Phlegra (XIV, 58). The story of the giants' rebellion against Jove is the pagan analog to Lucifer's story so that their presence here is another example of Dante's habit of pairing lessons with both a pagan and a Christian exemplum. Nimrod, who divides mankind by causing the confusion of language, is an Old Testament figure who repeats the motive of pride and the hopeless struggle to equal God. He also reminds us again of the issue of corrupt language and thought which will climax again in Canto XXXIII. Antaeus is a pagan figure who, "had he been at the high war" (119) of the rebellion of Ephialtes and Briareus, might have assured the defeat of the gods. He seems to be included to emphasize how dramatic Dante's vision of history is, how close defeat has always been in the struggle between good and evil. All of the giants are embedded in the rock up to their chests. Throughout Hell, the motive of the prominent chest has been a symbol of pride, from Farinata rising from his tomb to the centaurs to Satan who will repeat it in Canto XXXIV.

Why are the giants in Hell? They are not all alike. Ephialtes and Briareus were rebels, as, conceivably Nimrod could be said to be, but there is no hint of rebellion in the story of Antaeus. In Virgil's catalog we were lead to expect sinners here whose guilt had two elements, fraud and treason. In his first reference to the lowest part of Hell, Virgil speaks of fraud (XI, 25–27):

> "But because fraud is an evil peculiar
> to man, it more displeases God, and there-
> fore the fraudulent are the lower, and more
> pain assails them."

Later, he breaks fraud into categories and characterizes the worst of it as treason (XI, 52–66):

> "Fraud, which gnaws every conscience, a
> man may practice upon one who trusts in
> him, or upon one who reposes no confidence.
> This latter seems to sever the bond of
> love which nature makes; wherefore in the
> second circle hypocrisy, flatteries, sorcerers,
> falsity, theft, simony, panders, barratry, and
> like filth have their nest.
>
> "By the other way both that love which
> Nature makes is forgotten, and that also
> which is added to it and which creates a
> special trust; therefore in the smallest circle,
> at the center of the universe and the seat of
> Dis, every traitor is consumed eternally."

As we have seen, fraud requires deception, but this is not always the case with treason or rebellion. The giants may have rebelled, but they did so openly. Nimrod wanted to reach God, but the tower was not hidden. Here, as in the case of the schismatics, Dante's actual treatment of a category of sin seems to modify what Virgil's catalog would lead us to expect. In the next canto, few of the sinners are fraudulent. Most of them are simply open murderers of their relatives or outright political rebels. Those sinners in the absolute depths, Brutus, Cassius and Judas, do have an element of fraud in their stories. Of course Virgil did mention malice (XI, 22, 82) and the giants are certainly malicious. It might be important that Dante's loosening of Virgil's categories does not necessarily imply a rebuke of Aristotle who warns at the beginning of the *Nichomachaean Ethics* not to expect ethical issues to sort themselves out into absolute distinctions much in the way St. Thomas argued in his discussion of scandal and schism.

Like those schismatics and slanderers of Canto XXVIII, the giants seem to be in this arena for their general nature rather than for a specific type of sin. John Ciardi's comment on them captures part of their significance (Ciardi, 1954):

> These are the sons of earth, embodiments of
> elemental forces unbalanced by love, desire without
> restraint and without acknowledgement of moral and
> theological law. They are symbols of the earth-trace that
> every devout man must clear from his soul, the unchecked

> passions of the beast. Raised from the earth, they make the
> very gods tremble. Now they are returned to the darkness
> of their origins, guardians of earth's last depth.

What Ciardi does not say is that the natural passion of these beings is only one element of their sin. The other part comes from conscious mind not instinctual passion. Dante makes this very clear in what is one of the most important definitions of *Inferno* (49–57):

> Nature assuredly, when she gave up the art
> of making creatures such as these, did right
> well to deprive Mars of such executors; and
> though she repents not of elephants and
> whales, he who looks subtly holds here therein
> more just and more discreet, for where the
> instrument of the mind is added to an evil
> will and to great power, man can make no
> defense against it.

Evil will and great power directed by the mind equals the maximum danger for threatened humanity. Given Dante's Christian viewpoint it is easy to understand how he reasons that this kind of threat would take the form of intentional treason (whether fraudulent or not) and would be at the bottom of the pit: the first sin of all, that of Lucifer against God was a rebellion of a servant against a master, Adam in his fall mirrors and repeats that sin as does Judas in his gross error. We will see Lucifer and Judas, but not Adam. Although he is not far from our thoughts here and we anticipate seeing him eventually, we know from our visit to Limbo that his fate is bound up with the new beginning which Christ's resurrection represents.

The passage just cited speaks of size in this context, but it also invites us to look subtly. The size of the giant is indexed by the reference to the giant pine cone of St. Peter's at Rome (59) immediately suggesting the evil will, great power and conscious direction of the corrupt papacy, so that we see that size is not the real issue. This is another structural element. It is like the similar moment in Canto XVIII where we are reminded of the way the Romans arranged the passage of pilgrims across the bridge during the Jubilee. There we are reminded of Rome during the description of the seducers and panders suggesting the sexual corruption of the Roman "event." That was at the very beginning of the whole section of fraud.

Here at the end of the section of "simple fraud" a similar reminder of Papal corruption contributes to the symmetry of the poem.

The entire poem has been concerned with the causes and results of divisiveness and the giants and the reference to the papacy also refer to this. The rebellion of the giants disrupts the orderly governance of earth as does the greed of the papacy. Even Antaeus, not a rebel, is generally divisive. His brutal nature and violent acts simply disturb things. This, the general tone and lesson of the canto, is further set by the references to towers within it of which there are four. The first is while Dante and Virgil are still approaching the giants and Dante thinks that the giants *are* the towers of a city (21). This misperception is corrected by Virgil, "these are not towers, but giants" (31). The second reference to towers compares the circle of giants to a specific set of towers, "as on its round wall Montereggione crowns itself with towers, so here the horrible giants" (41–44). The third tower reference is by implication in the identification of Nimrod who, tradition says, built the Tower of Babel. The last tower reference is at the end of the canto in the description of Antaeus as he bends over (136–139):

> Such as the Garisenda seems to one's view
> beneath the leaning side, when a cloud is
> passing over it against the direction in which
> it leans, such did Antaeus seems to me.

Montereggione was a Sienese fortress which figures in the wars between the Guelphs and the Ghibellines which put at odds Florence and Siena (Singleton 1970). It is therefore a reference to political divisiveness between states. Nimrod's tower brings to mind the divisiveness and loss of reason caused by the corruption of language. The Garisenda was one of many towers built by the feuding families of Bologna as fortresses within the city as part of their constant internal wars.

The symbolism of the towers goes further, however, into the Christological theme. Cassell (1979) has shown that the entombed Satan of Canto XXXIV is imprisoned in a pit which has many similarities to the sepulchre of Christ of which there were many full size models in Dante's Italy. The Holy Sepulchre was the ideal goal of a pilgrimage and these models were built for those who could not attempt the journey to the real one. Dante himself made no pilgrimage, but the *Comedy* is a literary pilgrimage as we saw in Canto I which has many reminders of the sights and experiences of a devout traveler on the road to Jerusalem (Demaray 1969). According to Cassell, the real sepulchre was at one time surmounted by a modest tower. The huge giants are false towers which mark the way into Satan's tomb which is a false tomb in the sense that it is not the tomb true pilgrims seek. Satan is himself false, of course, and the frozen, lifeless water which traps him is a negative image of the living, flowing water of baptism which liberates the Christian.

The Poet speaks in retrospect of the fear he then had of the giants (109–111):

> Then more than ever did I fear death, and
> nothing else was wanted for it but the fear,
> had I not seen his bonds.

Later, while in the hand of Antaeus he comments, "it was such a moment that I should have wished to go by another road!" (140–141). This is physical fear of which he speaks and readers probably have trouble appreciating this kind of fear here since we know that on this divinely authorized journey no harm can come to him. This fear is, however, an element of the transition to Canto XXXII where it is spoken of again and in a way which makes us understand (XXXII, 1–6):

> If I had harsh and grating rhymes, as would
> befit the dismal hole on which all the other
> rocks converge and weigh, I would press out
> more fully the juice of my conception; but
> since I do not have them it is not without
> fear that I bring myself to speak.

We can now see the point, I think. The Poet reminds us that this vision of the bottom of Hell, of the ultimate evil, is his conception, not a description of a seen reality; that he is poet engaged in poetic creation, the making of metaphor that leads to truth. The fear he feels is that fear proper to such an undertaking, the fear of poetic failure (7–9):

>   for to
> describe the bottom of the whole universe is
> not an enterprise to be taken up in sport,

> nor for a tongue that cries mamma and
> daddy.

Dante's is indeed not a tongue that babbles baby talk (like Nimrod's nonsense or that of Plutus in Canto VII, see Hollander 1980), but this is going to take all his powers. Hence, there is a new invocation (10–12):

> But may those ladies aid my verse
> who aided Amphion to wall in Thebes, so
> that the telling may not be diverse from the
> fact.

This is the first invocation since the address to the muses and memory in Canto II. A new invocation here marks the special nature of what is to follow (Singleton 1970). "Those ladies" are also the muses. Amphion made the walls of Thebes by playing his lyre so sweetly that the stones arranged themselves. The implication is that since Dante lacks rhymes which are "harsh and grating" he will have to rely on the "music" of the muses. We must not expect a "realistic" description of Hell, but an artistic one which is, however, not "diverse from the fact." Singleton in his note on line 12 reminds us that already in the poem we have been warned of the discrepancy between the descriptions and the reality. In IV, speaking of those in Limbo, the Poet says (IV, 145–147):

> I cannot give
> full account of them all, for my long theme
> so drives me on, that many times the telling
> comes short of the fact.

This place of great difficulty is Cocytus, the ninth circle of Hell. We first learned that name in Canto XIV, 199 where it is given to us as the final destination of the tears of the Veglio. We heard the word again in XXXI, 123 where Virgil asks Antaeus to place the travelers there. The speech of the sinners and conversation with Virgil will reveal that Cocytus is subdivided into four areas holding types of sinners: Cäina (XXXII, 58), holding those who were treacherous to their kindred, Antenora (XXXII, 88), those who betrayed their country, Ptolomaea (XXXIII, 124) betrayers of guests, and Judecca (XXIV, 117) traitors to their lords.

The sinners here in Cäina and Antenora and at the end of Canto XXXIII in Ptolomaea are distinguished by their position in the ice even as the different practitioners of violence took different postures in the fire. Some of them have their faces downward so that their tears drain from their eyes before it can freeze, others, face up, are made to suffer the added pain of eyes encrusted by ice. The group cataloged in XXXII are all betrayers of either family members or political parties. Two of them, Mordred the killer of King Arthur and Ganelon who betrayed his stepson Roland, are either fictional or semifictional. The rest, eleven in all, are people who would be well known in the Italy of Dante's time. It is difficult at this remove of time and culture to feel strongly about their stories and the best we can do is to accept them as exemplars of a general class. It does help to remember how strongly family ties were felt by Italians of that day. Some evidence of that within the poem is the incident with Geri del Bello in Canto XXIX where Dante seems embarrassed that a member of his own family has been allowed to go unavenged, even though to take such vengeance would be a sin of violence.

To Dante the sinners on the list which he gives us in the bottom of Hell must be the most evil individuals he can muster and we cannot doubt that however distant they are from us that Dante felt strongly about them. One index of how far we have come into evil is the sudden reversal of the familiar motive of fame which has throughout Hell been a measure of comfort to so many of the damned. The Pilgrim and his guide have used the promise of keeping the memory of a sinner alive many times to induce speech or aid. Indeed, as recently as Canto XXXI the brutish Antaeus is made to cooperate by high flown flattery and the appeal to fame (XXI, 115-129):

> "O you that, in the fateful valley which
> made Scipio heir of glory, when Hannibal
> with his followers turned his back, did once
> take for prey a thousand lions, and through
> whom, had you been at the high war of
> your brothers, it seems that some still believe
> the sons of earth would have conquered, set
> us down below - and disdain not to do so -
> where the cold locks up Cocytus. Do not
> make us go to Tityus nor to Typhon: this
> man can give of that which is longed for

here. Bend down, therefore, and do not curl
your lip. He can yet restore your fame on
earth, for he lives and expects long life yet,
if grace does not untimely call him to itself."

To this appeal Antaeus responds "in haste" (130). How different the
response is once in Cocytus. Camiscion de Pazzi speaks only to make Dante
go away, "that you may not put me to further speech" (67). The next,
Bocca degli Abati, does not wish to speak and desires only to be forgotten.
Dante makes the standard appeal (91–96):

> "if you
> crave fame, it may be worth much to you that
> I note your name among the rest." And he
> to me, "The contrary is what I crave. Take
> yourself hence and trouble me no more, for
> ill do you know how to flatter in this depth."

The rules have obviously changed, but the worst is not mere sullenness and
is yet to come. Dante sees the two, the one gnawing the skull of the other,
and makes a modified version of the appeal (133–139):

> "O you who by so bestial a sign show
> hatred against him whom you devour, tell
> me the wherefore," I said, "on this condition
> that if you with reason complain of him, I,
> knowing who you are and his offence, may
> yet requite you in the world above, if that
> with which I speak does not dry up."

CHAPTER 24

Canto XXXIII

Ugolino: Pity's Final Assault

The appeal is not made in terms of fame, but of justice and amounts to a contract with the sinner: if he complains "with reason," the Pilgrim will make a case for him in the world of the living. The sinner agrees to speak in spite of the pain (XXXIII, 4–9):

> "You will
> have me renew desperate grief, which even
> to think of wrings my heart before I speak
> of it. But if my words are to be seed that
> may bear fruit of infamy to the traitor whom
> I gnaw, you shall see me speak and weep together."

The words are a paraphrase of Aeneas's words to Dido at the beginning of his retelling of the fall of Troy (*Aeneid*, II, 3–8):

> "Beyond all words, O Queen, is the grief thou
> bidst me revive, how the Greeks overthrew Troy's
> wealth and woeful realm - the sights most piteous
> that I myself saw and whereof I was no small part.
> What Myrmidon or Dolopian, or soldier of stern
> Ulysses could in telling such a tale refrain
> from tears?"

This passage has been paraphrased once before in Canto V by Francesca (V, 121–126):

> And she to me, "There is no greater sorrow
> than to recall, in wretchedness, the happy
> time; and this your teacher knows. But if you
> have such great desire to know the first root
> Of our love, I will tell as one who weeps and tells."

Francesca's canto establishes the pattern for so much of *Inferno*. From her we learned not to trust the speech of the damned, how much they desire pity and how little justified their appeal for it is. The reminder here of those lessons learned so long ago and seemingly so far away invite us to cast a long look backwards over the journey before we turn to face the last challenges. The repetition of the reminder of *Aeneid* not only puts us in mind of the pain of memory, but also of the other lessons of Hell. Ugolino is the last of the great "sympathetic" speakers of Hell. Like Francesca and Farinata, Pier della Vigne, Ulysses and others, he makes a strong claim on our emotions; our reason must be armed in our defense. Hence the pointed reminder of Francesca's deceptive speech. There are other reminders of Francesca. One is the fact that Ugolino is bound in Hell to another sinner with whom he was closely associated in life as Francesca with Paolo. I think it is intriguing that in both cases of paired sinners there is a kind of embrace, heads touch, in the one case in a kiss, in the other in a cannibalistic parody of a kiss.

The similarities of the situation prepare us to follow Dante's meaning, but the differences should be noted also. Francesca's openly speaks of her desire for pity. She would, she says, pray for the peace of God for Dante, "since you have pity on our perverse ill" (V, 93). Ugolino's approach is different. He says his goal is the "fruit of infamy" for Ruggieri, whose head he gnaws, a fiercer desire proper to a sinner who is much fiercer than Francesca. But we can see that his unstated desire for pity is also very strong.

Ugolino and Ruggieri show how mixed the classifications of the damned are in these extreme reaches. The details of the political intrigues which involve these figures are complicated, but worth the effort to sort out in outline. Ugolino was originally a Ghibelline (of the party of the Emperor), but had become a Guelph (of the party of the Pope) at a time (1285) when Guelph fortunes in Italy were high. His city of Pisa, traditionally a Ghibelline stronghold, was threatened by Guelph cities including Florence and Lucca. Since it was thought that Ugolino as a Guelph would be in a strong position to negotiate with Pisa's enemies, he was elected Podesta, chief executive, of the city. Following the wishes of the citizens he undertook a policy of compromise with the foreign Guelphs. His conciliatory acts included ceding to Florence and Lucca certain fortresses which Pisa held. These are the "castles" referred to in XXXIII, 88.

By 1288, Ugolino's son-in-law, Nino Visconti, began to conspire to obtain for himself the leadership of the Guelph party which for a long time had been in the hands of the Visconti family. This was not a betrayal of Ugolino, but rather an effort at an orderly succession as Ugolino was by this time about 68 years old. Ugolino was then allied with Nino both by ties of party and of family.

The Ghibelline opposition to the Guelphs was lead by Archbishop Ruggieri in alliance with the families of the Lanfranchi, the Gualandi and the Sismondi (named in line 32). The fortunes of the Ghibellines were now on the upswing and Ugolino secretly betrayed his son-in-law Nino to the Ghibellines by leaving the city himself with his personal supporters and going to his estate in the country. The Ghibellines, with a stronger force within the city, then exiled Nino who fled to Florence where he quite possibly met Dante.

After Nino departed, Ugolino returned to Pisa to find that Ruggieri had named himself Podesta in his place (this is Ruggieri's first betrayal of Ugolino). Ugolino, evidently not a trusting soul, had however with him 1000 men and with them he forced himself into the city to regain his position. Ruggieri then resorted to propaganda and charged that the cession of the castles to Florence and Lucca had been an act of treason (this lie is Ruggieri's second act of betrayal). The aroused populace captured Ugolino and Ruggieri imprisoned him in the tower "that has the title of Hunger" of line 23 and starved him to death with his children (a third betrayal). Ruggieri resigned his position as Podesta in favor of Guido da Montefeltro whom we met in Canto XXVII.

Those are the facts as well as they are known. What we must examine now is what Dante makes of them, remembering always that, as in the case of Francesca, absolute adherence to the facts is not required in the poetic approach to truth. Historically, Ugolino's children were grown men, probably as guilty as he was. It is important for Dante's point, however, that they be innocent children, even as it was important for his point in Canto V that Francesca speak in the language of courtly love.

It seems that Ugolino is in Antenora because he betrayed his party and his family. Performing either one of these acts by itself would seem to qualify one for Cäina which is largely populated by betrayers of party or family, one or the other, although even there we heard of Mordred who betrayed his country by usurping Arthur who was his uncle. Ruggieri, on the other hand, betrayed his ally who was his rightful lord in his role as Podesta. It has been argued that Ugolino was Ruggieri's guest when he reentered the city after the betrayal of Nino (Singleton 1970). This would make his placement here accord with the other sinners in this canto who did indeed betray guests. However, Ruggieri's sinfulness is obviously more complicated than merely that. In any case, it seems that what is meant is that absolute evil is a mixture of fraud, betrayal and counter betrayal and creates a situation in which men cannot tend either to their civic responsibilities, their families or their souls. It brings to mind Dorothy Sayers' comment, "Good is simple, evil complex."

Scholars have noted that the story of Ugolino as it is told here contains Christological elements, chiefly pertaining to the Last Supper with the disciples, the Crucifixion and the burial of Christ (Cook and Hertzman 1979, Freccero 1977, Hertzman 1980, Hollander 1984, Shapiro 1976, and others).

Ugolino identifies himself and Ruggieri and explains that since everyone knows the story related above, he will tell how cruel his death was and that it is in this that his claim against Ruggieri lies. Of course, to omit the story is to omit his own sins (he thinks), although in passing he can mention Ruggieri's "ill devising" and to imply that he was only trusting in his relations with him.

That he was locked up in a tower has a lot of meaning in the context of these last cantos as we have already seen. That it was a narrow hole (22) returns us to the image of the sepulchre of Christ which was also narrow (Cassell 1979). In all these references to the sepulchre the issue is that these tombs are permanent while Christ escaped from his. Ugolino's last days begin with a dream in his sepulchre. The form of the dream is quite literary and it is the first appearance of the motive of the prophetic dream which will be one of the most prominent formal features of *Purgatorio*. Of the several types of dreams in the medieval catalog this one is a *somnium* (Lewis 1971), that is, a dream which is an allegory of truth. The allegory, that of the Ghibelline hunters chasing the wolf pack of the Guelphs (Freccero 1977), is entirely appropriate to the reality. The dream is prophetic in that the hounds eventually catch and, with their teeth, tear (eat) the wolves. What is suggestive is that Ugolino says that Ruggieri appeared "as master and lord *to me*" (28).

Now, this statement contains the meaning for us within the allegory but it has a different meaning for Ugolino. For Ugolino, it is a vision of his last earthly experiences, for us it contains the explanation of the failure which leads Ugolino to Hell. In a very real sense, Ruggieri is Ugolino's "master and lord" and that sense is in that Ruggieri is an archbishop and thus charged with the salvation of souls and serving as Christ's representative. That he is personally faulty is irrelevant. Ugolino's failure, common in Hell, is that he does not see past the turmoil of earthly life to the eternal truths beyond it. Much like Pier della Vigne, for instance, he mistakes earthly accidents for final circumstances. This is why Ugolino spends eternity eating Ruggieri, a materialistic eating of the flesh in hatred instead of a spiritual eating of the flesh of Christ in love, as symbolized by the sacrament of the Eucharist. Hertzman, 1980, points out that the disciples who leave Christ when he commands them to eat his flesh do so because they fail to understand the spiritual meaning of the words and are repelled by the cannibalistic image (John 6:53):

> The Jews on that account argued with one another
> saying, "How can this man give us his flesh to eat?"

Jesus explains (61–64):

> "Does this scandalize you? What then if you should
> see the Son of Man ascending where he was before?
> It is the spirit that gives life; the flesh profits
> nothing. The words that I have spoken to you are
> spirit and life."

But it is not enough for some (67):

> From this time many of his disciples turned back
> and no longer went about with him.

The fact that Ugolino fails to see the spiritual meaning behind the material is the message of his reaction to the children's pleas, all of which clearly have spiritual implications which Ugolino ignores. The first occurs immediately upon awaking after the dream (37–39):

> "When I awoke before the dawn I heard
> my children, who were with me, crying in
> their sleep and asking for bread."

As the archbishop's proper reference is to Christ, so the children's appeal for earthly bread should have lead Ugolino to consider the spiritual bread which was their true need then, but it does not. Similarly, he fails to grasp the implications of the invitation to eat of his sons which is their response to his spiritual anguish which they mistake for physical hunger (58–63):

> "I bit both my hands
> for grief, and they, thinking I did it for
> hunger, suddenly rose up and said, ' Father,
> it will be far less painful to us if you eat of
> us; you did clothe us with this wretched
> flesh and do you strip us of it!'"

On their part this is a physical offering, but it is reminiscent of Christ's own spiritual offering to his Father (Luke 23, 46):

> "Father, into thy hands I commit my spirit!"

Gaddo's cry is also Christological (69):

> "Father, why do you not help me?"

echoing Christ (Matthew 27, 46):

> "My God, my God why hast thou forsaken me?"

(There are other scriptures to which this text refers, see Freccero 1977 and Hollander 1984.)

To all of this Ugolino is not merely blind, he is indifferent. Ugolino does not respond to the children, to the signs, but he challenges us to respond (40–42):

> "You are
> cruel indeed if you do not grieve already, to

think what my heart was foreboding; and if
you weep not, at what do you ever weep?"

Yet he does not weep, "I did not weep...I shed no tear." The children, "they wept." His only reaction is silence, "nor did I answer...That day and the next we stayed all silent."

Ugolino's speech ends with the line (75), "Then fasting did more than grief had done." I think most readers take this to mean that Ugolino overcome with hunger, the corpses of his children before him, performed the last orgy of Eucharistic inversion and ate of his sons. This interpretation is controversial. Singleton's (1970) rejection of it is significantly phrased:

> Some commentators have held the curious view that by this last line of Ugolino's narrative Dante meant to imply that the count, in the extremity of starvation, did actually attempt to prolong his life by feeding upon the bodies of his sons, as they had begged him to do while they were yet alive...that "hunger" prevailed over "grief" in that sense. But such a view of the meaning here is hardly worth a serious rebuttal.

Freccero (1977) and Hertzman (1980) reject Singleton's view while Hollander (1984) supports it. I side with Freccero and Hertzman. Singleton seems to reject the ideas of a father eating his son because it is simply too horrible, yet this is the bottom of Hell, a place not to be described by those who "cry mamma and daddy." Here the great Dante scholar and translator was overwhelmed by the intensity of his poet's language. How else to describe the bottom of the universe but in terms of an ultimately horrible act? This is especially so since only Ugolino's cannibalism could complete the inversion of the Christological reference. The line is ambiguous, of course, but this ambiguity only invites us to ponder and, finally, come to the horrible realization.

That we have reached the limits of purely human evil is shown by the fact that the next sinners we meet have an element of the demon in them. They merge with the purely demonic image of Satan.

The Pilgrim has a deal with Ugolino. If his case against Ruggieri is well founded, Dante will speak his case to the world. The Pilgrim decides against Ugolino, but he does speak the case of the children in the condemnation of Pisa in lines 79-90.

As in the case of Ugolino, Dante's interaction with the sinners of the second part of the canto is levered with an appeal. In this final instant of this particular formal device, its content promises neither fame, nor a chance at revenge, but only a temporary relief of some of the pain. These sinners who violated the sacred relationship between a host and his guests (see the chapter of the burning sands and the sodom imagery) are frozen in the ice so that their tears cannot fall from their eyes. The advance is made by the sinner, not the Pilgrim (109–117):

> And one of the wretches of the cold crust
> cried out to us, "O souls so cruel that the last
> station is given to you, lift from my face the
> hard veils so that, before the weeping freezes
> again, I may vent a little the misery that stuffs
> my heart." Wherefore I to him, "If you would
> have me help you, tell me who you are, and
> if I do not relieve you, may I have to go to
> the bottom of the ice."

Dante knows he will go to the bottom of the ice, although not as one of the damned as the sinner takes him to be, so already the Pilgrim's speech is deceptive. Even so, the promise to go to the bottom if he does not remove the crusts can mean little since the sinner already perceives that Dante is so bound. Perhaps the acceptance by the sinner of a contract based on such a slender reed is an index of how desperate he is, how little a soul in such torment has to lose.

The soul, Fra Alberigo, along with his companion Branca d'Oria has a body which is not yet dead, but which is inhabited by a demon. This is the punishment of those who violated the trust which their guest placed in them; the *contrapasso* is that they must now entertain a very unwelcome guest indeed. Note, though, that they were in charge of their bodies when the sins for which they are punished were committed. In Dante's theology, no one can plead that they were made to do something by a demon or someone else. This, remember, was Guido da Montefeltro's ploy. One can never escape the responsibility for possessing both reason and free will. Human will and reason, used in an evil manner, leads us to the very edge of the completely demonic represented in the next canto by Satan. To say Satan is wholly demonic is to say that he is a reversal or negative image of

Christ himself. This "reversal" element, crucial at the end of the canticle, is shown here by the Pilgrim's "fulfillment" of the contract with Fra Alberigo, who has performed his side of it, by an act which is itself a betrayal (148–150):

> "But now reach out your hand here: open my
> eyes"; and I opened them not for him - and
> to be rude to him was courtesy!

CHAPTER 25

Canto XXXIV

The Defeat of Satan

Canto XXXIV is perplexing even by the standards of the *Divine Comedy* which has perplexities by the multitude. Possibly the biggest problem is that Satan, whom we have long expected, seems anticlimactic and the impression of the reader, who has not yet read the whole of the *Divine Comedy*, is that the *Inferno* lacks a satisfactorily climactic conclusion. In the last chapter we discussed the fact that the end of *Inferno* isn't really an ending, but rather the sign of a new beginning and readers should be assured that if they do work their way through the whole poem, the fitness of the vision of Satan here will be abundantly clear to them. I don't want to describe in detail why this is so, since that would deprive readers of the pleasure of wonder while watching Dante work it out. This discussion will largely remain concerned with what is immediate in the canto.

It is possible that our expectations are so influenced by other visions of what the Devil should be like, ranging from modern Protestantism to Walt Disney, that our surprise is in some part that Dante's image is so different. Satan seems so helpless and undramatic, so stupid and pointless. Nevertheless, we are obliged by Virgil's exhortation and by the Poet's Address to the Reader to accept that the being actually is dangerous (XXXIV, 20–27):

> "Lo Dis! - and lo the place where you must arm
> yourself with fortitude."
>
> How frozen and faint I then became, ask
> it not, reader, for I do not write it, because
> all words would fail. I did not die and I did
> not remain alive: now think for yourself, if
> you have any wit, what I became, deprived
> alike of death and life!

Given that Satan is dangerous, we need to try to understand in what sense this is so. We can begin by acknowledging the obvious; that Satan

is overcome by Dante and Virgil and that his overcoming has an obvious
allegory. On the literal level, he is a physical object. The Poet emphasizes
his materiality by describing his gigantic size, larger than the giants by far.
This emphasis on the material nature of Satan is understandable if we take
him as the exemplar of the nature of Hell. Throughout *Inferno* we have been
repeatedly reminded of the physical, materialistic preoccupations of the
damned: Ciacco's indulgence in physical appetite and Pier della Vigne's
concentration on his earthly fate to the exclusion of any consideration of his
immortal soul, to choose from among many possible examples. Therefore,
it is appropriate that the very incarnation of evil should be primarily a
physical presence which Virgil conquers by coming into contact with him,
grappling the hair of Satan's flank and moving through space from tuft to
tuft. Virgil carries Dante on his back in a clear continuation of the allegory
of the role of reason. The two thus overcome the physical and Ciacco,
Francesca, Pier, Ugolino and the rest should have done.

That part seems clearly intended. Less obviously, Satan is also a
means to an end, a difficult ladder by means of which the evil which he
himself embodies is overcome (XXIV, 82–84):

> "Cling fast," said the master, panting like
> a man forspent, "for by such stairs as these
> we must depart from so much evil."

The explanation of this part of the allegory leads us a bit into Christian
theology and into what I take to be the major device of this canto: That it
contains a number of reversals in expectation and understanding which are
paradoxical in nature. Twice in the canto the Poet specifically challenges
our intelligence and ability to understand. The first we have already seen in
line 26 where the Poet describes his state of mind at the sight of Satan
"now think for yourself, if you have any with." The second is just after
Virgil and Dante dismount from Satan's flank (91–93), "if I became
perplexed then, let the dull crowd judge who do not see what is the point
that I had passed." With these clear warnings in mind, let us look for the
paradoxes.

Early commentators as well as modern scholars (Singleton 1958,
Freccero 1965b) have emphasized that the hymn parodied at the beginning
of the canto is a hymn of the Cross. In fact, it is a crusader's hymn and a
crusade is the highest type of pilgrimage and Dante's journey is an allegory

of a pilgrimage. The point of the hymn is that the crucifixion is the necessary means to eternal life and that the crucifixion involves a contradiction, a paradox. Here is the original of the first verse of the hymn with a literal prose translation:

> Vexilla Regis prodeunt: The banners of the King proceed,
> Fulget Crucis mysterium,   The mystery of the Cross shines forth
> Qua vita mortem pertulit,   On which Life suffered death,
> Et morte vitam protulit.   And by His death obtained life for us.

The paradox is, of course, in the last two lines. Life (Christ) must die in order for the Christian to obtain life. Life for humanity comes through death. Already we see some of the intent behind Virgil's statement that Satan, the very emblem of eternal death, is the means to defeat death. Of course Dante does not give us the entire hymn, but only the first line, and that distorted. Virgil phrases it "*Vexilla regis prodeunt inferni*," The banners of the King of Hell proceed. This is itself a reversal since we are not in the presence of the Cross of Christ which gives life, but the crucifixion of Satan, eternal death. Still, we know from our previous experience that when Dante refers to a text he expects us to know it, and our knowledge of this particular hymn must bring to mind the particular paradox of the Crucifixion. This paradox is the one meant by St. Paul when he writes in I Corinthians 22–23:

> For the Jews ask for signs, and the Greeks look for "wisdom"; but we, for our part, preach a crucified Christ - to the Jews indeed a stumbling-block and to the Gentiles foolishness.

It is a foolishness since it seems to defy logic. This point, that salvation is not reached through reason alone was referred to before in *Inferno* in the discussion of the Old Man of Crete in Canto XIV. The pagans had gods who died and were buried, but the Christian dies and lives forever, escaping the tomb.

Before we go on, here is a digression about hymns. The rest of the *Divine Comedy* contains many hymns which were well known in Dante's time. There are also many references to poets other than Dante throughout the rest of the work. There have already been two. We heard of Guido

Cavalcante in Canto X and Bertran de Born in Canto XXVIII. This the first hymn, however, although they are a prominent feature of *Purgatorio* and *Paradiso*. (It is important that the single hymn of Hell is given in a distorted form.) Hymns are written by poets, and, working on the theory that Dante expects us to know his sources, it may be that the citation of this one is intended to bring its author to mind. *Vexilla Regis prodeunt* was a favorite in Dante's age and survives in the church in our own time. It was written by Venantius Fortunatus (530–609) who was an Italian poet whose biography has some similarities with Dante's own. Early in life his failing vision was healed by St. Martin of Tours. Eventually Venantius undertook a pilgrimage to St. Martin's tomb to pay homage for the miracle. On the way, however, he took employment with the King of the Franks as a court poet. His duties were to write a sort of social poetry praising the king, the king's guests, the castles and the women of the court. It was this last aspect of his duties which makes him a part of the courtly love tradition of which Dante was the crown. Eventually, Venantius remembered his vow to St. Martin and completed his pilgrimage. He then went to Poitiers where Queen Radegunde had established herself in a monastery with her companion, Abbess Agnes. These lades, who lived lives of great sanctity, befriended Venantius who was frequently entertained at the monastery. Many of his poems of this period are, in fact, verses in praise of the meals the holy ladies gave him. Eventually, the story goes (Raby 1927), the good example of Radegunde and Agnes turned Venantius' thoughts again to God. Like Dante, Venantius had an experience early in life which turned him to God. Like Dante, he became distracted by secular affairs, in his case in the royal court while Dante was distracted by philosophy, but eventually, as Dante does in the *Comedy*, Venantius made his pilgrimage. Like Dante, the courtly poet was saved by the example of a woman. Venantius' poetry became serious. In addition to *Vexilla regis*, he is also the author of the *Pange lingua*, another very popular hymn. Venantius Fortunatus became Bishop of Poitiers shortly before his death. How much about Venantius Dante knew is not known, but his literary estate was kept at Ravenna where Dante is reputed to have studied at the university, so he could have seen the works there. It is intriguing that in this canto of "reversals" two poets whose lives "reverse" are brought to our attention.

To return to the canto's paradoxes and reversals, however, the fact that Satan is himself a kind of reversal is shown by the two references to the fact that he is not now what he once was, that is, beautiful. The first mention of the "creature who was once so fair" in line 18 is followed by Dante's statement of wonder in lines 33–36:

> If he was once as beautiful as he is ugly
> now, and lifted up his brows against his
> Maker, well may all sorrow proceed from him.

Satan's movement from beauty to ugliness mirrors his role in the universe; he is the opposite of everything which God is. Originally next to God in beauty and power, he now is the lowest thing in the universe. If God is light, Satan is darkness. If God is warm and attractive, Satan is cold (hence the ice at the bottom of the world rather than the fires of more traditional imagery) and repulsive. Most important, if God is power, then Satan is weakness and this last explains the brisk treatment which he receives from Virgil whose only words about him are to identify the archtraitors he chews and to urge Dante to move on in a manner reminiscent of the way he has previously dismissed sinners who were beneath contempt (61–69):

> "The soul up there that has the greatest
> punishment," said the master, "is Judas
> Iscariot, who has his head within and plies
> his legs outside. Of the other two who have
> their heads below, the one that hangs from
> the black muzzle is Brutus: see how he
> writhes and utters not a word; that other is
> Cassius who seems so stark of limb. But night
> is rising again, and now we must depart, for
> we have seen the whole."

We have been following Freccero and Hollander in their explanation of these last few cantos as containing reminders of the last events in the life of Christ. His suspension here is like a permanent crucifixion in a hole which is like the tomb from which Christ escaped. Singleton (1958) addresses the fact that Satan's three heads, joined at the crown into one entity, parody the Trinity itself and that the colors of the faces, yellow, red and black are the colors which in medieval tradition are associated with decay, but that white, the color of rebirth, is absent. To those things we can add a discussion of the description of Dante's state of mind confronted with the negativeness of the Devil (22-27):

> How frozen and faint I then became, ask
> it not, reader, for I do not write it, because
> all words would fail. I did not die and I did
> not remain alive: now think for yourself, if
> you have any wit, what I became, deprived
> alike of death and life!

To be deprived of life and death alike would be a terribly empty experience. To be frozen and faint at the same time would be to be in much the state of Satan. Ugolino was frozen, vacuous, when his children asked him to respond and now he is frozen in Hell. The situation is similar with Satan who had been so full, and that state of emptiness is his crucifixion. Dante is about to emerge from Hell as Christ did and to be reborn on the foot of the slopes of the mountain of Purgatory. This moment of spiritual and intellectual nonbeing is perhaps the Pilgrim's own crucifixion, his death from which to be reborn. In a way, it too is a kind of reversal. All along the journey our Pilgrim has grown in power and understanding, yet knowledge and understanding is not enough. It seems there must be this instant of emptiness for the true conversion to occur.

That Dante changes here is the burden of the allegory of the climb down Satan's flank. Virgil makes a tremendous effort, places his head where his feet had been and what was down becomes up and what was evening (68) becomes morning (96) in the final reversal image of the canto. Dante has passed the midpoint of the earth, the spot to which all evil tends and now he is faced with a climb, up through half the earth, to escape. Previously his journey was down, but now he understands that he only had to go down in order to be able to make the climb up. Since the direct climb up was denied the Pilgrim by the fierce three beasts of Canto I, he has had to make what appeared to be this long detour, irrational like the Crucifixion, but which turns out to be the proper route any way.

The last few lines of the poem record the travelers' ascent (which is fully as far as the distance of their descent, half the diameter of the earth) to make their appearance under the morning stars Easter morning, 1300. This completes the Pilgrim's journey in imitation of Christ's entombment and the harrowing of Hell. In the course of the journey, he has been reversed, but unlike Satan, he is not a reversal, but is now straight on the road to God.

SELECTED BIBLIOGRAPHY

Armour, Peter. 1983. "Dante's Brunetto: The Paternal Paternine?" *Italian Studies*. 38: 1–38.

Atchity, Kenneth John. 1969. "*Inferno VII*. The Idea of Order." *Italian Quarterly*. 12: 5–62.

Baird, Julian. 1967. "Principles of Violence in *Inferno XIII*." *Italian Quarterly*. 10: 63–80.

Baker, David J. 1974. "The Winter Simile in *Inferno XXIV*." *Dante Studies*. 92: 77–91.

Baldassaro, Lawrence. 1974. "Dante as Pilgrim: Everyman as Sinner." *Dante Studies*. 92: 63–76.

_____. 1981. "Metamorphosis as Punishment and Redemption in *Inferno XXIV*." *Dante Studies*. 99: 89–112.

Barnes, J. C. 1981. "Inferno XIII." *Dante Soundings: Eight Literary and Historical Essays.* David Nolan, ed., Dublin: Irish Academic Press. 28–58.

Barolini, Teodolinda. 1979. "Bertran de Born and Sordello: The Poetry of Politics in Dante's Comedy." *PMLA*. 94: 395–405.

Beall, Chandler. 1979. "Dante and his Reader." *Forum Italicum*. 13: 299–343.

Brown, Merle E. 1971. "A Reading of *Inferno X*." *Italica*. 68: 315–333.

Burckhardt, Jacop. 1954. *The Civilization of the Renaissance in Italy.* New York: Modern Library.

Cambon, Glauco. 1970. "Synesthesia in the *Divine Comedy*." *Dante Studies*. 88: 1–16.

Cassell, Anthony K. 1976. "Failure, Pride and Conversion in *Inferno I*: A Reinterpretation." *Dante Studies*. 94: 1–24.

_____. 1977. "Dante's Farinata and the Image of the Arca." *Yale Italian Studies*. 1: 335–370.

_____. 1979. "The Tomb, the Tower and the Pit: Dante's Satan." *Italica*. 56: 331–351.

_____. 1981a. "The Lesson of Ulysses." *Dante Studies*. 99: 113–131.

_____. 1981b. "Ulisseana: A Bibliography of Dante's Ulysses to 1981." *Italian Culture*. 3: 23–45.

_____. 1984. *Dante's Fearful Art of Justice*. Toronto Press.

Ciardi, John (trans.). 1954. *Dante Alighieri, The Inferno*. New York: Mentor.

Cook, William R. and Ronald D. Hertzman. 1979. "*Inferno XXXIII*: The Past and the Present in Dante's Imagery of Betrayal." *Italica*. 56: 377–383.

Davis, Charles T. 1975. "Dante's Vision of History." *Dante Studies*. 93: 143–160.

Della Terza, Dante. 1981. "*Inferno V*. Tradition and Exegesis." *Dante Studies*. 99: 49–66.

Demaray, John B. 1969. "The Pilgrim Texts and Dante's Three Beasts: *Inferno I*." *Italica*. 69: 233–241.

Diorio, Dorothy. 1978. "Dante's Condemnation of Usury." *Re Artes Liberales*. 5: 17–25.

Donno, Daniel J. 1977. "Moral Hydrography: Dante's Rivers. *MLN*. 92: 130–139.

Economou, George D. 1976. "The Pastoral Similie of *Inferno XXIV* and the Unquiet Heart of the Christian Pilgrim." *Speculum*. 51: 637–646.

Elwert, Theodore W. 1971. "*Inferno*, Canto III." *Italian Studies*. 15: 23–45.

Ferrante, Joan M. 1967. "*Malebolgia (Inferno XVIII–XXX)* as the Key to the Structure of Dante's *Inferno*." *Romance Philology*. 20: 456–466.

_____. 1969. "The Relation of Speech to Sin in the *Inferno*." *Dante Studies*. 87: 33–46.

Fido, Franco. 1986. "Writing Like God--or Better?: Symmetries in Dante's 26th and 27th Cantos." *Italica*. 63. 250–264.

Friedman, John Block. 1972. "Antichrist and the Iconography of Dante's Geryon." *Journal of the Warburg and Courtauld Institute*. 25: 108–122.

Freccero, John. 1977. "Bestial Sign and Bread of Angels (*Inferno 32–33*)." *Vale Italian Studies*. 1: 53–66.

_____. 1959. "Dante's Firm Foot and the Journey Without a Guide." *Harvard Theological Review*. 52: 245–281.

_____. 1961. "Dante's Pilgrim in a Gyre." *PMLA*. 76: 168–181.

_____. 1965a. "Infernal Inversion and Christian Conversion (*Inferno XXIV*)." *Italica*. 42: 35–41.

_____. 1965b. "The Sign of Satan." *MLN*. 80: 11–26.

_____. 1972. "Medusa, The Letter and the Spirit." *Yearbook of Italian Studies*. 2: 1–18.

_____. 1986. *Dante: The Poetics of Conversion*. Cambridge. Harvard University Press.

Glickman, Enrica. 1968. "Human Dignity in Dante's *Inferno*." *Laurentian University Review*. 2: 33–44.

Guzzardo, John D. 1979. "The Noble Castle and the Eighth Gate." *MLN*. 94 (No. 1): 137–145.

Hatcher, Anna and Mark Musa. 1968. "*Inferno V* and the Old French Prose *Lancelot*." *Comparative Literature*. 20: 97–109.

_____. 1970. "Aristotle's *Matta Bestialitade* in Dante's *Inferno*." *Italica*. 47: 366–372.

Hatcher, Anna. 1970. "Dante's Ulysses and Guido da Montefeltro." *Dante Studies*. 88: 109–117.

Heilbronn, Denise. 1983. "Master Adam and the Fat-Bellied Lute (*Inf. XXX*)." *Dante Studies*. 101: 51–65.

Hertzman, Ronald B. and William A. Stephany. 1978. "'O miseri seguaci': Sacramental Inversion in *Inferno XIX*." *Dante Studies*. 96: 39–66.

Hertzman, Ronald B. 1980. "Cannibalism and Communion in Inferno XXXIII." *Dante Studies*. 98: 53–78.

Higgins, David H. 1975. "Cicero, Aquinas, and St. Matthew in *Inferno XIII*." *Dante Studies*. 93: 61–94.

Hollander, Robert L. 1968. "Dante's Use of *Aeneid I* in *Inferno I* and *II.*" *Comparative Literature.* 20: 142–156.

_____. 1973. "The Invocations of the Comedy." *Yearbook of Italian Studies.* 235–240.

_____. 1982. "Dante's 'Book of the Dead': A Note on *Inferno XXIX,* 57." *Studie Danteschi.* 54: 31–51.

_____. 1983. "'Ad ira parea mosso': God's Voice in the Garden (*Inf. XXIV,* 69)." *Dante Studies.* 101: 27–49.

_____. 1984a. "Dante on Horseback: (*Inferno XII,* 19–126)." *Italica.* 61: 187–296.

_____. 1984b. "*Inferno XXXIII,* 37–74: Ugolino's Importunity." *Speculum.* 59: 549–555.

_____. 1980. *Studies in Dante.* Ravenna: Longo Editore.

Huizinga, Johan. 1921. *Herfsttij der Middeleeuwen.* Haarlem: H. D. Tjeewk Willink.

Iannucci, Amilcare. 1980. "Limbo: The Emptiness of Time." *Studie Danteschi.* 52: 69–128.

Kay, Richard. 1978. *Dante's Swift and Strong: Essays on Inferno XV.* Lawrence: Regents Press of Kansas.

Kenny, Anthony. 1980. *Aquinas.* New York: Hill and Wang.

Kleinhenz, Christopher. 1979. "Plutus, Fortune and Michael: The Eternal Triangle." *Dante Studies.* 97: 35–52.

_____. 1986. "Dante and the Bible: Intertextual Approaches to the *Divine Comedy.*" *Italica.* 63: 225–236.

Lansing, Richard H. 1974. "Two Similes in Dante's Commedia: The Shipwrecked Swimmer and Elijah's Ascent." *Romance Philology*. 28: 161–177.

_____. 1981. "Dante's Concept of Violence and the Chain of Being." *Dante Studies*. 99: 67–87.

Levenson, Jon D. 1972. "The Grundworte of Pier della Vigne." *Forum Italicum*. 5: 499–513.

Lewis, C.S. 1971. *The Discarded Image*. Cambridge: Cambridge University Press.

Limentani, Uberto (ed.). 1985. *Dante's Comedy: Introductory Readings of Selected Cantos*. Cambridge: Cambridge University Press.

Lovejoy, A. O. 1936. *The Great Chain of Being: A Study of the History of an Idea*. Cambridge: Harvard University Press.

Mansfield, Margaret Nossel. 1970. "Dante and the Gorgon Within." *Italica*. 47: 143–160.

Markulin, Joseph. 1982. "Dante's Guido da Montefeltro: A Reconsideration." *Dante Studies*. 100: 25–40.

Mayer, Sharon E. 1969. "Dante's Alchemists." *Italian Quarterly*. 12: 185–200.

Musa, Mark. 1974. *"Advent at the Gates: Dante's Comedy."* Bloomington: Indiana University Press.

_____. 1977. "Virgil Reads the Pilgrim's Mind." *Dante Studies*. 95: 149–152.

_____. 1978. "Virgil's Ulysses and Ulysses' Diomedes." *Dante Studies*. 96: 187–194.

_____. 1983. "Filling the gap with *consiglio frodolente.*" *Italian Culture.* 3: 11–21.

Mussetter, Sally. 1978. *"Inferno XXX* Dante's Counterfeit Adam." *Traditio.* 34: 427–435.

_____. 1984. "Ritonare a lo suo principio: Dante and the Sin of Brunetto Latini." *Philological Quarterly,* 63: 431–448.

Nokes, Susan. 1968. "Dino Compagni and the Vow in San Giovanni." *Dante Studies.* 86: 41–63.

Popolizio, Stephen. 1980. "Literary Reminiscences and the Act of Reading in *Inferno V." Dante Studies.* 98: 19–33.

Raby, F. J. E. 1927. *"A History of Christian-Latin Poetry from the Beginnings to the Close of the Middle Ages."* Oxford: Clarendon Press.

Rolfs, Daniel. 1974. "Dante and the Problem of Suicide." *Michigan Academician.* 6: 367–376.

Ryan, C. J. 1982. *"Inferno XXI.* Virgil and Dante: A Study in Contrasts." *Italica.* 59: 16–31.

Ryan, Lawrence V. 1976. *"Stornei, gru, colombe.* The Bird Images in *Inferno V." Dante Studies.* 94: 25–45.

Scott, John S. 1970. "The Rock of Peter and *Inferno XIX." Romance Philology.* 23: 462–479.

Shapiro, Marianne. 1974a. "The Fictionalization of Bertran de Born (*Inf. XXVIII*)." *Dante Studies.* 92: 107–116.

_____. 1974b. "An Old French Source for Ugolino?" *Dante Studies.* 92: 107–116.

_____. 1975A. "Semiramis in *Inferno V*." *Romance Notes*. 2: 455–456.

_____. 1975b. *Women, Earthly and Divine in the Comedy of Dante*. Lesington: University of Kentucky Press.

_____. 1976. "Addendum: Christological Language in *Inferno XXXIII*." *Dante Studies*. 94: 141–143.

Sheehan, David. 1972. "The Control of Feeling: A Rhetorical Analysis of *Inferno XIII*." *Italica*. 51: 193–206.

Silverstein, Theodore. 1937. "Did Dante Know the Vision of St. Paul?" *Harvard Studies and Notes in Philology and Literature*. 19: 231–247.

Singleton, Charles S. 1958. *Dante Studies 2: Journey to Beatrice*. Cambridge: Harvard University Press.

_____. 1965. *"Inferno XIX*: O Simon Mago!" *MLN*. 80: 92–99.

_____. 1957. "The Irreducible Dove". *Comparative Literature*. 9: 129.

Spraycar, Rudy S. 1978. "Dante's Lago del Cor." *Dante Studies*. 96: 1–19.

Stephany, William A. 1982. "Pier Della Vigne's Self-Fulfilling Prophecies: The *Eulogy* of Frederick II and *Inferno 13*." *Traditio*. 28: 193–212.

_____. 1985. "Dante's Harpies: 'tristo annunzio di futuro danno.'" *Italica*. 62: 24–33.

Sturm, Sara. 1974. "Structure and Meaning in *Inferno XXVI*." *Dante Studies*. 92: 93–106.

Suther, Judith D. and R. V. Giffin. 1979. "Dante's Use of the Gorgon Medusa in *Inferno IX*." *Kentucky Romance Quarterly*. 27: 69–84.

Tatlock, J. S. P. 1932. "Mohammed and His Followers in Dante." *Modern Literary Review*. 27: 186–195.

Thompson, David. 1967. "Dante's Ulysses and the Allegorical Journey." *Dante Studies*. 85: 33–58.

_____. 1974. "A Note on Fraudulent Counsel." *Dante Studies*. 92: 149–152.

Triolo, Alfred A. 1968. "*Matta Bestialita in Dante's Inferno*: Theory and Image." *Traditio*. 24: 247–292.

Truscott, James G. 1973. "Ulysses and Guido (*Inf. XXVI-XVIII*)." *Dante Studies*. 91: 47–72.

Valency, Maurice. 1961. *In Praise of Love*. New York: The Macmillan Company.

Walker, D. P. 1964. *The Decline of Hell: Seventeenth-Century Discussions of Eternal Torment*. Chicago: The University of Chicago Press.

Wenzel, Siegfried. 1967. *The Sin of Sloth: "Acedia in Medieval Thought and Literature"*. Chapel Hill: University of North Carolina Press.

Wingell, Albert E. 1981. "The Forested Mountaintop in Augustine and Dante." *Dante Studies*. 99: 9–48.

Wolff, Hope Nash. 1969. "A Study of Dante's Distance from the Creatures of Twenty-One and Two of the *Inferno* and Its Relation to the Use of Animals in Preceding Cantos." *Italian Quarterly*. 12: 239–251.

Yates, Frances A.   1966.   *The Art of Memory*.   Chicago: The University of Chicago Press.